WHAT YOUR COLLEAGUES ARE SAYING . . .

Rachel Lambert skillfully delivers cogent background and advice for addressing the complexity of teaching mathematics to students with disabilities. By contextualizing all approaches in an environment of high expectations, trust, and strengths-based instructional approaches, she suggests a carefully crafted continuum to spur one to rethink what mathematics educators and special educators do. Every individual engaged in working with K–8 learners needs to delve into this critical information. Let the sense-making begin.

Karen Karp
Professor, John Hopkins University
Baltimore, MD

This book by Rachel Lambert, a leading expert in special education and mathematics education, is an invaluable contribution to our thinking and knowledge of the best ways to support students with learning differences in their understanding of mathematics. A must-read for any educator or parent.

Jo Boaler
Nomellini-Olivier Professor, Stanford
Stanford, CA

This book is long overdue! I applaud Lambert for challenging mathematics educators to reimagine what students with disabilities are capable of in mathematics. Lambert confronts the deficit perspectives that have permeated the way many educators think about students with disabilities in mathematics. Lambert also provides specific examples that show that students with disabilities can engage in rich, cognitively demanding mathematics when given the proper support and guidance.

Kyndall Brown
Executive Director, California Mathematics Project
Los Angeles, CA

All too often in my career, I've heard neurodiverse students discussed in deficit ways in terms of their opportunities to know and do mathematics. Lambert's book provides shining examples of strategies we can use to empower and provide access to neurodiverse students so that they can demonstrate their full mathematical brilliance in math class. The strategies described are simultaneously revelatory and straightforward to implement.

Michael D. Steele
Professor, Ball State University
Muncie, IN

UDL can now truly become a tool that mathematics educators can use to change how they go about designing mathematics experiences for disabled students.

John Staley
Past President, NCSM
Coordinator, Baltimore County Public Schools
Randallstown, MD

This book is a transformer! *Rethinking Disabilities and Mathematics* is a must-read for all educators. Dr. Lambert provides insight into different types of disabilities and strategies to implement UDL Math to engage and support learners in developing positive mathematics identities. She goes beyond strategies and instruction, giving us clarity through the lens of different perspectives that will make educators rethink disability.

Joleigh Honey
Past President, Association of State Supervisor of Mathematics
Author/Consultant, OpenUp Resource High School Mathematics
Executive Committee, Mathematical Sciences (CBMS)
Sandy, UT

As I read this extraordinary book, it felt like I was having a conversation with Rachel Lambert. Connecting with my innermost being in a deep and meaningful way; this is what is needed to change mindsets and practices. The vignettes, coupled with well-documented research, allow the reader to reflect on their own experiences and teaching schema with practical transformative methods from the perspective of not only researchers but also authentically from teachers.

Christina Lincoln-Moore
Elementary Mathematics Coordinator,
Los Angeles County Office of Education
Downey, CA

The word "strength" rarely makes its way into conversations about students' disabilities in school buildings. In Lambert's work, strength is a basic tenet of students with disabilities. From classroom visits to conversations with mathematicians with disabilities, Lambert unveils a landscape of possible math learning with a UDL Math framework and strengths-based pedagogies because disabled learners were never the problem to be fixed in math education, the system is.

Fawn Nguyen
Math Teaching and Learning Specialist, Amplify
Oak View, CA

If there is one book you need to read about the field of special education and mathematics, this is it. Rachel Lambert has torn apart our old tapestry of beliefs and teaching practices and rewoven another with clarity, powerful examples, and research. This book breaks new ground.

Catherine Fosnot
Professor Emerita of Education, City College of New York
Founder, Mathematics in the City
New York, NY

This is a groundbreaking exploration that transcends traditional teaching paradigms and revolutionizes our perspectives on disability in mathematics education. With insightful chapters exploring the brilliance of diverse learners, real-life stories, and rigorous research on UDL, it empowers educators with a strengths-based approach. A transformative guide, it ignites introspection and catalyzes action, shaping a more inclusive mathematical landscape.

Ma Bernadette Andres-Salgarino
Assistant Director, iSTEAM, SCCOE
President, CMC (2024–2025)
San Jose, CA

This is the book I've been hoping for for so long! Lambert dares us to think radically about and reimagine math instruction and disability, while also giving us the practical, classroom-tested tools to bring these bold dreams to life. I feel both inspired and equipped to make real progress in my district with this trusted guide at my side.

Tracy Johnston Zager
Math Coach
and Author of *Becoming the Math Teacher You Wish You'd Had*
Portland, ME

Rethinking
DISABILITY and
MATHEMATICS

To my father, who taught me that normal was boring.
To Dina Williams, who welcomed me to the math community
in Los Angeles.

Rethinking DISABILITY and MATHEMATICS

A UDL Math Classroom Guide for Grades K-8

RACHEL LAMBERT

Foreword by Megan Franke

CORWIN Mathematics

For information:

Corwin
A SAGE Company
2455 Teller Road
Thousand Oaks, California 91320
(800) 233-9936
www.corwin.com

SAGE Publications Ltd.
1 Oliver's Yard
55 City Road
London, EC1Y 1SP
United Kingdom

SAGE Publications India Pvt. Ltd.
Unit No 323-333, Third Floor,
F-Block
International Trade Tower Nehru
Place
New Delhi – 110 019
India

SAGE Publications
Asia-Pacific Pte. Ltd.
18 Cross Street #10-10/11/12
China Square Central
Singapore 048423

Vice President and Editorial Director:
   Monica Eckman
Acquisitions Editor: Debbie Hardin
Senior Editorial Assistant:
   Nyle De Leon
Production Editor: Tori Mirsadjadi
Copy Editor: Sheree Van Vreede
Typesetter: Integra
Proofreader: Barbara Coster
Indexer: Integra
Illustrator: Avery McNiff
Cover Artist: Rasha Hamid
Cover Designer: Gail Buschman
Marketing Manager:
   Margaret O'Connor

Printed in the United States of America.

Paperback ISBN 978-1-0719-2603-1

This book is printed on acid-free paper.

24 25 26 27 28 10 9 8 7 6 5 4 3 2

CONTENTS

Note From the Publisher: The author has provided video and web content throughout the book that is available to you through QR (quick response) codes. To read a QR code, you must have a smartphone or tablet with a camera. We recommend that you download a QR code reader app that is made specifically for your phone or tablet brand.

FOREWORD
By Megan Franke

A number of years ago I was involved in a large-scale study investigating how teachers could use research about the development of students' algebraic thinking to support their classroom practice and student learning. As a part of the study, we individually assessed six randomly selected students in third- through fifth-grade classrooms. When I approached one of the fifth-grade teachers to share the list of students who had been randomly selected, she pointed to the name of one student and told me that I did not want to assess Jayden because he was in special education and struggled with mathematics. I asked if it would be okay if I started our assessment and if Jayden seemed uncomfortable or could not engage the tasks, I would end the assessment and bring him back to class. The teacher agreed.

I discovered that Jayden's solutions were mathematically sophisticated and beyond what we heard from most of the other students I assessed at the school. He could engage in what we term *relational thinking*—when asked to solve a problem like 47 + 35 = _____ + 45 he could say that 45 is 2 less than 47 so the answer has to be 2 more than 35. He thought like this consistently throughout the assessment. I sometimes had to ask him to repeat himself as the numbers he was saying seemed to fly out of his mouth so quickly that I was not quite sure how he was solving the problem and needed to hear it again; but every time, he explained he used relational thinking in mathematically elegant ways. It is not surprising that those working with him at school did not know that he could think in these mathematical ways. School would be teaching Jayden to use the standard algorithm to add 47 and 35 and then subtract 45. Teachers would be working hard to get him to learn it this way, which likely would lead to confusion for Jayden because it is not how he was thinking about the solution to the problem. In fact, how Jayden was thinking about the problem was more efficient, mathematically more sophisticated, and better connected to what he needed for his future mathematical work in algebra.

Schools often do not allow space for students like Jayden to share what they know or solve math problems in ways that make sense to them. This is a challenge of schooling, not of a single teacher, but a challenge that extends to how teaching and learning occurs in classrooms. We expect all students to think the same way, solve problems the same way, use tools in the same way, and all at the same time. Doing so means school only works for certain students—students who think the way the curriculum is asking, are thinking that way when the teacher lands on that page, and they can share what they know in the way the curriculum is asking. This approach provides an extreme challenge for students who work differently, process differently, share what they know differently, and so on. It also provides a challenge for the teachers who work with these students.

In *Rethinking Disability and Mathematics: A UDL Math Classroom Guide for Grades K–8,* Dr. Lambert asks us to disrupt this approach to schooling in mathematics and prompts us instead to see the breadth and depth of students' mathematical capabilities. Students may not know the math that school wants them to know or be able to show what they know in the way school expects, but they know valuable mathematics—such as how to build a Lego structure, draw a picture of their family, or organize their collection of toy cars by type and color. They may know that 4 quarters is a dollar and that means 4 one-fourths is one whole or that you can double a number and then double it again and again and again. Seeing and hearing what young people bring to math class feels like a tall order when working with students with disabilities. I often hear the worry that students with disabilities are behind and cannot participate in the ways we are asking of them. Many educators note that it can be hard to figure out what they know. We worry that we will ask too much of the students and they will get quickly frustrated. In a well-intentioned effort to help students, we reduce the options (fewer tools, less complexity in the task, more practice) and show students what to do. However, reducing options leads us to underestimate students and provide them with little agency. Dr. Lambert provides a vision and practical ways of enacting that vision that move beyond typical schooling responses by centering students and helping us see how to build on what they know and can do.

Dr. Lambert challenges all of us to consider what it means to see, hear, and support students with disabilities in our mathematics classrooms. She asks us to reflect on our views of students with disabilities and their capabilities. She helps us see how much schooling shapes how we think about both what counts as student success and what it means to do mathematics. Yet, she also provides a vision of what classroom mathematics can look like that supports students with disabilities. She provides many real-life vignettes that get to the heart of interaction in math classrooms and what it would look and feel like to support a range of student participation, enable students to share what they know, allow them to take the lead mathematically, and do so in inclusive classrooms.

Brilliance, patience, support, and differential participation come up over and over throughout this book. But so does the reality of schooling for students with disabilities and the challenges that emerge. Dr. Lambert brings forth the voices of teachers and students in classrooms to help all of us see what it means to support students with disabilities and reminds us that supporting students with disabilities means understanding the assets the student brings along with developing particular strategies for supporting them. Dr. Lambert repeatedly reminds us that our challenge as educators is to move beyond seeing what students know as isolated and random ideas but as knowledge that draws on valuable spatial, number, and grouping (and so on) understandings. This groundbreaking book will help educators recognize what students know and can do mathematically as an important part of the development of their mathematical thinking and ultimately what we want them to learn in school mathematics.

PREFACE

I wrote this book because of a puzzle I had as a classroom teacher. I taught for 6 years at River East Elementary School in East Harlem, New York City. It was a progressive, teacher-run school that gave teachers the freedom to develop curriculum. I was initially a special education co-teacher and then took over the classroom teaching for a multi-age, inclusive fifth/sixth-grade classroom. I noticed again and again that students came into my class telling me they were "bad at math" and then began to love the subject once they were allowed to think. I found this particularly true for the students with disabilities in my classroom.

My puzzle emerged once I started reading research on special education and math. I was shocked by what I found. Article after article focused on deficits. Some articles explicitly claimed that students with disabilities should not be exposed to inquiry mathematics and implicitly said that these students did not know how to think on their own.

I knew this was wrong. As a person who had grown up with neurodiversity in my family, friends, church, and community, this deficit attitude toward the potential of neurodiverse and disabled people angered me. This deficit attitude particularly angered me since my students were not only in special education but also Black and Latino/a, and thus they should be offered more educational opportunity, not less. The research seemed to contradict everything I was experiencing as my students grew in their confidence as mathematicians.

This puzzle motivated me to leave the classroom after 10 years and become an educational researcher in meaningful mathematics for students with disabilities, with a particular focus on neurodiverse students of color. My problem of practice has been to better understand the experiences of disabled and neurodiverse students learning mathematics through sense-making.

This book is an existence proof; students with disabilities can and do become confident mathematical thinkers. Teachers all over the world are doing the hard work of making this happen. I am here to share these stories. This book has grown out of 15 years of research, as well as out of continued work in schools doing professional development. Teachers from research projects, whose identity I need to protect as part of the terms of research, are given pseudonyms (i.e., Mr. Jay and Ms. Rey). Teachers from my professional development work are referred to by their first names. All students, whether I met them in a visit to a class or in a research project, are given pseudonyms. I use line drawings taken from photographs to show how students and teachers engaged with each other while preserving anonymity.

NOTES ON LANGUAGE

Writing a book about disability means dealing with complexity in terms of language. First, for advocates in the Disability Rights Movement and academics in disability studies, the word *disability* is not a negative word but a word that is rich with political power. I often get asked why I don't use *differently abled*, *special needs*, *dis/ability*, or some other "nicer" term. These alternative terms are almost always created by nondisabled adults to refer to children with disabilities. Some disabled adults find these kinds of euphemisms insulting, so I do not use them.

I use both person-first language and identity-first language in this book. Person-first language puts the person first and the disability second, such as *person with autism*. This approach is often preferred by those with intellectual disabilities (*a person with an intellectual disability*). Other disability communities tend to prefer identity-first language, such as *autistic person*. Increasingly, identity-first language such as *disabled person* is used by disabled people with pride as it emphasizes how disability does not reside within the individual, but in the environment. I use both kinds of language in this book to respect multiple points of view. Just as in any other social justice movement, people have the right to name themselves, and I try to respect that with my language. While at times in this book I am writing about the many different categories that we currently understand as disability, including sensory disabilities or mobility disabilities, I primarily focus on neurodiversity in this book. At times I discuss disability and neurodiversity, and at other times I use disability as an all-encompassing word that includes neurodiversity.

ACKNOWLEDGMENTS

This book relies on the generosity of teachers who have let me into their classrooms to see the way they empower students with disabilities to be mathematical thinkers: Sussan De Matta, Hannah Benavidez, Kayla Martinez, Dina Williams, Kit Golan, Suzanne Huerta, and all those teachers who collaborated with me on research that led to this book. Much of this book comes from a collaboration with the Downey Unified School District, particularly with Melissa Canham, who trusted me to work with special education teachers in her district. Another valued partner has been the Santa Barbara Unified School District. Others I cannot name because the research agreements protect the district's privacy, but I want to thank all these educators from teachers to administrators for collaborating with me.

To Tracy Zager, who helped me dream up a book like this with Andrew Gael many moons ago. It has changed shape, but the initial vision was collective. I would not have persevered without your support through years and years, Tracy!

For Debbie Hardin at Corwin who has coached me through this process with kindness and flexibility. Thank you for being my guide to writing my first book.

I also thank the participants in two courses on Design Thinking and Universal Design for Learning, as well as Kara Imm for our long-time collaboration that has taught me so much.

I thank my research colleagues, particularly my students who have worked with me on so many of these projects: Avery McNiff, Tomy Nguyen, Monica Mendoza, Rachel Schuck, and Sunghee Chao. I thank my colleagues on the project with Ms. Rey: Shayne Brophy, Trisha Sugita, Cathery Yeh, and Jessica Hunt. I also am particularly indebted to the work of Marilyn Monroy Castro and Rebeca Mireles-Rios for the chapters on Mr. Jay. My dissertation chair, Wendy Luttrell, helped me see Luis and Ms. Marquez. And I am grateful for my collaborations with colleagues Edmund Harriss, Paulo Tan, Alexis Padilla, Katherine Lewis, and David Hernández-Saca who have all influenced this book.

Further thanks go to colleagues at the California Mathematics Project, particularly those at the University of California, Santa Barbara (UCSB) Math Project. Also, my colleagues at the University of California, Los Angeles Math Project who have accepted me into the math community here in Los Angeles.

Much of what I share here came from teaching at River East, a small teacher-run progressive elementary school in East Harlem, New York. I am forever grateful for my innovative colleagues there, as well as for the children and families who taught me so much.

A special thank-you to Avery McNiff for taking research photographs and turning them into art. Rasha Hamid, whom I taught with in New York City, created the cover art for this book. Special thanks go to them both.

Funding for the projects included came from the Spencer Foundation, UCSB Academic Senate, Chapman University Faculty Grants, California Partnership for Math and Science Education, and the Santa Barbara Unified School District.

Finally, I want to thank my family growing up, who taught me about neurodiversity. I owe a lot to what I learned from my friend Ali. I am grateful beyond words for Kevin, Rufus, Jack, and Ruby who supported me to write, write, write!

PUBLISHER'S ACKNOWLEDGMENTS

Corwin gratefully acknowledges the contributions of the following reviewers:

Jennifer Hein deMause
Math and Special Education Specialist
San Francisco, CA

Jody Guarino
Math Coordinator, Orange County Department of Education
San Clemente, CA

Joanna Hayman
K–5 Math Coach, UCLA Mathematics Project
Redondo Beach, CA

P. Renee Hill-Cunningham
Associate Professor of Mathematics Education, University of Mississippi
Houston, MS

ACKNOWLEDGMENTS

Joleigh D. Honey
Past President, Association of State Supervisors of Mathematics
Author & Consultant, OpenUp Resources High School Mathematics
Executive Committee, Conference Board of the Mathematical
Sciences (CBMS)
Sandy, UT

Rosa Serratore
PreK–12 district mathematics coordinator
NCSM regional director
CMC board member
Santa Monica, CA

John William Staley
Past President NCSM
Coordinator, Baltimore County Public Schools
Randallstown, MD

Michael D. Steele
Professor, Ball State University
Zionsville, IN

Catherine Anne Vittorio
Principal, Etiwanda School District
Etwinda, CA

ABOUT THE AUTHOR

**Rachel Lambert** is an associate professor in special education and mathematics education at the University of California, Santa Barbara. Before becoming a professor, she worked for more than 10 years as both a special education and a general education inclusion teacher in New York City, San Francisco, and Los Angeles. Dr. Lambert researches how students of color with disabilities construct identities as math learners and the role of emotions in mathematics. She also researches UDL in the area of mathematics, as well as neurodiversity in mathematics. Her goal is to increase access to meaningful mathematics for students with disabilities.

CHAPTER 1

TRUST IN THEIR THINKING

IN THIS CHAPTER, WE WILL...

- Visit a fifth-grade special education classroom in which students are engaged in meaningful mathematical inquiry
- Provide an overview of this book

Trust has been my key to becoming an effective math teacher. I trust that my students have the ability to make sense of math. I trust that they will arrive at the understandings they need at their pace. Trusting my students has empowered them. In my classroom, students know that I will not be coming to the rescue at the first sign of trouble because I believe in their own abilities. When they get stuck I redirect them back to themselves, "What do you know about numbers that can help you?" "It's hard," they tell me. "Yup, but you'll figure it out," and eventually they do. They do because through my trust, they trust themselves. We need to empower students to trust themselves.

Figure 1.1 • *Sussan De Matta, fifth-grade special education teacher*

—Sussan De Matta, fifth-grade special education teacher (Figure 1.1) ●

I begin this book with this idea, expressed by this exceptional math teacher, that when we as teachers trust in the thinking of our students, especially our students with disabilities, we create the conditions our students need to trust themselves as mathematical thinkers. When we, their teachers, believe that our students can and will solve complex problems, they will be able to.

In my work for almost 30 years in education, first as a general education and special education classroom teacher and now as a teacher educator and researcher, I have seen students with disabilities underestimated and over-scaffolded. These students are conceptualized as broken, as needing to be fixed. Their mathematical thinking is not trusted. Deficit conceptions of learners turn into deficit pedagogies that assume students cannot think for themselves. And these problems become intensified for students with disabilities who are Black, Latino/a, Indigenous, and/or multilingual.

This book is dedicated to overturning deficit pedagogies and returning mathematical agency to all students with disabilities. Mathematics can and should be a transformative space for these students, where they can discover their power and potential.

In this book, you will be invited into classrooms like Sussan's that provide students the space and support to allow students with disabilities to thrive as mathematical sense-makers. We will meet teachers who believe that all their students are mathematical thinkers and who design classrooms to build on students' thinking. We will highlight the mathematical thinking and brilliance of students with disabilities. We will frame these classrooms using Universal Design for Learning in Mathematics (UDL Math), which applies the theoretical framework of UDL to research in meaningful mathematics.

Before we jump into Sussan's classroom, you need to do some math! In order to appreciate the mathematical brilliance of the children, you need to tackle the problem first. So grab some scratch paper and get started. I recommend starting off, as children most often do, by drawing.

Try It

1. I have 12 cans of paint. I need $\frac{1}{4}$th of a can of paint to paint one chair. How many chairs can I paint?

2. What if it takes $\frac{3}{4}$ths of a can of paint to paint one chair? How many chairs can I paint with 12 cans of paint?

What did you notice about this problem? It's a tricky one, for sure. Some might start by drawing paint cans and chairs and then distributing $\frac{1}{4}$th of each can of paint to each chair. Some might find a ratio and work from there. Maybe some might think: If $\frac{1}{4}$th of a can of paint will cover 1 chair, then $\frac{4}{4}$ths of a can of paint will cover 4 chairs, and then they could multiply 4×12 to get the total. Some might have added or skip-counted the $\frac{1}{4}$ths until they got to 48. In that case, you might have seen this situation as

$$\frac{1}{4} + \frac{1}{4} + \frac{1}{4} + \frac{1}{4} + \frac{1}{4} + \frac{1}{4} + \frac{1}{4} + \frac{1}{4} + \frac{1}{4} + \frac{1}{4} + \frac{1}{4} + \frac{1}{4} + \frac{1}{4} + \frac{1}{4} + \frac{1}{4} + \frac{1}{4} = 48$$

Or perhaps as $12 \div \frac{1}{4} = 48$, thinking about it as how many groups of $\frac{1}{4}$ths fit into 12?

Although this is a division of fractions problem, that is often not initially obvious to either children or adults. The first two strategies I described use multiplication to figure out how many groups of $\frac{1}{4}$th. For a problem like this, which Susan Empson and Linda Levi (2011) call a *Multiple Groups Problem (Division)*, kids usually draw it out to understand the relationships involved. I am not embarrassed to say that I do the same when I am multiplying or dividing with fractions. I always need to see the situation in a model before I understand exactly what is happening. In this way, I am like most students, who begin with *direct modeling*, a term from cognitively guided instruction (CGI, Carpenter et al., 2015) that simply means that a student chooses to represent each item in a problem to solve it, either with manipulatives or through drawing.

This kind of fraction division problem is included in the fifth grade in the Common Core State Standards (CCSS; National Governors Association Center for Best Practices & Council of Chief State School Officers, 2010)—students are asked to solve real-world fraction division problems like the one in this case, a whole number divided by a unit fraction ($12 \div \frac{1}{4}$). The standards set the expectation that students will begin by using visual models to solve these problems, drawing on their knowledge of both fractions and how multiplication and division are related. As we will see, Sussan offered her special education students the choice of solving with either $\frac{1}{4}$ths or $\frac{3}{4}$ths, the first option meeting grade-level standards and the second number choice (a common fraction with a number other than 1 in the numerator) going beyond them.

SUSSAN'S FIFTH-GRADE SPECIAL EDUCATION CLASS

Sussan taught a fifth-grade special education class, in which all the students received special education services. The students in Sussan's class had IEPs for either learning disabilities or autism, with multiple students also receiving speech and language services. Her students were primarily Latino/a, and several were multilingual learners. She teaches all subjects to the students, who move in and out of the room as some attend general education for certain subjects.

Through multiple conversations with Sussan, I learned that her ultimate goal in her mathematics teaching is for her students to see themselves as successful mathematics learners, to be able to solve problems and persevere, to engage in mathematical discussions, and to reason quantitatively. Beginning with grade-level standards, she flexibly designs her curriculum based on what her kids are currently thinking and doing, using her professional development work in CGI with her district to help her notice and build on student thinking. Throughout, she has a focus on helping her students become strategic learners.

I VISITED HER class with a group of special educators from her district who were interested in teaching mathematics through problem-solving. Sussan started with a warm-up in which she showed four images of fractions and asked students the question, "Which One Doesn't Belong?" (which she found on the website Fraction Talks [https://bit.ly/3EVJJG6]). She started by giving a little independent think time; then the students talked in pairs about what they noticed; and then they shared with the whole group. She annotated the image, using a tablet that was connected to the classroom projector. She added both the words students used and the way they named the fractions (Figure 1.2).

> ## Try It
>
> Which one doesn't belong? Why? Can you make an argument for each shape in Figure 1.2?

Discussion of this image was short, no more than 7 minutes, but it was a lovely way to get ready for a longer fraction problem. A student volunteered the upper right image of a hexagon (B) as the one that did not belong, as it was a different fraction, $\frac{2}{6}$s versus $\frac{1}{3}$rd. Other students disagreed, arguing that since those fractions were equivalent, this one did belong! When one student proposed that the bottom left triangle (C) did not belong, others nodded. This

Figure 1.2 · *Which One Doesn't Belong image*

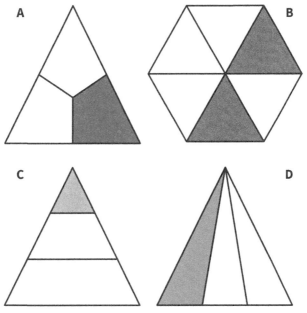

SOURCE: Reprinted with permission from Nat Bantling at FractionTalks.com. Image created by Denise Gaskins.

was the only fraction that was not equal to $\frac{1}{3}$. One student argued that it wasn't a fraction at all because it was "uneven." Sussan designed this discussion as a warm-up and as a chance to use some vocabulary around fractions (equivalence, equal shares). I noticed that these students had a strong grasp of the fundamentals of fractional equivalence.

Next, Sussan moved to the story problem that was the main focus of the class. She started by introducing students to the context of painting chairs, showing a funny GIF about painting. She asked the students what they knew about painting at home. She gestured painting a chair while she showed multiple images of painting a chair and cans of paint. Students talked in pairs about what they knew about painting. When she felt sure they all understood the context of painting furniture using cans of paint, she introduced the 12 chairs problem. She showed the following slide, reading the text out loud twice. While keeping 12 chairs constant, she gave two number choices, either $\frac{1}{4}$th or $\frac{3}{4}$ths a can of paint for each chair.

Your parents have asked you to help them paint some chairs. You have 12 cans of paint. If you need _____ cans of paint to paint a chair, how many chairs can you paint?

$$[\frac{1}{4} \text{ or } \frac{3}{4}]$$

SOURCE: istock.com/anchiy

As the students went off to work, scattering around the classroom into desks, or sprawling out on the carpet, Sussan and her two paraprofessionals supported students. One paraprofessional helped a student who wanted to use manipulatives. This drew me over to watch as I am always fascinated/ frightened when kids use manipulatives for fractional share problems. Take a moment and think about how you might use Cuisenaire rods to solve this problem. Confusing? Yes. Using manipulatives means that the kids need to assign a fractional value to a piece, and then make sense of the problem, almost creating another layer to their proportional thinking. I noticed that the paraprofessional did not dissuade the student, who counted out 12 rods, looked at them, looked at his paper, and then changed his mind and drew out the problem instead. Another paraprofessional was supporting a student who asked her to scribe for her. As the student verbally explained her strategy, the paraprofessional wrote down her words.

I became fascinated watching one girl, who we will call Amaris, who drew 12 boxes, which represented the cans of paint. She partitioned them into fourths and then seemed to be stuck. After a moment or so looking at the paper, she started drawing chairs (a reconstruction of her work can be seen in Figure 1.3). She meticulously drew each chair as she connected each chair to a $\frac{1}{4}$th of a can of paint. She eventually drew each of the 48 chairs necessary for her number choice. It was quite something to watch her. I looked around and saw four other teachers gathered, all of us seemingly spellbound by her work (Figure 1.3).

Figure 1.3 · *Amaris's strategy for 12 chairs and $\frac{1}{4}$th a can of paint*

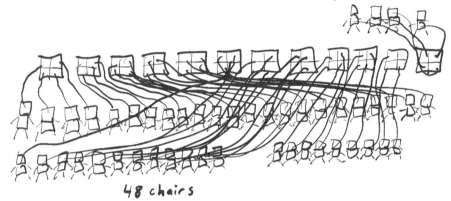

Later, I asked Sussan if Amaris did this kind of modeling every time. Sussan told me that in Amaris's previous classrooms, she had not been given access to solving problems on her own, and so it had taken her a few months to feel comfortable making sense of a problem. At the beginning of the year, she would ask Sussan to tell her how to solve every problem. Again and again, Sussan encouraged her to draw it out or to use manipulatives. It took time and a lot of patience for both teacher and student, but Amaris was now learning how to direct model through drawing. It took time for her to trust herself, and we were honored to be able to see her just beginning to trust that she could figure it out herself.

Sussan walked around the room, observing students quietly from a little distance. At times, she would bend down to a child and ask a few questions about what they were thinking. Her presence communicated a very quiet support, a sense that she believed these students could solve this complex problem.

Although most kids in the class choose $\frac{1}{4}$th, one child, Marty, immediately chose $\frac{3}{4}$ths as his number choice. He solved it by drawing the cans of paint, partitioning them into fourths, and grouping the fractional parts into $\frac{3}{4}$ths (Figure 1.4).

Figure 1.4 • *Marty's strategy for 12 chairs and $\frac{3}{4}$th a can of paint*

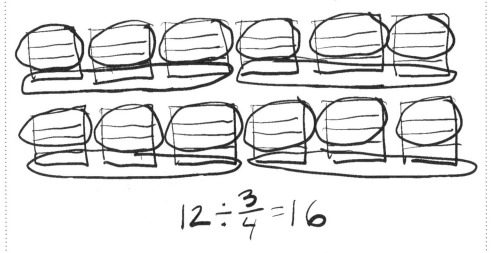

I noticed that Marty immediately wrote an equation to describe the problem, correctly identifying the problem as division.

Another student, Erica, chose $\frac{1}{4}$th. She partitioned one can of paint, finding that one can of paint worked for four chairs. She then skip-counted by four 12 times to get her answer (Figure 1.5).

Figure 1.5 • *Erica's strategy for 12 chairs and $\frac{1}{4}$th a can of paint*

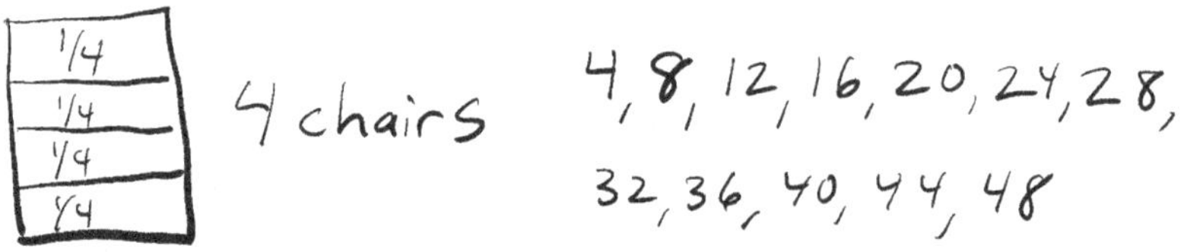

As the class gathered for a share on the rug, Sussan joined their circle, arm in a brace. She first had all the students turn and talk, explaining their strategy to a partner. She listened in on these shares. Afterward, Susan asked Marty to share. As he shared, she rewrote his strategy on her tablet, which was projected onto a screen in the front of the room. He did so confidently, sharing his thinking with little prompting from his teacher. After he had shared through his process once, she had him talk through it again, stopping at several points for students to turn and talk about what he had done. Next, she had Erica share. Again, the student shared once all the way through and then again more slowly with time for students to restate to their partners. At the end of the discussion, Sussan summarized the mathematical strategies used by students. She asked them to raise their hand to indicate which strategy they used. Sussan would remind them of these strategies the next day as they tackled a similar problem (Figure 1.6).

Figure 1.6 • *Sussan listens as her students share their strategies*

I noticed that Sussan was engaged in coaching her students not only on the math, but also in developing their own metacognition, including understanding and regulating their emotional response. For example, she listened in on one child, Johan, as he shared his thinking with his partner. As Johan shared, he kept recounting the number of shares, losing track several times of his count. He looked up at Sussan, clearly frustrated, and no longer sure of his answer. Sussan said, "It seems like you are now revising your thinking. What could help you be more sure of your answer?" The student thought and then said, "Recounting by myself." Sussan nodded, and the student got up and went to the back of the room and began recounting by himself. When he returned to his partner, he was now confident of his answer. He also had practiced noticing his own emotional response and finding a way to become emotionally and mathematically sure of his answer. I saw this kind of strategic coaching multiple times across visits to Sussan's classroom.

I noticed that some of Sussan's students had different ways of communicating their thinking. Although most students were sitting on the rug during the launch and share, one student, we will call Francisco, was sitting at his own table, a tablet in hand. He appeared to be concentrating on that tablet during the discussion, yet he would occasionally shout out comments that were connected to the problem without raising his hand. Many teachers would have considered his behavior inappropriate. For Sussan, his different way of engaging did not seem to be a problem. She did not call attention to it, but sometimes she ignored his comments and at other times incorporated them into the discussion, restating what he said.

When we debriefed, Francisco's previous special education teacher, who was observing with me, was blown away by this child's engagement, a dramatic improvement from when he was in her class. According to her, Francisco had previously not engaged in any math work that was not one-on-one with a paraprofessional. Francisco solved the problem and was consistently engaged. His engagement just looked different than other kids' engagement. And when seen in the context of his development as an individual, it was something to celebrate indeed! ●

MATHEMATICAL PEDAGOGY OF TRUST

Some fifth-grade teachers would have balked at giving such a challenging problem to their students. In particular, some teachers would worry about giving it to students with disabilities. They might wonder whether the problem somehow had too much language, which would confuse the students. Some teachers would preteach, giving the students a specific procedure to use to solve. Or they would walk them through the problem, step by step. Imagine for a moment how this lesson would have been different if the students were asked to use a procedure for dividing fractions. I remember learning the phrase, "Ours is not to wonder why, just invert and multiply," along with the procedure. In this case, for $\frac{3}{4}$ths, students would be taught to do the following:

$$12 \div \frac{3}{4} = 12 \times \frac{4}{3} = \frac{48}{3} = 16$$

Does this procedure match how these students were thinking? Forcing students to use this particular procedure, which many students (and adults) do not understand, would shut down the beautiful proportional and relational thinking that emerged from this problem quite naturally. Sussan believes that sense-making comes first. She trusts in the thinking of her students. She knew they could solve this problem using their mathematical intuition and what they already knew about fractions.

Sussan uses Story Problems as an almost daily routine (Carpenter et al., 2015). She chooses a problem designed to help students explore important grade-level mathematics, as in how to model and understand fraction division. For several days in a row, she gives increasingly complex Story Problems. For more about Story Problems designed to develop deep understanding of fractions, see "Unpacking a Core Idea: Developing Fractional Understanding Through Story Problems" (p. 210).

This routine has a consistent structure that helps students understand and meet expectations for behavior (Table 1.1).

Table 1.1 · *Teacher and student actions during Story Problems*

Story Problems	Teachers are:	Students are:
Launch	Introducing the story problem in an engaging, comprehensible way using visuals and storytelling.	Listening and restating aspects of the story situation.
Work Time	Conferencing with students as needed to support their thinking, gathering information for the share.	Solving the problems using methods of their choice, talking with peers about their solutions.
Share	Leading a share, ending with consolidation of concepts and/or student strategies.	Sharing (2–3 students) their thinking, either rewriting their own solution or having the teacher do so.

For more about facilitating Story Problems, see the Teaching Practice Guides on CGI Story Problems online, as well as Chapters 8 and 12.

Online Teaching Practice Guide

qrs.ly/l7f7rwq

To read a QR code, you must have a smartphone or tablet with a camera. We recommend that you download a QR code reader app that is made specifically for your phone or tablet brand.

Sussan's classroom is a powerful counterargument to circulating deficit myths about the mathematical potential of students with disabilities. I hear sometimes from educators (and researchers) that students with disabilities cannot "handle" inquiry-based teaching, that these students are not capable of developing their own strategies, and that these students need to be told how to think.

This brings me to perhaps the most important idea in this book. I strongly believe that students with disabilities are underperforming in mathematics in part because we don't trust in their thinking. In fact, we have created *deficit mythologies* about the mathematical capacities of students with disabilities. I write about how these deficit mythologies have emerged and about how we have created systems that perpetuate them. The opposite of deficit thinking is trusting in our students' thinking.

> **I strongly believe that students with disabilities**
> **are underperforming in mathematics in part**
> **because we don't trust in their thinking.**

Trust is communicated through the choice of problem, the choice in how to solve it, and the time Sussan gives them to think. Each time I am in Sussan's classroom, I am struck by her silences, her wait time. When she asks a question, she waits. When a student is thinking about what to say, clearly needing an additional minute to formulate their thoughts, she waits. There is no edge to her waiting, no sense that she is anxious to move on. I very much wish that I had this quality as a teacher and a parent. Many of her students have language processing differences, so it might take longer for them to be able to think out a strategy in their mind, or be able to process what she or another student has said. Her waiting—patient, not rushing, kind—was the secret sauce to her students' exceptional engagement in her class.

THIS BOOK

This book offers a vision of how we can design our math classrooms to become spaces in which students with disabilities thrive as mathematical thinkers, spaces that also become more flexible, more supportive, and more welcoming of all of our learners. When we design from the margins, we can transform our classrooms and our schools. A key idea of this book is that what students with disabilities need to succeed in math is not qualitatively different than what all kids need. It is not as if students (without disabilities) all learn one way, and then students with disabilities all learn another way. Instead, ALL learners are variable. Some students, with and without disabilities, have a particularly hard time paying attention in lectures. That describes a very wide swath of the population, actually. The people with the most challenges in attention might identify as having Attention Deficit Hyperactivity Disorder (ADHD). Since differences in attention occur across everyone, adapting classrooms to work for students with ADHD will not just help those students, but all of us. This is a key idea of Universal Design for Learning (UDL; Meyer et al., 2014), which we explore throughout the book.

> A key idea of this book is that what students with disabilities need to succeed in math is not qualitatively different than what all kids need.

The first big idea of the book is that **it matters how we think about disability.** It matters because kids take up how we frame them, and it matters because if educators think students with disabilities cannot do something, they won't give them opportunities to try. In Chapter 2, we will explore different models for understanding disability, such as the medical model, social model, and neurodiversity. We will also explore learner variability, the model for understanding learners used in UDL. Reframing students with disabilities from deficit to asset models is a necessary precondition to trusting their thinking.

Next we explore how **it matters how we think about the goal of mathematics itself**. Mathematics is not just memorizing. We should not make kids wait to have fun in mathematics until they have endured school mathematics. Math is and can be joyful, creative, and meaningful. Chapter 3 explores these ideas through a study with dyslexic mathematicians.

Deficit thinking about kids leads to deficit pedagogies, which is explored in Chapter 4. This chapter explores the differences between inquiry and explicit instruction, why explicit instruction is recommended so often for students with disabilities, and how to make informed choices about pedagogy. We move beyond seeing these two pedagogies as a binary, and instead we think about how great teachers combine elements of both using a middle school math teacher named Mr. Jay.

The next section of the book provides an in-depth exploration of UDL Math (Lambert, 2021). I have long loved UDL, which is a research-based approach to understanding classrooms and pedagogy grounded in the learning sciences and neuroscience (Meyer et al., 2014). UDL Math is my version of UDL that is based in research in the learning and teaching of mathematics, as well as in student voice. The big idea in these chapters is that **we can design math classrooms that work for variability by designing from the margins.** Math classrooms focused on meaning-making can be flexible, can be multimodal, and can support strategic development. Chapter 5 is an introduction to UDL Math, including a history of Universal Design. Chapter 6 follows two early childhood teachers, Ms. Diaz and Ms. Murphy, as they redesign group work in Ms. Diaz's inclusive second-grade classroom. They use a simple process that is described in three gestures with my hands (Table 1.2).

Table 1.2 • *UDL Math process*

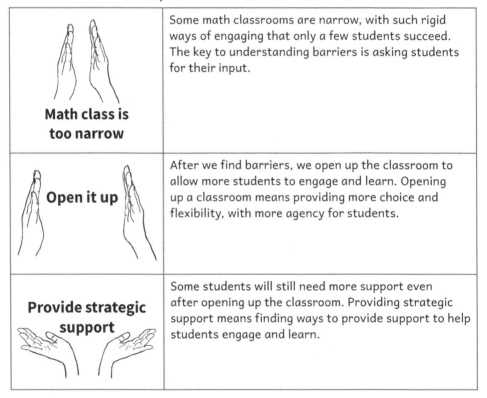

Math class is too narrow	Some math classrooms are narrow, with such rigid ways of engaging that only a few students succeed. The key to understanding barriers is asking students for their input.
Open it up	After we find barriers, we open up the classroom to allow more students to engage and learn. Opening up a classroom means providing more choice and flexibility, with more agency for students.
Provide strategic support	Some students will still need more support even after opening up the classroom. Providing strategic support means finding ways to provide support to help students engage and learn.

The final section of the book is a series of classroom stories. We meet teachers as they engage in redesigning some aspect of their practice to better serve disabled and/or neurodiverse students. These chapters are sequenced by the math content the teachers are working on, so that as a reader, you begin with children learning to count and finish with students learning algebra and fractions. Throughout, we visit classrooms that are inclusive, where the teacher is a general education teacher, as well as special education classrooms, where the teacher is a special education teacher. The teachers are a talented and diverse group, including teachers who identify as neurodiverse or disabled.

In Chapter 7, we explore how to invest time in core ideas. We see the power of repeated engagement in a routine like Counting Collections that helps students develop core ideas about number in a K–1 special education classroom taught by Hannah Benavidez. Special education teacher Kayla Martinez shows how to engage a special education class (K–3) in story problems, while supporting students with language processing challenges (Chapter 8). Dina Williams, teaching an inclusive second-grade classroom, engages in a carefully designed sequence to develop her students' understanding of the open number line and multidigit addition (Chapter 9).

The next two chapters are about students developing understanding of multiplication and division, and both come from my own research on agentic intervention in multiplicative thinking. In Chapter 10, I explore my experience designing multiplication intervention for two boys in fourth and fifth grade, with a focus on math fact fluency. Chapter 11 tells the story of Yola, an undergraduate researcher who finds a way to increase the participation and the understanding of Inez, a fourth-grade girl, in a number strings routine.

In Chapter 12, we enter Ms. Rey's inclusive fifth-grade classroom to learn how she creates a classroom environment that supports neurodiverse students, as well as her use of equal sharing fraction problems. In Chapter 13, we follow Kit Golan and their class as they take us through a Connecting Representations Instructional Routine (Kelemanik et al., 2016) in which students connect double number lines with algebraic expressions.

The last two chapters relate to assessment. In Chapter 14, we return to Mr. Jay's classroom to follow his experiments in assessment and grading in his seventh- and eighth-grade classrooms. Finally, in Chapter 15, we follow special educator Suzanne Huerta as she rethinks Individualized Education Program (IEP) goals in math for her fifth graders.

As you read, you may want to know more about the mathematics content of the chapter. Each classroom chapter (Chapters 7–15) ends with a feature on the math content. If you want to learn more about a particular teaching practice, such as Which One Doesn't Belong or Story Problems, I have created Teaching Practice Guides on my website (mathematizing4all.com) which have links to resources. Also at my website, you can find my research articles in open access format.

 mathematizing4all.com

REFLECTION QUESTIONS

1. What have been your experiences teaching students with disabilities or being a disabled student learning mathematics? What brought you to this book?

2. What did you notice and wonder about Sussan's class doing the 12 chairs problem? What questions would you want to ask her or the students?

3. What do you wonder about doing a story problem in your classroom?

4. What questions do you have about teaching math to disabled students that you hope I answer in this book?

PART 1

SHIFTING OUR CONCEPTIONS

CHAPTER 2

RETHINKING DISABILITY

IN THIS CHAPTER, WE WILL...

- Meet Luis and his teachers
- Explore why it matters *how* we think about disability
- Investigate multiple ways disability is framed and how this matters in math
- Learn from an insider perspective on dyscalculia

I FIRST MET Luis in his sixth-grade math classroom, co-taught by Mr. Pierce, his math teacher, and Ms. Scott, his special education teacher. I watched as Luis walked into the classroom of approximately 24 students, grabbed a chair and a desk, and pulled them away from the other students. As the class began, I saw him working studiously on a challenging math problem, head bent over his work. After about 20 minutes, he looked up and got the attention of Ms. Scott, who immediately walked over. The pair of them spent the next 30 minutes deep in conversation about his unique strategy of adding fractions. Luis was exploring what it meant to share across numerators and denominators and whether the answer had the same ratio.

Mr. Pierce called the class to attention to discuss the answers. There was no discussion of students' strategies, just students offering answers for each problem. The same few students were raising their hands, their answers all correct. Ms. Scott broke in, asking whether Luis could share his strategy of adding fractions. Luis then went up to the board and showed how he tried to share across the numerators of fractions with dissimilar denominators. It was a lengthy explanation, and it seemed as if Mr. Pierce was not sure how to respond. Luis's strategy did not yet work. It was also completely unrelated to the common denominator strategy that Mr. Pierce had demonstrated at the beginning of the class. Nevertheless, Luis was exploring the relationships between the numerators and the denominators, a complex undertaking with rich mathematical possibility. I wondered how uncomfortable Mr. Pierce might have felt: Was Luis confusing not only himself but also the rest of the class? Not sure what to do, Mr. Pierce thanked Luis for sharing and then moved on. ●

As part of my ongoing research on how students with learning disabilities experience math class (Lambert, 2015), I brought Luis up in an interview later that day with these two co-teachers. It became quite clear that Mr. Pierce and Ms. Scott had very different perspectives on Luis. Ms. Scott spoke about how Luis would never give up when solving a math problem and how much mathematical knowledge his unique strategies revealed. Mr. Pierce nodded but added, "But his strategies sometimes don't work." He also talked about Luis's low score on the math standardized test and how Luis never seemed to memorize the procedures that Mr. Pierce taught. Ms. Scott appeared to feel defensive on Luis's behalf, insisting, "If I have one student in my career who actually becomes a mathematician, it will be Luis." Mr. Pierce did not disagree, but he looked quizzical and asked a question about Luis's learning disability and related difficulties.

How can two teachers have such different conceptions of a student's mathematical aptitude? For Ms. Scott, Luis is an iconoclastic mathematical innovator, a potential mathematician. For Mr. Pierce, Luis is barely able to replicate procedures. Is this about Luis? Or do these teachers have different ideas about ability and disability in mathematics? Do they even agree about what mathematics is?

A caring, gentle math teacher, Mr. Pierce taught in a traditional fashion, demonstrating procedures, providing examples, asking students to complete worksheets, and then sharing answers. He wanted to learn more about teaching inquiry-based mathematics, but he was hesitant. He worried that students may not learn what they needed to pass the state tests if he no longer modeled particular procedures. Ms. Scott, a special educator, saw her work in the math classroom as developing students' confidence in mathematics. Ms. Scott valued Luis's creativity and engagement in problem solving since that was her goal as a math teacher. Mr. Pierce, on the other hand, had goals focused on students learning the procedures needed on tests. Since that goal was challenging for Luis, Mr. Pierce saw him as a problem to be fixed and hoped that Ms. Scott could do so with her expertise. For him the goal was procedures first and problem solving second. For Ms. Scott, problem solving was the primary goal. So not only did they see Luis differently, but they also saw mathematics differently.

But how did Luis see himself? Luis persisted in seeing himself as a mathematical thinker, all through the 3 years of middle school through which I followed him. In seventh grade, he told me that he liked "problems that give me problems," which he compared to worksheets, "which are nothing." I saw him hide interesting math tasks under his textbook and keep working on them in secret. When I asked him what kind of math learner he was, he responded immediately, "The talking kind," and went on to tell me that what he valued about himself was how he continually questioned mathematics, always looking for another way. Despite a challenging relationship with his eighth-grade math teacher, when I asked him at the end of the year how he felt about math, he smiled and told me, "I still love math."

DISABILITY IS COMPLEX

Disability is a very broad concept, including multiple kinds of cognitive, mobility, and other differences. Figure 2.1 approximates how complex the category of disability is (not every disability is represented).

Figure 2.1 · *The concept of disability*

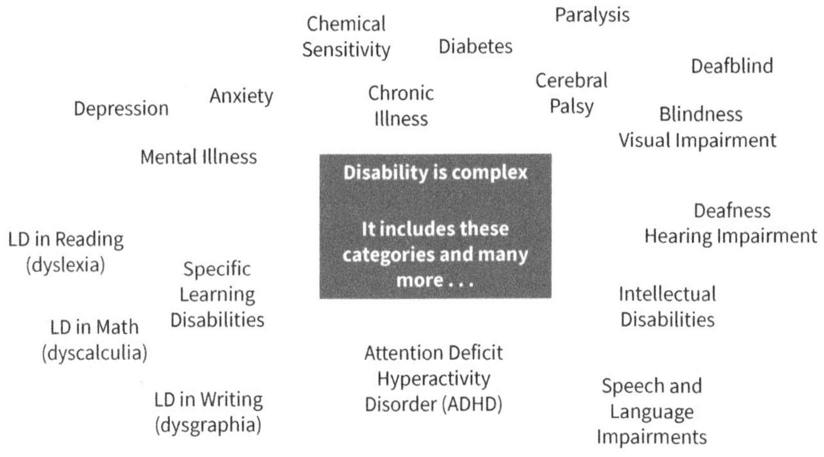

Disability includes sensory differences, such as visual and hearing impairments. Other disabilities include cerebral palsy and other mobility differences. Disability includes anxiety and depression, two very common human differences. It also includes cognitive differences, known as neurodiversity, which include learning disabilities, intellectual disabilities, autism, and Attention Deficit Hyperactivity Disorder (ADHD). Learning disability (LD) is an umbrella category that includes difficulties in reading, writing, and math, often known, respectively, as dyslexia, dysgraphia, and dyscalculia. This chapter and the next are focused on dyslexia and dyscalculia, which we will explore in depth.

Disability Is All Around Us

Disability is part of the human condition. More than 20% of people in the United States have disabilities, a number that has increased since the coronavirus 2019 (COVID-19) pandemic began. Many teachers have disabilities. Disability is something I grew up with: kids in the neighborhood and at church, adults, my childhood best friend, multiple members of my family. To me, and to most of us, these are natural parts of life. Yet I noticed as a child that one neighborhood friend, who had Down syndrome, was in separate classes held in the basement of our high school. I remember wondering why.

Individuals with disabilities often identify in multiple categories. For example, it is common for a person with LD to also have a diagnosis of ADHD. Each category holds tremendous diversity; ADHD, for example, can be experienced quite differently by different individuals. And some communities do not identify as disabled, particularly the Deaf community. Instead, the community understands itself as a language minority.

People with disabilities are as diverse and complex as the rest of the human population, including race, gender, and linguistic diversity. All disabled people are intersectional in their identities, meaning that they are complex, whole human beings. Autism and dyslexia are predominately associated with white males, despite the diversity that exists in these disability categories. Although as a whole, students with disabilities comprise 15% of the school population, 19% of Native American students and 17% of Black students received special education services in 2022, meaning that these students are more likely to be in special education than other students (NAEP Office of Special Education Programs, 2023). Special education has not meaningfully dealt with these issues, and as a field, it tends to be color-evasive, assuming that disability is the most important focus and minimizing the role of race (Annamma et al., 2018).

Yet race and other aspects of culture and identity matter tremendously for disabled youth. In middle school, Luis was labeled as having a learning disability in reading—what would be known now as dyslexia but was not named as such in the school system he attended at that time. That was not the only disability label Luis had been given in school. In elementary school, his Individualized Education Program (IEP) had the primary disability listed as behavior disorder, with LD secondary. But when he was in fifth grade and moving to middle school, his teachers and family held an IEP meeting. They decided to remove the label of behavior disorder both because he no longer had those difficulties, and because it was far too risky for him to have the behavior disorder label as a Latino. Latinos with this label are three times as likely as white boys with the same label to be placed in special-education-only settings (Skiba et al., 2011). In this large, urban school system, this label would most likely remove him from access to general education. Race, disability, and gender matter for access to educational opportunity.

Both learning disabilities and behavior/emotional disabilities are known as judgmental categories, meaning that they are not diagnosable by a measurable biomarker. In practice, this means that there have been decades of debate about how best to diagnose them, particularly learning disabilities (McFarland et al., 2013). It also means that the bias of teachers or psychologists can also affect outcomes (Artiles et al., 2002). It does not mean, however, that learning disabilities and/or dyslexia do not exist, not at all, but that since there is no single way to diagnose an LD and dyslexia, there are students who are misidentified.

How We Define the Problem Matters

One helpful exercise in understanding any complex problem is to try to identify how the problem is framed. Think about why you have chosen to read this book. Did you do so because you saw a problem? If so, how would you name that problem?

Think About It

Start by looking at the data on reading scores in both fourth and eighth grades, compared for students with and without disabilities in the United States. Take a minute and predict what you will see in the same type of graph for math scores. What do you notice and wonder about this data?

Percentage at Basic-Advanced Levels in Reading

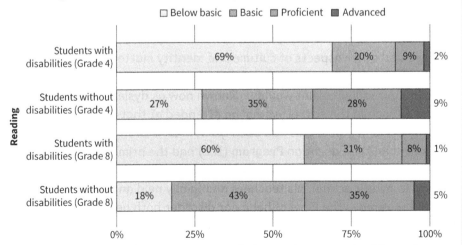

SOURCE: U.S. Department of Education, Institute of Education Sciences, National Center for Education Statistics, National Assessment of Educational Progress (NAEP), 2013. NAEP Office of Special Education Programs, Individuals with Disabilities Education Act (IDEA) database, 2023.

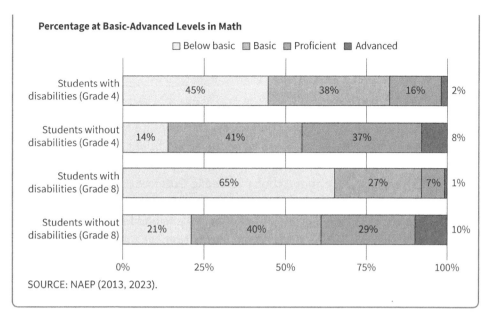

Percentage at Basic-Advanced Levels in Math

□ Below basic ■ Basic ■ Proficient ■ Advanced

Students with disabilities (Grade 4)	45%	38%	16%	2%
Students without disabilities (Grade 4)	14%	41%	37%	8%
Students with disabilities (Grade 8)	65%	27%	7%	1%
Students without disabilities (Grade 8)	21%	40%	29%	10%

0%   25%   50%   75%   100%

SOURCE: NAEP (2013, 2023).

Reading scores seem to improve from fourth to eighth grade for both groups. But for math, scores decline over time: All students do worse in eighth grade compared with fourth grade. For disabled students, the gap between these scores becomes *much* wider. In reading, students with disabilities improve in comparison with nondisabled peers over time in school. But in math, the longer students are in school, the larger the gap between disabled and nondisabled students becomes. Why would the situation be so different in math compared with reading?

When I show these graphs to teachers, I have heard them observe that reading instruction gets more attention and time compared to math. Others note that math gets much more abstract after fourth grade. Others wonder if mathematics teachers in secondary school teach more traditionally. Other teachers bring up their experiences that students with disabilities are often taken out of general education classes in middle school and exposed to a more procedural curriculum in separate special education classes.

Studies support these assertions, documenting that students with disabilities are offered fewer opportunities to engage in conceptual and standards-based mathematics in both special education and general education settings (Jackson & Neel, 2006; Kurz et al., 2014). Students with disabilities have fewer opportunities to solve open-ended problems and to engage in sustained mathematical thinking. This lack of opportunity could be a major piece of the puzzle in the graph we just examined.

Perhaps discrimination is part of the problem. One study found that students with disabilities were not placed in algebra at the same rate as nondisabled peers, even when controlling for achievement (Faulkner et al., 2013). The simple fact of being a child in the special education system meant that children were less likely to be placed in the most challenging math class available, no matter their previous grades in math.

Or maybe we are thinking about the problem all wrong. Perhaps the problem is not about test scores but about a lack of participation in STEM majors and careers for disabled students. Despite documented talent, students with disabilities are not represented proportionally in STEM fields (Dunn et al., 2012). Mathematics education scholar Rochelle Gutierrez (2002) has written that students of color not only need math, but also math needs the brilliance of students of color. When groups of people are excluded from fields such as math and other STEM fields that rely on innovation, we all suffer. Students with disabilities need math, but math needs them too (Tan & Kastberg, 2017)! Students with disabilities should have equal access to STEM careers, as well as to success in STEM classes. All of these analyses move away from focusing on the possible deficits of individual children with disabilities and onto the systems in which these students learn.

MODELS OF DISABILITY

To understand how we can reframe "the problem" of disability and mathematics, let's turn to how we understand disability itself. Specifically, let's look at four different ways of thinking about disability:

- ▸ The medical model
- ▸ The social model
- ▸ Neurodiversity
- ▸ Vygotsky's model of access

These different ways of understanding disability offer different possibilities in our work as math teachers to students with disabilities, different ways for us to imagine what disability is and how it connects to mathematics.

Medical Model of Disability

Understanding of disabilities in Western culture has emerged from the medical system. Disabilities are understood as individual problems that should be fixed through medical intervention. When we have a medical problem, we go to a doctor, explain the problem, and hope to hear a solution, a cure, a fix to the problem.

When we apply the medical model to education, we see disability as something to be fixed, eradicated, removed. When students are understood primarily through their deficits, the solution from a medical model perspective is to remediate those deficits through targeted intervention. Students undergo treatments designed to fix them. From a medical model perspective, the solution is an intense focus on deficits. Discussion of strengths is seen as not relevant to the problem.

Let's think about the medical model of disability in connection with Luis. Luis had an IEP for a learning disability in the area of reading, now more commonly known as dyslexia. Dyslexia is actually a far older term for this cognitive difference, but it fell out of favor in educational psychology and special education in favor of the broader category of learning disabilities. Currently, *specific learning disabilities* is the umbrella term used in U.S. law for students with dyslexia (LD in reading), dyscalculia or a mathematical learning disability (LD in math or MLD), and dysgraphia (LD in writing) (there are other subcategories under this umbrella term as well). Much of the research in LD and math is focused on students with dyscalculia or MLDs, which can be described as significant difficulty learning mathematics. However, students with LD as a whole, with by far the most common subgroup as dyslexia/reading LD, also significantly underperform as a group in mathematics (Wei et al., 2013). In addition, students can have both reading and math as significant challenges.

Understood from a medical model perspective, dyslexia is a hereditary neurobiological disability characterized by difficulties in reading, writing, and spelling, often unexpected in comparison with other academic skills (Lyon et al., 2003). Although the primary difficulty for individuals with dyslexia is phonemic processing, which affects learning how to read, there are also often patterns of difficulties in language processing, executive functioning, working memory, and difficulty with memorizing facts and procedures (Cortiella & Horowitz, 2014). Of course, not all people with dyslexia/LD experience all these challenges.

One challenge that matters in mathematics is issues with memorization of facts and procedures. Students with dyslexia are challenged by the memorization of disconnected facts (De Clercq-Quaegebeur et al., 2018). Adults with dyslexia continue to have challenges with memorizing multiplication facts (Simmons & Singleton, 2006). Students with LD who construct connections between facts are better able to remember them than those students who use memorization as a strategy (Erenberg, 1995).

In my first 2 years of observing Luis in both his sixth- and his seventh-grade math classes, I can attest to his difficulty with memorized procedures. Mr. Pierce noted it as a challenge in sixth grade. In his seventh-grade year, Luis had a teacher named Ms. Marquez, an excellent mathematics teacher who was able to teach both problem-solving and procedures within her daily 90-minute block. In the fall of his seventh-grade year, Ms. Marquez described Luis as one of her top students and often called on him to explain his unusual strategies. However, in the spring of that year, Ms. Marquez eliminated the inquiry-based problem solving that had been a big part of the class in the fall. She did so to focus on teaching the procedures called for on the state exam. In the spring, Luis was asked to solve problems like operations with negative numbers using memorized rules. He either could not or would not do so, no matter how many times he was taught the rules. Ms. Marquez told me that Luis "cannot do rote" and began to worry about him.

Using the medical model, we might assume that Luis has deficits in his memory that might have affected his ability to memorize the rules for adding and subtracting integers. Using a deficit thinking model, we might then focus only on procedures and memorization with Luis, providing intensive instruction in exactly what he is most challenged by.

But if his weakness is memorizing rules, why would we teach him through memorizing rules? One day, deep into the spring with its memorized procedures, Luis was easily finishing a worksheet on adding and subtracting integers. I asked him about his strategy. He smiled broadly and then whispered to me that he was using "the giant number line in my head." Luis teaches us that he can use his strengths in visual processing to imagine a number line and use it to find answers elegantly. Why would we not build on this, his unique strength? Focusing on deficits, rather than on strengths, can be a counterproductive strategy.

> **Focusing on deficits, rather than on strengths,
> can be a counterproductive strategy.**

Social Model of Disability

Our next model of disability was created by disabled people themselves. The modern Disability Rights movement was built on a fundamental shift away from medical, individual models of disability toward social models (Linton, 1998). Developed by disabled activists in England (Oliver, 2009), the social model recognizes that disabled people may have actual biological, neurological, or physical differences, but the model reserves the term *disability* for the disabling aspects of both society and an inaccessible built environment. A shift to the social model of disability means a shift toward accessibility rather than remediation alone. The social model asks us to look closely not at the students but at the classrooms, curriculum, and systems that surround the student. Can a classroom disable a student?

Let's return to the example of Luis. His seventh-grade teacher, Ms. Marquez, saw Luis as a "top conceptual student" in the fall when she valued inquiry-based instruction. When she shifted to explicit, procedural instruction in which students needed to memorize particular rules, Luis became a major concern for her since he could not or would not use certain methods, preferring ones he developed himself. Luis was understood as a mathematical innovator when mathematics was seen as inquiry based and as disabled when mathematics was about memorization of previously determined procedures. In this comparison, we can see how the social model of disability matters in a math classroom. Luis has stayed very much the same. Different ways of teaching mathematics make him seem mathematically brilliant or in trouble.

Another student in Luis's classroom had the opposite trajectory. Ana also had a label of a learning disability but was a very different learner than Luis. While Luis had attended a progressive elementary school with an inquiry-based mathematics curriculum, Ana had only experienced traditional mathematics until she got to Ms. Marquez's seventh-grade classroom. In the first half of the year, Ana was a concern for Ms. Marquez, who said that Ana was "not good at that side," meaning the inquiry-based problem solving. Ana told me in interviews that her way of doing math was to "just learn whatever [my teacher] is saying, I learn everything from there." Ana also said that when problems were different from what the teacher said, she would get "confused." Ana also described intense feelings of math anxiety that she felt when taking tests in class and particularly as she prepared for the high-stakes standardized tests in the spring. As their math instruction shifted to prepare for these tests, it became entirely memorization of specific procedures. Now that what was valued was memorization, Ana became a top student despite her increasing anxiety in mathematics.

In most ways, Ana and Luis stay the same as math learners in their seventh-grade year. But as what is valued in math class shifts, they are seen as more or less competent in math. Disability seems to not only be part of an individual student but also what is valued in their math class, demonstrating how disability can be constructed socially in mathematics classrooms (Lambert, 2015).

> **Disability seems to not only be part of an individual student but also what is valued in their math class, demonstrating how disability can be constructed socially in mathematics classrooms.**

Neurodiversity Model of Disability

Another model for disability is *neurodiversity*, a social justice movement that developed from the activism of autistic people (Robertson & Ne'eman, 2008). Starting in the 1990s, autistic activists began advocating for a new way to think about autism. They argue that autism comes with a set of challenges, yes, but also with a set of strengths. Instead of being understood as a problem, these activists argue that they need to be seen as the complex individuals they are. Neurodiverse individuals are demanding to be seen not as deficient but as *different*: part of the natural and beneficial cognitive diversity of society. Here is an excerpt of a description of autism, made not by a diagnostic manual, but by the Autistic Self Advocacy Network (ASAN), an autism organization led by autistic people.

> **Neurodiverse individuals are demanding to be seen not as deficient but as *different*: part of the natural and beneficial cognitive diversity of society.**

About Autism by ASAN (excerpt)

Every autistic person experiences autism differently, but there are some things that many of us have in common.

1. **We think differently.** We may have very strong interests in things other people don't understand or seem to care about. We might be great problem-solvers, or pay close attention to detail. It might take us longer to think about things. . . .
2. **We process our senses differently.** We might be extra sensitive to things like bright lights or loud sounds. We might have trouble understanding what we hear or what our senses tell us. We might not notice if we are in pain or hungry. We might do the same movement over and over again. This is called "stimming," and it helps us regulate our senses. . . .
3. **We move differently.** We might have trouble with fine motor skills or coordination. . . . Speech can be extra hard because it requires a lot of coordination. . . .

4. **We communicate differently.** We might talk using echolalia (repeating things we have heard before), or by scripting out what we want to say. Some autistic people use Augmentative and Alternative Communication (AAC) to communicate.... Some people may also communicate with behavior or the way we act. Not every autistic person can talk, but we all have important things to say.

5. **We socialize differently.** Some of us might not understand or follow social rules that non-autistic people made up. We might be more direct than other people. Eye contact might make us uncomfortable.... Some of us might not be able to guess how people feel. This doesn't mean we don't care how people feel! ... Some autistic people are extra sensitive to other people's feelings.

(This is an excerpt from ASAN's short definition of autism, Welcome To The Autistic Community!)

Think About It

What do you notice and wonder about this definition of autism? How is it different than ways you have seen autism defined in the past? Do you think it matters that this description was written by autistic people?

Neurodiversity arose in the autistic community, but it has been taken up by individuals with dyslexia, Tourette syndrome, ADHD, and mental illness. There has long been a movement in the mental illness community called *Mad Pride*, dating back to the 1970s to destigmatize differences such as depression, schizophrenia, and bipolar disorder. Individuals with intellectual disabilities have also been a part of the neurodiversity community.

Neurodiversity is also scientific fact: All humans ARE different, unique, individual, and brains change based on experience (Cantor et al., 2019). Every human brain is different from the next. This natural human variability is called *learner variability* in the learning sciences, one of the foundations of Universal Design for Learning (Rose, 2017).

Neurodiversity is a strengths-based (or asset-based) way to think about cognitive differences that has overlaps with the social model of disability. Activists for neurodiversity advocate for accessibility rather than for remediation, or just being "fixed." Just as in the social model, the problem is located in inaccessible contexts, institutions, practices, and systems. In the next section, we return to dyslexia, reviewing research on dyslexic strengths.

Neurodiversity in Action: Strengths in Dyslexia

Discussion of the possible visual–spatial strengths associated with dyslexia has been around for almost 100 years, dating back to 1925 (Schneps et al., 2007). One strength associated with dyslexia in several research studies is 3-D spatial thinking (von Károlyi & Winner, 2004), which is connected to strengths in mechanics and complex visualization (Attree et al., 2009). Another strength seen in people with dyslexia is in the category of interconnected reasoning. This means seeing the BIG PICTURE, focusing on patterns (Eide & Eide, 2012). One final documented strength is creative thinking; students with dyslexia scored higher than did those without dyslexia on measures of original thinking (Akhavan Tafti et al., 2009) and on tasks requiring novel and creative solutions (Everatt et al., 1999). Again, not all people with dyslexia and/or a learning disability in the area of reading have this set of strengths; it varies by individual. In addition, there is much less research in the area of strengths than deficits, making the research field as a whole less robust.

Taylor and Vestergaard (2022) proposed that the set of strengths and challenges in dyslexia could be understood as an evolutionary strength toward *exploratory search*, a cognitive style of exploration and making connections across ideas, which comes with trade-offs in automatization or routine thinking. They discussed how evolution moves toward variability itself as humans work together best with varied skill sets. How might evolutionary search matter in mathematics?

> **Taylor and Vestergaard (2022) proposed that the set of strengths and challenges in dyslexia could be understood as an evolutionary strength toward *exploratory search*, a cognitive style of exploration and making connections across ideas, which comes with trade-offs in automatization or routine thinking.**

OTHER STRENGTHS-BASED MODELS

Deaf Gain

Although neurodiversity developed in the autistic community, different theories that focus on strengths have emerged from other communities. A critical concept in Deaf studies is Deaf Gain (the opposite of "hearing loss"), or "the unique cognitive, creative, and cultural gains manifested through deaf ways of being in the world" (Bauman & Murray, 2014, p. xv). Research has begun to investigate strengths associated with deafness, more specifically, these strengths are associated with use of signed languages. Studies have found deaf strengths in visual attention and visual memory (Craig et al., 2022) and peripheral visual reaction time (also found in sign language interpreters) (Codina et al., 2017). Other work has found that signed language fluency correlated with mental rotation skills (Kubicek & Quandt, 2021). Theories about these strengths for those who use signed languages are that these languages are inherently visuospatial, where communication is about transforming visual images in space and time. How might these strengths matter in mathematics?

Vygotsky's Theories of Access

Lev Vygotsky, one of the most important educational theorists of the 20th century, paid attention to disability in a radical way despite working almost 100 years ago. Writing at the end of the 1920s, he rejected the idea of disability as within the individual alone (Vygotsky, 1993). Similar to the social model of disability, he separated the disabling condition from the "defect" or the impairment. Just as he saw learning as mediated by interactions with others and with educational tools, he saw disability not as internal within one person but as created when an individual cannot access interaction with others and/or cultural tools. So, for example, a person who is blind cannot access written text on a page. Is that a problem within the person? Vygotsky would say no, the problem is in the access to the tool. He noted that these problems of access can be solved by new tools, such as the creation of Braille or text to speech. If a person continues to have access to the important cultural tool (text), their individual difference (blindness) does not matter.

Vygotsky (1993) noted that disabled people seemed to find ways to use (or invent) new mediational tools, which can have new affordances for learning. This is not overcoming one's disability; rather, it is about finding ways to compensate for it, to adapt to make your way in the world. It is a creative act, redesigning one's environment to make it more accessible, making or finding new tools when others do not work for you.

Dylan Lynn and Access to Mathematics

In a collaborative research project, Dr. Katherine Lewis and Dylan Lynn (2018) used this approach to understand dyscalculia. Dylan Lynn was an undergraduate statistics major at the University of California, Berkeley, and worked as a data analyst after graduation. She also has dyscalculia. Together with Dr. Lewis, they studied the ways in which Dylan made higher mathematics accessible for herself (Lewis & Lynn, 2018).

Let's define dyscalculia. The term *dyscalculia* applies when a learner has an exceptionally hard time with math but not necessarily with other subjects. It can also be called an "MLD" or a "mathematical learning disability." Researchers estimate that 6% of the population may have dyscalculia (Shalev, 2007). Dyscalculia is marked by difficulty with mathematical representations and symbolism, such as connecting numbers with amounts or the perceptual recognition of quantity (Butterworth, 2010). Learners with dyscalculia also tend to have difficulty becoming fluent with basic mathematics, such as addition and multiplication math facts. Some believe that there is a single "core deficit" responsible for dyscalculia; others believe that since mathematics is made of multiple kinds of cognitive tasks, there are myriad ways an individual learner can have significant difficulties with mathematics (Dowker, 2019).

It is important to note that we have a lot more to learn about dyscalculia. Almost all the research on dyscalculia is on deficits in basic mathematics, so we know little about the strengths of people with dyscalculia, as well as about how they might perform in higher mathematics. This is why the research by Lewis and Lynn (2018) is so important.

In assessments she took as an adult, Dylan took much longer than others to do numerical computation, which qualified her for disability services as an undergraduate. Yet Dylan described her biggest barrier in mathematics as working with abstract symbols (Lewis & Lynn, 2018). During her undergraduate degree in statistics, Dylan would rewrite equations in a precise way onto graph paper, adding words to describe symbols, and making sure all the notation was clear. She also made sure to always ground procedures in real-life contexts, which was why she liked statistics so much— she could understand its relationship to real-world contexts.

Dylan identified what her issues of access were: the abstract nature of mathematical symbols. She created a system in which she found ways to work around what was challenging for her. Despite these workarounds, Dylan still faced many barriers to achieving her goal of a statistics degree. Quoted in an interview with Dr. Lewis, Dylan said:

> It's really really unfortunate to me, I think that, in mathematics, it's not just that you understand the concept. It's not just that you can get a correct answer, you also have to do it in a certain amount of time, which inevitably is like this really bizarre artificial constraint. Especially now that I've worked in industry at [*sic*] as a data analyst. And yes, I had time constraints, I had to get a report done in this amount of time or whatnot. It's nothing like sitting down for a test and

> you have 60 min to do this insane page of stuff and this huge mental
> dump, where these kinds of rewriting things would really become
> problematic, I would just flat-out run out of time. (2018, p. 14)

Dylan provided the following suggestions that she used in her work tutoring
students with dyscalculia (Lewis & Lynn, 2018).

▶ Have students identify their own "issues of access."

▶ Identify and build on strengths.

▶ Connect the mathematics to real life.

▶ Encourage multiple solution paths.

▶ Give students agency over deciding what works for them.

Much more still needs to be learned about dyscalculia. But I wonder why
research focuses so heavily on what learners like Dylan can't do rather than
adding to our knowledge of what they can do.

It matters how we as teachers think about disability. We can use the medical
model, as many educational settings do. But we can also use the innovations
of the social model, neurodiversity, Deaf Gain, and access models, which
challenge us to see disabilities as both strengths and challenges, to change
the classroom, not the kid. This makes our mission clear: How can we create
classroom environments that would enable, not disable, kids like Luis and
adults like Dylan Lynn?

> **This makes our mission clear: How can
> we create classroom environments that
> would enable, not disable, kids.**

REFLECTION QUESTIONS

1. Have you ever had a student like Luis? What did you learn from
   that student?

2. What experiences have you had with disability in your life? From a
   first-hand perspective? In your family and friends? As a professional?
   What have you learned from your experiences with disability that
   you wish other teachers knew?

3. As you read about the different ways to think about disability, what
   were your thoughts? Which model resonated with you? Why?

CHAPTER 3

RETHINKING MATHEMATICS

IN THIS CHAPTER, WE WILL . . .

- Reevaluate our definition of math
- Learn from a study on dyslexia and mathematics at the university level
- Reconceptualize mathematical development as multiple pathways
- Understand that neurodiversity can mean unusual ways of moving through mathematics

AS THIS CHAPTER is about what mathematics is, real mathematics, I want to begin with a story that a mathematician, Edmund Harriss (Figure 3.1), told me. It starts in France, with Edmund riding a bus, head filled with ideas after an interesting math talk. He had a flash of insight about how that talk related to another problem he was working on, on tiling a plane. This mathematics required shifting methods designed for understanding space in three dimensions to four dimensions. When first he tried to explain the connections across topics, his colleagues did not understand his thinking, probably because, as he said, "I did not yet understand it myself."

Figure 3.1 • *Edmund, mathematician and artist, holding a mathematical toy of his own creation*

SOURCE: Asa Harriss

Cut to 2 years later. Edmund was now in Japan, working with the same group of colleagues to solve this same problem, holed up in a room with a whiteboard. He described their process like this:

> Edmund: One person would go up, talk until they got stuck, sit down, and immediately someone else had the next piece. And the whole process, basically the heart of the paper, over about

> 3 hours, went from something unknown to something which we all felt we had a fairly solid understanding of. And then 2 years later there was actually a paper that described that result.

Rachel: When you came in, did you just explain your ideas or did you write something on the board? What else was happening?

Edmund: So I was basically drawing sketches on the board and the understanding that I'd brought to it was thinking about this problem in four-dimensional space and seeing how it related to . . . so instead of looking at the values of the matrix, you have to look at what the matrix does to area.

A little later in the interview, Edmund started talking about how he thinks of himself as a mathematician.

Edmund: I have lots of ideas. In fact, at that same time, my Japanese colleague said, "I like you Edmund because most of your ideas are bad but when you have a good one it's really worth listening to. So it's worth listening to all the bad ideas in order to get the different one." And I'm probably a bit slower as a mathematician than many.

Rachel: What do you mean by you're "a bit slower" than other mathematicians?

Edmund: In terms of doing computation or just taking an idea and seeing what it actually means and how it. . . Once you've got the idea, how do you do all the routine manipulation of that idea before you need to have another idea?

Rachel: I like this phrase "routine manipulation." Because it's beyond computation at the level you're at, it's like you have to apply things to it about what already exists in mathematics to see if it works, right? . . . What are you good at in mathematics?

Edmund: Coming out with the idea that pushes you beyond that routine. So thinking about things, especially visual or spatial ideas. Questioning and poking at the routine to say how do we express this idea. So sort of coming up with ideas that are not in that routine, especially things that are related to images. And then when things can get translated into images, I have a lot of facility there to do stuff. I can do immensely technical work in images that others can do in language. ●

REEVALUATING OUR DEFINITION OF MATH

We are led to believe from an early age that mathematics is noncreative, a chore. We are taught that it is a calling for the few, and that the few are a very narrow group of people that excludes most of humanity, excluding women, people of color, and disabled people. We are taught that being good at math is memorizing the digits of pi, and being fast at multiplication. Few of us are given access to the beauty and creativity of math. I had no idea I loved mathematics until I started teaching it, as well as started working with professional developers who gave me problems to think about that obsessed and intrigued me.

Working with mathematicians has also changed my mind, particularly my work with Edmund Harriss, both a mathematician and a working artist, currently a professor in both mathematics and art at the University of Arkansas. Edmund is a geometer, meaning that he studies the mathematics of three-dimensional shifting shapes. He is known for helping develop the field of illustrating mathematics, connecting mathematics to art to help researchers challenge the boundaries of the subject. This leads him to think about math communication broadly, especially how it connects to art, creativity, and neurodiversity. Edmund has co-written a mathematical coloring book (Bellow & Harriss, 2015) and has developed mathematical toys such as the Penrose tiles (https://bit .ly/46c3V2w).

Edmund has taught me that math can be a creative, artistic, joyful calling; that math is about finding what you love to do, and doing it; and that math is not just for those who are good at what matters in elementary school: memorizing. And he has also taught me that mathematical development is not a ladder, not step by step, but a much more complex web of connections and concepts, and that sometimes the simplest parts of math seem the hardest. And, also, Edmund was identified with dyslexia as a boy growing up in England. So as we explore his story, we can explore the radical potential of mathematics for creativity and joy for neurodiverse minds.

Think About It

Think about this story of Edmund's, an international saga of mathematical discovery, across 4 years and three continents. With this in mind, what is mathematics? How do we do mathematics? How does this compare with the mathematics we teach at school?

Edmund's work is about innovation, about creating new knowledge, here finding a way to tile a two-dimensional plane by adapting the mathematics of four, five, or higher dimensional spaces (see Figure 3.2). That takes insight, what Edmund calls "technical work in images." It also needs to hold up to the critique of routine manipulation—in other words, does this idea work with the rest of the mathematical rules we have created?

Figure 3.2 · *Penrose tiles for mathematical play designed by Edmund*

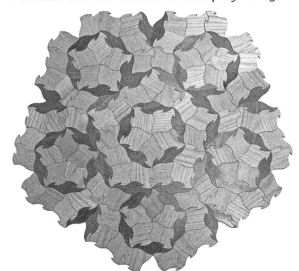

SOURCE: Reprinted with permission from Edmund Harriss.

Such complex mathematics is done most often in teams, with people who gather to think together about a problem each had thought about individually. Together, sharing new ideas, they each talk until, as Edmund noted, "they were stuck" and then the next one speaks. Their collaboration is scaffolded by the images on the whiteboard as they talk. So if we are to define "real" mathematics, as described by Edmund, it is creative, multimodal, collaborative. Being stuck is a natural part of the process, and we move out of being stuck by talking through ideas with others.

ENGAGING IN THE PRACTICES OF REAL MATHEMATICS

One important innovation in mathematics education has been to try to better connect school mathematics to the academic field of mathematics itself. Perhaps the most important innovation in connecting school mathematics to mathematics as a field is the part of the Common Core State Standards (CCSS) known as the Standards of Mathematical Practice, better known as the SMPs (National Governors Association Center for Best Practices

& Council of Chief State School Officers, 2010). These standards were developed through work by both math educators and mathematicians, using research and their own experiences to design a set of practices used by research mathematicians. To learn mathematics includes both content (what you are learning) and practices (what you are learning to do). For too many kids, school math is content only. The goal is test scores and high grades, determined by how much a student can memorize.

This approach can cause several problems. For example, students who are good at school math can run into problems at college because mathematics changes into a more creative, open-ended field where the work is more similar to what Edmund and his colleagues do (Boaler & Greeno, 2000). Such students may have the content knowledge, but they might not have the habits of mind to succeed in higher math.

Standards for Mathematical Practice

1. Make sense of problems and persevere in solving them.
2. Reason abstractly and quantitatively.
3. Construct viable arguments and critique the reasoning of others.
4. Model with mathematics.
5. Use appropriate tools strategically.
6. Attend to precision.
7. Look for and make use of structure.
8. Look for and express regularity in repeated reasoning.

The bigger problem is for the many. Mathematics that is only about memorization is less compelling for students, more likely to induce boredom, and makes students less happy (e.g., Sengupta-Irving & Enyedy, 2015). How can we possibly expect students to persevere in math that is boring, repetitive, and allows for little agency and engagement?

> ## Think About It
>
> Take a moment to look again at the SMPs (in the box that preceded this). Which of these did Edmund engage in when thinking about tiling a sphere?

Certainly Edmund engaged in SMP 1: *Make sense of problems and persevere in solving them.* Excelling at mathematics at the highest levels includes taking 4 years to solve a math problem. Mathematicians may work decades on a problem and *not solve it.*

Edmund even identifies himself as slow, not to disparage himself, but to be clear about his strengths and his challenges. This is one of the gifts of a neurodiversity perspective—it is not about being either good or bad at math but about being strong in some ways, challenged in others, and learning to adapt accordingly.

Edmund also excels at SMP 2: *Reason abstractly and quantitatively*. This SMP is about thinking mathematically, which means thinking across concrete, representational, and abstract situations, as well as across different kinds of representations. Here Edmund and his colleagues are extending the mathematics of dimensions, which is necessarily asking them to make connections across concepts and think both abstractly (equations) and concretely (the physical model of the expanding sphere).

I also see evidence of SMP 3: *Construct viable arguments and critique the arguments of others*. Edmund and his colleagues work both alone and together. When working apart, they communicate in writing, and when working together, as on that day in France, they talk and share and critique each other's thinking. The final product of their work is a mathematical paper (Arnoux et al., 2011).

A RESEARCH STUDY ON DYSLEXIA AND MATHEMATICS

The interview between myself and Edmund was part of our research project (Lambert & Harriss, 2022). We were both interested to learn more about the thought processes and careers of dyslexic mathematics. Edmund and I interviewed five research mathematicians who identified as dyslexic (including Edmund himself). All were working at universities, with mathematical foci in the following areas: real analysis, three-dimensional geometry, topology, and algebraic topology. This was an exploratory study—we don't claim that we now have definitive answers about the strengths or challenges of dyslexic mathematicians—but what we found reveals some interesting patterns that we think are quite useful for those teaching math to students with dyslexia.

Considering how much dyslexia—having difficulty learning how to read—can affect your school years, how did each of these people become mathematicians? The life narratives of these research mathematicians describe a nondirect pathway to becoming a research mathematician. They describe barriers that could have limited their process, particularly math classes focused on memorization. All participants noted that they moved forward in mathematics once they reached a place in which they were completely fascinated by the problems, most often, a visual–spatial set of problems to solve.

Some of our participants were concerned about being recognized and perhaps penalized in their departments if it was commonly known that they are dyslexic. For that reason, we describe the mathematicians with gender-neutral names and they/their pronouns, and we don't connect details about their specialties to their quotes. This preference to remain anonymous despite their enormous success reminds us of how damaging deficit conceptions of disability are, even to those at the top of mathematics. Of the five mathematicians, two were women. Next let's look at some findings from our study.

Mathematics Requires Resilience

Our dyslexic research participants noted that working through the challenges of dyslexia made them more resilient, which became a considerable strength for them in higher mathematics. When asked what a strength of dyslexia is, a mathematician we are calling Dakota said, "Resiliency, I guess. Just being able to kind of overcome things that are not necessarily the easiest for you." Success in mathematics, participants noted, comes with hard work. Because math gets hard for everyone at some point in their math studies, understanding what to do when that happens is a gift for any mathematician.

> **Because math gets hard for everyone at some point in their math studies, understanding what to do when that happens is a gift for any mathematician.**

Multimodal Thinking

Mathematics is multimodal. Edmund taught me quite a bit about the difference between a mathematics focused on algebra, which is primarily symbolic, and the mathematics of space or geometry. He often sees mathematicians with an inclination toward one or the other, and many core mathematical problems are about mapping the connections between the two.

In our study, we found a strong visual–spatial thinking bent in the dyslexic mathematicians. Four out of five participants identified as visual and/or geometric mathematical thinkers. Some of their comments:

▸ "I learn through geometry first, thinking through space."

▸ "My entire memory is sort of visual, it's like playing back little snippets of film."

▸ "I am both a details kind of thinker and like a visual thinker. I can't get interested in the details unless I have the picture that I think I'm working out the details for. But, once I have a picture of what I think should be going on, then the details become interesting. . . . It's not the other way around."

Another connection across the dyslexic mathematicians was the importance of intuition in their problem-solving process, including how challenging that sometimes is for mathematical collaborators:

> "I talk in ghosts and mists. My brain seems to be really, really comfortable with just throwing out ideas. It just really is very flexible. And so, I get a sense that something is true, or something that I want, I need, is there. And then my brain really doesn't get bothered by the fact that some ideas don't work, it just will throw out lots and lots of ideas and sort of wander. And that drives co-authors nuts, because they'll say, 'Oh, I see? That idea doesn't work.' And it doesn't slow me down one bit. My brain just has like five other weird ideas, two of which you can throw out immediately, and the three others you have to spend time on."

This quote resonates also with the way that Edmund described his collaborations, in which he felt his strength was contributing innovative ideas.

Multiple participants described how mathematics was impossible without visuals. A participant named Atlas described how challenging it was when mathematician colleagues at conferences just talked about math, without any visuals.

> Atlas: This even happens when I'm with mathematician friends and they'll be vocalizing an argument. There's no whiteboard, and they'll say, you do this and then you. . . Yeah, I'm not necessarily going to follow the point. But, I'll go back to my [hotel] room later and I'll remember enough of the points that they were trying to make that I'll get it. And, I'm okay with that; I don't have to be as quick-witted as some of my colleagues are in mathematics, and I don't mind that.
>
> Rachel: So, it's really different for you if there's paper or there's a whiteboard?
>
> Atlas: Yeah, if I can visualize things I'm much better off.

If it is difficult for a professional mathematician to follow the math solely through verbal language, we can assume it is exceptionally challenging for many kids.

Math Is Collaborative

In Edmund's story, we can see how mathematical discovery is about collaboration and communication. Other research participants also stressed this aspect of mathematics. For several, collaboration at the graduate level is what attracted them to mathematics as a field. One used the term "feeling comfortable" as they described the collaboration in their master's program, which felt so engaging and supportive they decided to continue to get a doctorate.

Collaboration is critical for solving complex mathematical problems as multiple perspectives are often needed to develop ideas and critique them until they are well developed. We saw this process at work in Edmund's story about mathematical creativity, so closely connected to collaboration.

Challenges With Memorization

When asked to think back on K–12 school, the research participants discussed having no particular challenge with the concepts but lots of trouble with memorization, particularly difficulty with the times tables and/or memorizing mathematical procedures. Dakota told us:

> I've never been good at memorizing things, just like I couldn't memorize how to spell words, I couldn't memorize facts in math. So I paid attention in class, and I had good enough teachers that they derived everything. And I figured out how to derive everything I needed to know.

Another noted that their mother taught the multiplication tables through using a smaller set of memorized facts, specifically the squares, and then encouraging them to build equations through the distributive property from known facts. Participants noted the difficulty of any kind of memorization "without structure." Edmund said:

> That is one of the reasons I'm slower. I have really good memory for connected facts. I can't remember phone numbers at all. Learning foreign languages was the one bit of school that I hated because you have this long list of words that had no connection to anything. So memorization without structure. So I memorized the structure.

Atlas told us that they had a history of understanding "concepts" in mathematics and struggling with "the details." When we asked what they meant by details, they told a story about being negatively judged for their lack of memorization of the multiplication tables in elementary school:

> I could've explained to you with a picture why nine times five was 45, and my friends could tell you that it was 45 but they couldn't tell

> you why. And it struck me *as* really upsetting that someone who, just memorizing that number, was valued more than me understanding *why* that was the right answer. And it's always been a problem. But it just seems to me that why something is true is much more important than knowing that it is true.

Not only was memorization without structure very challenging, participants were asked to do this task under time pressure, which made it impossible. Edmund, who attended school in the United Kingdom, noted:

> The high school calculus in the U.S., I think I wouldn't be a mathematician if I'd taken that because it so emphasized fast, technical things. . . . And I make a lot of errors when doing calculation, and when you have a test which is multiple choice which is designed to map you into all your errors, I would have got very poor scores.

STRENGTHS AND CHALLENGES WITH DYSLEXIA AND MATH

Students with learning disabilities (LDs) and/or dyslexia are variable, with individual sets of strengths and challenges. Yet if we collect those that have been investigated in research for this group of learners, we can do some analysis on how the strengths and challenges might matter in mathematics.

Challenges associated with LD/dyslexia	Strengths associated with LD/dyslexia
• Language processing • Phonological processing • Memory for disconnected facts and procedures • Working memory • Executive functioning (planning, organization)	• Visual–spatial thinking • Creativity • Pattern finding • Interconnected reasoning • Exploratory search

Think About It

What does this list of possible strengths and challenges mean for mathematics? What did you see reflected in the stories of dyslexic mathematicians? What kinds of activities might be challenging in our math classes? What kinds of activities might leverage student strengths?

Strengths and Challenges

Our collaboration (myself and Edmund) has the goal of leveraging understanding of dyslexia and mathematics in mathematical research to create better conditions for learning for dyslexic students in K–12 settings. We can offer multimodal mathematics and support challenges with memorization. Students with these challenges CAN develop fluency with multiplication facts through reasoning strategies that draw on their strengths with interconnected reasoning, as we explore in Chapter 10. We can create the conditions to support mathematics as a calling for all of our students.

We dream of exploring the mathematical ways of mathematicians with other disabilities. Although people with autism are less likely to attend college than people without autism, the ones who do attend are more likely to choose STEM fields (Wei et al., 2013). Yet little research has documented the strengths of autism in mathematics. One study (Truman, 2017) analyzed the mathematical problem solving of three undergraduate students with autism, illustrating strengths in solving paradoxical problems. The researcher also noted the variety of problem-solving styles, with one student strongly preferring visual and geometric strategies, and the other two preferring numerical strategies. There is so much more to be learned about autistic strengths in mathematics.

Blind mathematicians have been important mathematical innovators, including the prolific mathematician Leonhard Euler (1707–1783). Jackson (2002) profiled Bernard Morin, who was discouraged from pursuing mathematics because of his blindness, yet contributed to theories of sphere inversion, or how 3-D spheres can turn inside out. To communicate with sighted colleagues, Morin created clay models of the shapes he imaged in his mind. He reported that his way of seeing—in his mind and with his hands—allowed him to see both the inside and the outside of an object at the same time. Recent research on blind mathematicians found that they processed mathematics in the same area as nonblind mathematicians: one generally associated with visualization (occipital cortex; Amalric et al., 2018). This finding included a mathematician who was blind since birth, suggesting that we use this part of the brain not just for seeing but also for imagining objects in space.

Jackson (2002) profiled multiple blind mathematicians who worked in geometry in addition to Morin. But other blind mathematicians had different ways of thinking, including Lawrence Baggett, who was well known for his talent of holding and manipulating long numeric sequences in his mind.

A critical issue for blind learners in mathematics is creating tools to allow access to mathematics for those whose vision is impaired (Ahmed & Chao, 2018).

These authors insist that access to mathematics is not just access to alternative versions of visuals, such as a textbook, but also access to real mathematical collaboration. It is not enough to be able to imagine what your collaborators can see, you need to be able to collectively manipulate representations in order to mathematically collaborate.

Rethinking Slow

Mathematics has long been assumed to be a subject in which speed equals success. Yet we heard multiple mathematicians in our study describe themselves as slow. I have heard the same from neurodiverse middle school students I have interviewed. One girl in Luis's class (see Chapter 2), Desi, who had a label of LD and identified as having Attention Deficit Hyperactivity Disorder (ADHD), told me she was "slow" in math. She did not mean it to disparage herself but to explain that she needed extra time. As a strong self-advocate for herself and other students with disabilities, Desi let me know that there should be space in her classroom for those who were slower, and that speed did not equal mathematical competence (Lambert, 2019).

Educator Perspective: Rethinking Slow

The following narrative comes from an interview I had with Berkeley Everett (Figure 3.3), the creator of Math Flips and Math Visuals (mathvisuals.wordpress.com). In discussing mathematics and neurodiversity, he told me that he was identified as a "slow processor." I asked him to reflect on his current thinking about the relationship between this way of thinking and his passion for math.

Figure 3.3 • *Berkeley, mathematics educator*

SOURCE: Natalia Kaminska-Palarczyk

I AM A "slow processor." School math was thoroughly disconnected from my curiosity, creativity, and imagination. Now, as a math coach and designer of digital tools, I am beginning to consider the way we use time and space in math class to include, or exclude, people like me.

Slow processing is a superpower. It gives me the desire and patience to look at one idea from many angles. I pull on loose ends, toy with parameters, and bend it until it breaks.

Consider 6 × 7. Do you see where it appears in "Twinkle Twinkle Little Star"? Do you see how the 7 is often shorthand for a ratio? Do you see how it is similar to $n(n + 1) = n^2 + n$? New connections float into my mind with enough space and time.

You can unlock the potential of students like me. Pose problems with an inviting on-ramp and a chance for generalization, like: "What patterns do you notice when you multiply by 4?" Find out what we like and where we excel. Music is my secret mathematical playground—something I wish my teachers knew. What untapped passion and potential might your "slow processors" have? How might they contribute to a rich understanding for everyone? ●

Think About It

What do you learn from Berkeley's story? How can we tap into the gifts of slow processors as he suggests?

NEURODIVERSITY AND MATHEMATICAL DEVELOPMENT

Mathematics itself is creative, collaborative, and multimodal as we have seen from our study of mathematicians. What about mathematical development, or how we conceptualize how children learn mathematical concepts? I will argue that neurodiversity challenges traditional notions of development.

SOURCE: istock.com/Sergey Tinayakov

Understanding mathematical knowledge as a set of subskills on a linear trajectory, a ladder ascending to the sky, is probably the most common way of understanding mathematical learning, as discussed by Paul Lockhart (2009). Using this metaphor, children who have difficulty with some of the skills at the lower rungs of the ladder cannot/should not progress until they master the "basics."

Neurodiversity directly challenges linear ideas of development like the ladder. In my work with special education teachers, I often hear about students who are unusual in their mathematical development. During one professional development, an experienced elementary special education teacher asked me, "What do I do with a child who does not know their addition and subtraction facts in fourth grade but can multiply two-digit numbers?" The room was full of special educators who nodded, telling their own stories of their students who seemed to struggle with the basics but could do more complex mathematics.

The students she was speaking of had a diagnosis of autism. I have often heard the term "splinter skills" to describe the skills of those with autism when such skills are not consistent across mathematics (or other areas). Unfortunately, the term can be used as a way to devalue what the student CAN do: "It's just a splinter skill." But what if these unusual higher-level skills are giving us clues that there is a different way that this student is thinking? Maybe multiplication is easier for the child than addition and subtraction? For many kids, it is! Maybe the child learned multiplication in a particularly supportive context, or from a particularly supportive adult, and thus the child remembered it? Or maybe the child gets bored with addition and subtraction?

In my experience, neurodiverse students are often particularly unusual in their learning trajectories. Often the easiest thing seems the most challenging for them. I have known multiple students who cannot count objects reliably but can work with numbers in more sophisticated ways. I have worked with students with intellectual disabilities who understand the concepts behind counting (cardinality and one-to-one correspondence) but struggle to remember the order of the numbers. I also have worked with students with intellectual disabilities who could count to infinity (if one could) but have challenges with counting concepts. Knowing the number sequence requires memorization, while understanding one-to-one correspondence and cardinality is a conceptual understanding. Students' variability in these tasks can be partially related to what kinds of mathematical activity they prefer, plus their previous experiences with counting, all within their particular set of strengths and challenges related to their neurodiversity.

> **In my experience, neurodiverse students are often particularly unusual in their learning trajectories.**

Neurodiversity tends to help us notice these different pathways, but variability in how we learn even something as fundamental as counting exists across ALL our students. Using data from 478 interviews with preschool students doing counting, Nick Johnson and colleagues (2019) found that significant variability existed in how students learned how to count objects. The researchers gave students three different interview tasks that assessed counting in different ways (see sidebar: Three Counting Tasks).

Three Counting Tasks

1. <u>Counting out loud</u>
   The interviewer asks the child to count as high as they can starting at 1 (no objects involved). The student can count in whatever language they prefer. If the student stops counting before making an error, the interviewer can do one prompt to ask if they can keep going.

2. <u>Counting bears</u>
   The interviewer sets up eight bears in a neat row and asks the student, "How many bears?" After the student has counted, even if the student has said a final number, the interviewer asks again, "How many bears?" Keep note of (a) student use of number names, (b) student use of one-to-one correspondence, and (c) cardinality. One way to assess cardinality is whether the student seems confident that the last number they counted to is the number of bears. If you are using this task, you can use any kind of object for students to count, but make all the objects the same (in size and color).

3. <u>Counting pennies</u>
   The interviewer pours 31 pennies out in front of the child in a purposefully disorganized pile. The child is then asked, "How many pennies?" After the student has counted, even if the student has said a final number, the

interviewer asks again, "How many pennies?" Keep note of (a) student use of number names, (b) student use of one-to-one correspondence, and (c) cardinality. One way to assess cardinality is whether the student seems confident that the last number they counted to is the number of pennies. If you are using this task, you can use any kind of object for students to count, but again keep the objects the same.

Think About It

Think about these three tasks. Which do you think preschool students would be more successful at? Why? If you can, I encourage you to stop and give similar tasks to a child who is still learning to count.

The researchers were looking for evidence of students' understandings of number sequence (how high a student can count out loud), one-to-one correspondence (assigning one number to one object), and cardinality (understanding that the last number in the count describes the quantity of the set) (for more, see "Unpacking a Core Idea: The Development of Counting" on p. 126). In terms of these three tasks, I think most of us would assume that students would be able to count the farthest when just counting out loud. We would probably also assume that only children who were able to count the bears correctly would be able to count the pennies.

The actual results of their research showed that children were developing this important knowledge about counting in nonlinear ways. Some kids showed one-to-one correspondence on the pennies task but not on the bears. Others were the opposite. Other kids showed evidence of cardinality on the pennies task and not on the bears task, and others the reverse. Some children counted farther on the first task, and others when they were counting pennies. Looking across all three tasks, the children showed a wide variability in their development of the three counting principles. Some had strong number sequence but difficulty with cardinality. Some had understanding of cardinality but a limited knowledge of number sequence.

If math development were a ladder, we might assume that these three counting principles would always be sequential—in other words, that first, all children would learn the counting sequence, then all would develop one-to-one correspondence, and then finally they all would understand the more abstract idea of cardinality. And that was true for some students but not all. Yet educators are often taught about early number development as if there were set sequences for students in developing their understandings, usually that knowing the number sequence comes first. Sometimes ideas of learning progressions can become rigid little ladders of their own.

This particular study did not collect any data on the disability categories of the students, as they actually picked students at random in each preschool classroom. But the study reminds us that *all* students are variable in how they learn to count. Perhaps some of the students who had an unusual trajectory through counting were neurodiverse but certainly not all. However, neurodiversity is useful to challenge our understanding of development as linear, as a ladder. Embracing neurodiverse students in our math classrooms means seeing the possibilities of what they can do, not only their challenges. It means supporting students to engage in grade-level (or beyond!) mathematics, while working on the most important concept they need.

In fact, students don't develop unless given challenging problems. Zhang and colleagues (2014) found that students with mathematical learning disabilities only developed a more complex strategy for multiplication when given problems of bigger magnitude—students only grow when challenged, including neurodiverse students. We can use standards not as a ladder, holding students back, but as a map to a landscape where our fundamental goal is providing access to grade-level work and, through that, an identity as a mathematical thinker. The metaphor of a learning landscape, in fact, can help us see that all students have unique ways through mathematics (Fosnot, 2010).

> Students only grow when challenged,
> including neurodiverse students.

In summary, in this chapter, we explored how dyslexia/LD, the most widespread disability category in our schools, can be connected to strengths in mathematics at the highest levels, such as complex visual thinking and mathematical intuition. The dyslexic adults Edmund and I spoke with describe becoming interested in math once they saw it as a creative, visual, collaborative field. As math teachers, we can build from student strengths, leaning into the kinds of visual challenges many of our students enjoy.

Each one of the dyslexic mathematicians also noted that they had significant challenges in math as memorization of disconnected facts as it was taught in schools. Building mathematical understanding through "structure," as Edmund notes, is the way to long-lasting understanding. A mathematics of memorization is a barrier for these students. It makes me wonder: How many students like Luis in Chapter 2, with uncommon ways of mathematical thinking, are held back in mathematics because of memorization?

REFLECTION QUESTIONS

1. What have been your experiences with mathematics as a learner? Have you had opportunities to engage in challenging, engaging mathematics? What makes you "feel comfortable" solving complex math problems?

2. Thinking about the experiences of these dyslexic mathematicians, what implications might this have for your students with LD/dyslexia? How might you design from student strengths?

3. What metaphor for mathematical development resonates with you? How do these different metaphors affect our work as teachers?

CHAPTER 4

BEYOND THE BINARY OF INQUIRY VERSUS EXPLICIT INSTRUCTION

IN THIS CHAPTER, WE WILL . . .

- Meet Mr. Jay's eighth-grade inclusive classroom and solve a Visual Pattern Task
- Move beyond oversimplified debates about inquiry versus explicit instruction
- Develop understanding of the research across special education and mathematics education

AS THE EIGHTH-GRADE students filed into Mr. Jay's classroom, he handed out a playing card to each one. As they entered a bright, portable classroom with whiteboards covering two full sides of the class, the students moved toward the table with the card that matches their own (Figure 4.1).

Figure 4.1 • *Mr. Jay, seventh- and eighth-grade teacher, talking with a student*

Mr. Jay moved to the front of the board and greeted his class. His manner was friendly, unassuming. He let them know that they would be doing a Visual Pattern Task, and some students smiled, one even let out a quiet "yes." I can tell they have done this kind of task before. Mr. Jay gave a very short set of directions: "Here are the first four terms of the sequence. Your job is to find out how this pattern works. What would be the next term? How many blocks would it be? Can you find a way to find the number of blocks for any term?"

Try It

Before you see student work, take some time to play with this problem yourself (see Figure 4.2).

How many blocks are in Term 5? Term 10? Term 43? Can you write an equation for the number of blocks in any term? Please don't skip this problem because it seems far out of your grade level. These are wonderfully rich ways to engage kids (and adults!) in the mathematics of algebra. Give it a go!

Figure 4.2 · *Pattern #225*

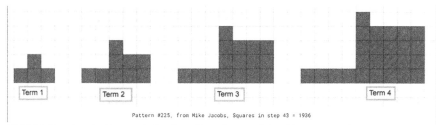

Pattern #225, from Mike Jacobs, Squares in step 43 = 1936

SOURCE: Reprinted with permission from Fawn Nguyen (VisualPatterns.org).

And before you finish, did you see the pattern in chunks? If you had to describe in words how the pattern changed, what would you say? Can you imagine multiple ways to see this pattern?

This task comes from the website Visual Patterns created by math educator Fawn Nguyen. Her website (https://www.visualpatterns.org/) is a collection of similar visual tasks that get students thinking about variables and equivalence. Mr. Jay has used many of these kinds of tasks with his middle school students. He finds that they are low-floor, high-ceiling tasks, meaning that every kid can find a way to start, and students get right to work on them. They allow students to explore algebraic equivalence as there are multiple ways to see and symbolize the pattern. I would consider visual pattern tasks to be great accessible math tasks because they are accessible (low-floor), extendable (high-ceiling), multimodal, and there are multiple solution paths. (For more on Visual Pattern tasks, see the online Teaching Practice Guide.)

Online Teaching Practice Guide
https://qrs.ly/l7f7rwq

Back in the classroom, students moved from their desks to the whiteboard walls that line the classroom. The groups seemed to start with redrawing each term of the pattern. Students had clearly done this before because they jumped right into discussion of how the pattern is changing, even as one student was drawing it. Students started chunking particular pieces of the pattern together.

The two boys in Figure 4.3 are discussing how the pattern works and finding the "chunks" that they see repeated across the pattern. The boy who is pointing noticed the "tail," as he calls it, and is looking at how it grows.

Figure 4.3 · *Two boys discuss the pattern*

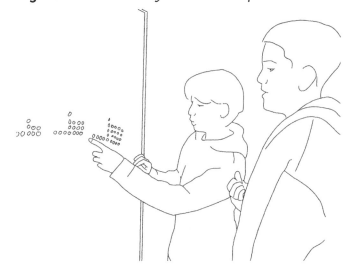

I notice how engaged they are, as well as how connected to the problem.

These two students in Figure 4.4 saw the pattern differently. The girl in front sees the chunks that she has outlined, and she sees them as x^2, and is trying to figure out how to explain the extra pieces.

Figure 4.4 • *Two students discuss finding a square in the growing pattern*

Here is an annotation of her thinking:

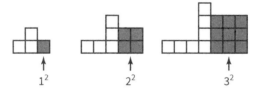

1^2 2^2 3^2

The boy she is working with sees it differently. He makes a second rectangle outside of hers, showing how one can take the piece sticking out and move it to the top, thus making a square. At this exact moment, he has explained his thinking to her, and she is clearly thinking about it. Here is an annotation of his thinking:

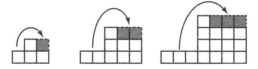

As I was watching them work, I heard him tell her that he had no idea how to write this in algebra because "I don't get algebra." She laughed, as he is quite the joker, and then together they started working on how to algebraize his elegant strategy. At this moment, he had a visual insight, and she had strengths in symbolic representation, so their group benefited from their different strengths.

Another student left her group and walked up to the SmartBoard at the front of the class to start working alone. She was so enthusiastic about her pattern that she wanted to share it on the teacher's board (Figure 4.5). She started explaining to me how she saw the pattern as two groups of x^2, with a few left over. See her arrows?

Figure 4.5 • *A girl works on the SmartBoard*

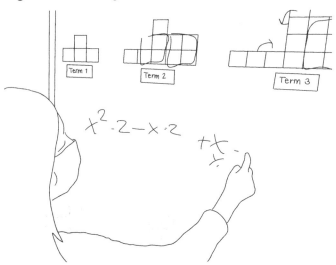

She is shown here working on an algebraic expression of the pattern, not yet complete.

While the students worked, Mr. Jay circulated. When asked a question, he often posed another question or asked if they had discussed this as a group. He watched, collecting strategies students were using and assessment data. When a group had written an equation that they could defend, Mr. Jay asked them to first walk around the room and check out the work of their peers. If they finished, he has another visual pattern ready for them.

Mr. Jay ended the class by briefly comparing the different ways that students saw it, and raising the question of whether the different equations were equivalent (Figure 4.6). He said, "That's what is cool about it. If you take each of these ways to write it and simplify them, you find the same expression, x plus 1 squared."

Figure 4.6 · *Mr. Jay leads a final discussion*

During one of these lessons, which I was observing for a research project,[1] my co-researcher turned to me and said, "I can't imagine how far I might have gone in math if I had a math teacher like this." I could only nod in agreement. ●

Think About It

Are these expressions of the problem equivalent? Are they all equivalent to $(x + 1)^2$?

MR. JAY'S PEDAGOGICAL DECISION-MAKING

Mr. Jay teaches at a school that is almost 100% Latino/a, in a rural/suburban mixed community, where most families have incomes below the poverty line. The school is a dual language school focused on developing student agency and engagement. This class includes multilingual learners who are

---

[1] These data were collected and analyzed with the assistance of my colleagues Marilyn Monroy Castro and Rebeca Mireles-Rios.

also students with disabilities. Before this task, Mr. Jay did not preteach anything, although he did know that students were comfortable with the concept of a variable (something he attributed to lots of visual pattern tasks!). This was near the end of 2 years of visits to his classroom for a research project.

In one of my first interviews with Mr. Jay, he told me that working as a middle school math teacher used to leave him exhausted at the end of the day. He felt as if he had been performing all day, working double time to get his often reluctant students to engage in the complex mathematics of middle school. As he told me:

> I used to think that I was doing the right thing if I was just handing them the information and spoon-feeding them every inch along the way. And then at the end of the day, I would feel exhausted. And I would think they knew it. They knew the math because I told them every little step. But what I've learned is that doesn't work. That doesn't mean my kids have actually learned anything.

He felt that increasing student engagement in problem solving was the primary problem of practice for his work. He wanted to facilitate a shift from perfunctory participation for some and not all, to getting *all* of his students to deeply engage in problem solving. Mr. Jay had already worked hard on creating a positive classroom community. His gentle and yet funny nature, his strong relationships with students, and his natural flexibility with his kids were a strong foundation. But it did not feel like enough. Mr. Jay described his thinking about math teaching as beginning with the goal of developing "problem-solving thinkers" before skills and standards. Another focus was on building student confidence, supporting them to "believe in themselves."

Because of this desire to increase student engagement, Mr. Jay had spent the last 2 years experimenting with strategies for engagement in problem solving developed by Peter Liljedahl in his book *The Thinking Classroom* (2020). For Mr. Jay, integrating three elements of *The Thinking Classroom* made a big difference: (a) putting students into visibly random groups (making sure the students *know* the groups are random), (b) providing vertical nonpermanent surfaces (in this case, whiteboards), and (c) giving them great, accessible tasks to work on (Table 4.1), starting with noncurricular tasks (thinking tasks that are not connected to the standards of the grade; for more on the Thinking Classrooms, see the online Teaching Practice Guide).

As the year progressed, Mr. Jay integrated problem sequences including those from Illustrative Mathematics and Desmos to cover the grade-level content of algebra.

Table 4.1 · *Features of a great accessible math task*

Features	Description	Example from Mr. Jay's Visual Pattern Task
Accessible: Low Floor	Students can engage in the problem even if they have limited knowledge of the topic. There is a way in for everybody.	Students can count the boxes to find how many for each term. They can begin their work by drawing the next terms, which may be more accessible than creating the algebraic expression.
Adaptable: High Ceiling	The problem has extensions and pedagogical possibilities that allow for extensions into more complex mathematical topics.	Mr. Jay prompted some students to focus on equivalence across different algebraic expressions.
Multimodal	The problem is visual/geometric, numeric, and symbolic, in both solution paths and representations.	Students need to turn a visual pattern into expressions using symbolic notation (variables and exponents). The task asks them to move between two modalities.
Multiple solution paths	There are multiple ways to solve the problem.	Students could conceptualize the "chunks" that they then represented algebraically in multiple ways, which all were different (equivalent) algebraic expressions.

So far we have a beautiful story of a teacher who learned how to facilitate meaningful inquiry-based instruction in eighth grade for a class that successfully included students with disabilities. And yes, this is why Mr. Jay's class was so inspiring to be a part of, and why I enjoyed visiting so much. Yet as I visited across this school year, I also saw Mr. Jay use more structured pedagogy. While in this lesson he completely trusted the students to get there on their own, in other lessons, he offered more scaffolds for students. At the same time, I was observing a rehash of the old argument: whether inquiry-based instruction or explicit instruction was more effective in math. I could see that a great teacher like Mr. Jay had moved well beyond that tired binary.

Mr. Jay always began a new topic with inquiry tasks. However, he shared that for some of the topics he was teaching, he moved into a more explicit kind of pedagogy but one that did not return to the entirely explicit instruction of his past. For the rules for exponents, for example, he began the topic with an open-ended exploration of squares and cubes, to make sure students could visualize what exponents meant. But for the rules for addition and multiplication of exponents, he presented the students with equations using exponents that highlighted patterns. He then led a discussion on what they noticed about the patterns. He then carefully discussed each rule, how to apply it, and gave them plenty of practice with feedback. Students took notes, which they could refer to in the future. As he told me, "It just feels like a rule," he said, "and so I teach it as a rule." He tried to keep these moments short and only use this kind of instruction when the topic clearly called for it.

He was also more explicit with students in individual moments, just as students needed it. One topic he taught was solving linear equations. I saw him in the middle of the year, giving a seventh-grade class a series of problems to work on solving linear equations. He told me that on the previous day's assessment, too many students in this class had not been able to remember the procedure, so he was returning to it. He did not use any whole-group explicit instruction, but he put students in groups to work together. He walked around the classroom and provided just-in-time support for students who asked.

I noticed that Araceli, a student with an Individualized Education Program (IEP) for a learning disability, had moved away from her group and was working at a whiteboard on a problem. The problem was $-9x = -81$. Araceli wrote the problem on the whiteboard and was able to divide both sides by -9 but seemed stuck past that.

As she stood there, Mr. Jay came over. He quietly asked her if she wanted to talk about the problem, and she nodded "yes." I listened as he tried to figure out what part of the problem had her stumped. He started with why she would be dividing by -9; she seemed to get that, understanding that $-9/-9$ would be one, and that her goal was to keep both sides equivalent. He then started talking about the rules for multiplying negative numbers, and he wrote out a visual to help her remember (a positive x a positive is a positive, and so on). He created this visual with her, asking her to recall as best she could the rules as he scribed them. He did not tell her the answers, but he prompted her both verbally and visually, and then waited. After they created this visual, Araceli wrote $x = 9$, successfully applying the rules. She then started on the next problem –x = 11 = 35. Here is what the board looked like at the end of their conversation:

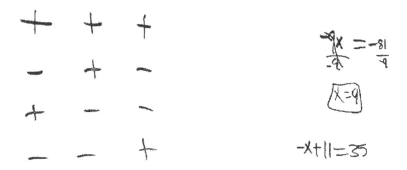

Let's unpack this interaction. First, Mr. Jay did not take over Araceli's thinking. He waited to get a better understanding of what she knew and did not know before he jumped in. With the visual for multiplication with signed numbers, he was not giving her the answer but co-creating a visual that she could use to get to the answer. He scaffolded her answer, providing strategic coaching just as necessary but always starting with questions and giving her enough space to remember if she could.

In an interview with our research team a few months later, we asked Araceli about this moment. She remembered it and explained how she liked how Mr. Jay would talk to her "one on one" when she wasn't sure what to do. She also noted that he gave her enough time to think, and "he doesn't give you the answer but he like explains it more better than the paper." Araceli was critical of teachers who give too much help, as well as of those who give too little. Mr. Jay had found the sweet spot, giving just enough support that she could figure it out herself. In my research projects, I have heard multiple students with IEPs tell me that they particularly appreciate when a teacher comes to them and respectfully gives them the individualized assistance they need.

Finally, we saw one more way in which students in Mr. Jay's class got more explicit kinds of instruction: student-to-student coaching. Since his class was so focused on group work, we saw many instances of students coaching other students. Just as Mr. Jay made this visual to support Araceli, we saw students making visuals for other students to support them. We saw students with and without disabilities being the coach for other students. In interviews, students were very appreciative of this coaching from other students.

UNDERSTANDING EXPLICIT AND INQUIRY INSTRUCTION

So when do we use inquiry-based instruction? When do we use explicit instruction? And why are people still arguing about this? Let's dig into these questions for the remainder of the chapter, starting with defining the two.

Explicit Instruction

Explicit instruction is a set of practices that include clearly defined goals, well-paced instruction with opportunities for student interaction, feedback, and practice. It developed from direct instruction, a specific set of instructional practices that developed in the 1970s to teach all subjects (Hughes et al., 2017). Explicit instruction is also connected with I Do (teacher models), We Do (students try with significant guidance from the teacher), and You Do (students practice independently). Explicit instruction has been defined as the following sequence (Doabler & Fien, 2013):

1. the teacher modeling a new concept or skill,
2. the teacher providing guided practice opportunities,
3. the teacher checking for student understanding,
4. the teacher providing academic feedback, and
5. the students engaging in independent practice.

There is nothing necessarily wrong with direct instruction or explicit instruction, if it matches our goals. I find this kind of pedagogy useful when students need to learn a specific skill or procedure and the best way to learn it is to practice.

But I do worry quite a bit when teachers are told that explicit instruction is the *only* effective way to teach students math, something I hear often about students with disabilities. This belief is highly problematic because explicit instruction is not designed to develop mathematical sense-making. Explicit instruction tells students how to think and exactly how to solve problems. It could affect student ability to learn how to solve nonroutine problems, as well as to develop mathematical intuition (National Mathematics Advisory Panel, 2008). It may affect students' sense of agency and thus their developing identities as mathematicians. A meal of only explicit instruction in procedures is not a well-rounded mathematical diet, depriving students of the opportunity to solve complex, authentic problems.

> **A meal of only explicit instruction in procedures is not a well-rounded mathematical diet, depriving students of the opportunity to solve complex, authentic problems.**

Another of my concerns with explicit instruction exclusively is that this mode of teaching does not allow for the possibility of students uncovering their own misconceptions and building new ideas. Explicit instruction is about learning a predetermined procedure, and there is not often consideration for the ideas that the learner already has. Yet all our learners have ideas. Some are problematic and potentially confusing. When students are allowed to think, allowed to share their thinking, their ideas become visible to them, both what works and what needs to change. The power is in the hands of the student, guided by a teacher. When students are taught procedures and not allowed to think about why they work, students can develop "buggy algorithms," in which they misapply the procedures (Hurst & Huntley, 2018).

Another concern is how targeted this instruction needs to be to be effective. Explicit instruction is designed to carefully build on prior knowledge of procedures. We would not use explicit instruction to teach the multiplication algorithm for students who did not have mastery of subtraction with regrouping. The multiplication algorithm builds on the subtraction procedure, so students need to already know it. This is why much of the research on explicit instruction in math education is done one on one, so that the researchers can be sure that the instruction is targeted to the student. Thus, it is a difficult pedagogy to apply in classrooms as our students are often in different places in terms of prior skills.

Inquiry-Based Instruction

Inquiry-based instruction refers to a much broader range of pedagogical practices than explicit instruction: most broadly, students learning mathematics through solving problems without being told how to do so ahead of time. It comes from constructivist theories of learning in which we all learn through experience and our reflections on these experiences.

Sometimes when I hear arguments against inquiry-based learning, I can see that the arguments are really against *discovery learning*. An older concept from the 1960s, discovery learning is a more extreme form of constructivism in which students are given problems and the freedom to discover mathematics completely on their own without *any* teacher support. This is not what most teachers do when teaching mathematics, including when giving inquiry problems. Mr. Jay is not just giving students problems and going out to lunch! He, like all the teachers in this book, are working super hard to design purposefully designed and sequenced tasks, as well as to provide support in the form of teacher questioning, verbal discussion, and attention to generalization of new ideas. In fact, I know that inquiry instruction can go wrong for students when they are not provided with enough support for participation, or with enough support to remember and generalize the understandings that develop. Great inquiry math teaching includes plenty of scaffolds and supports for students.

What Are Our Goals?

I believe that the problem is that we have framed this debate about which approach to teaching "works" without considering that they both work for different goals. Cognitive scientists Daniel Schwartz and colleagues (2016) described this problem in a way that might move us beyond the either/ or approach. Using concepts from cognitive science, they described how knowledge itself (in all content areas) has tension between *efficiency* and *innovation*. Innovation refers to preparing learners to solve complex and new problems in their fields. Efficiency refers to preparing learners to efficiently solve the kinds of problems that already exist. Both goals are laudable, but they are often in tension as we plan. If we focus too much on preparing for innovation, students may not get enough time preparing for efficiency. Yet a focus on efficiency can be counterproductive to innovation. Cognitive scientists describe *adaptive expertise* as the goal for students across subjects, which means being able to adapt and strategize for new, unfamiliar problems (innovation) using knowledge (efficiency) (Hatano & Inagaki, 1986).

> **Innovation refers to preparing learners to solve complex and new problems in their fields. Efficiency refers to preparing learners to efficiently solve the kinds of problems that already exist.**

Let's put this discussion in another context. Think about soccer games as opportunities for innovation in mathematics. A soccer game asks kids to innovate based on changing conditions—a nonroutine task. And it is (hopefully!) fun. Soccer practice is a different kind of activity. During practice, students do routine activities designed to build their skills. Can you imagine only playing games with no practice? Kids may not have the skills they need to innovate successfully during the games. And what about practice with no games? Kids would lose interest, as well as the ability to think on their feet for nonroutine problems.

SOURCE: istock.com/FatCamera; istock.com/AzmanJaka

In math, students need to develop skills and strategies alongside experience in complex problem solving. Adaptive expertise in mathematics is richly connected procedural (strategic) and conceptual knowledge that can be flexibly applied in new contexts (Baroody, 2003). Table 4.2 applies these ideas from Schwartz et al. (2016) to mathematics to create a chart that contrasts innovation with efficiency. These authors cautioned that we should not focus on one column to the exclusion of the other; these kinds of knowledges are best developed iteratively. We should not wait until undergraduate mathematics to let students play with mathematics, nor should we fail to provide opportunities for students to develop efficiency.

Table 4.2 · *Goals of innovation activities versus goals of efficient knowledge activities*

Goals of innovation knowledge activities in mathematics (playing the game)	Goals of efficient knowledge activities in mathematics (focused practice)
• Develop understandings of the structure and variation of mathematics • Explore the problems that need to be solved in mathematics • Pose problems that can be solved in mathematics that matter to you • Be part of a learning community where making mistakes is part of the process • Play with mathematics • Foster intrinsic satisfaction • Learn to hold mathematical conjectures lightly and seek feedback • Develop a productive disposition • Engage in the practices of mathematics, such as modeling and discussion (SMPs) • See the relevance of mathematics to one's own identity and community	• Be exposed to the solutions of others • Learn why those solutions work • Practice with the goal of efficiency • Solve problems under different conditions toward generalization • Refine problem solving and strategies • Feel a sense of competence through skilled performance

> **Think About It**
>
> Reflecting on Table 4.2, what matters to us as teachers? Which statements did you feel a particular connection toward? What do we do in our classrooms to support both kinds of knowledge development?

Reflecting Back on Mr. Jay's Goals

Let's return to Mr. Jay's goals as a teacher for his inclusive class: first, developing "problem-solving thinkers" before skills and standards. His second focus was on building student confidence, supporting them to "believe in themselves." Mr. Jay believed that to accomplish these goals, his students needed plenty of opportunities to engage in meaningful inquiry. And he believed they needed to start the year fully in problem solving inquiry mode. Efficiency would come, but first he needed to get them to believe in themselves as problem solvers. They needed to get into the habit of sense-making.

Mr. Jay does not believe that his students with disabilities need something completely different than other students. If all students need to have a strong investment in meaningful problem solving, then so do his students with disabilities. If all students also need instruction that leads to efficiency, then so do his students with disabilities. This is a key equity argument. A key aim of inclusive education is to provide access to participation in general education for students with disabilities, what is called the "least restrictive environment." In mathematics, that principle means students with disabilities should have access to the same kind of mathematics as general education students are given, or the least restrictive curriculum. To assume that certain students cannot do this kind of math, because they cannot think and thus need to be given mathematical procedures only, is ableist and destructive.

UNDERSTANDING THE CLAIMS ABOUT EXPLICIT INSTRUCTION AND STUDENTS WITH DISABILITIES

So where does this come from, this idea that inquiry-based instruction is not appropriate for students with disabilities? To understand, we need to spend a little time comparing the research in mathematics education with research on math in special education.

Beginning in the 1950s, both mathematics and special education were heavily influenced by behaviorism, or the idea that we should focus on observable behaviors. Research in this tradition is focused on directly measurable skills such as accuracy of memorization of facts or replication of procedures. Direct instruction, and explicit instruction, is the pedagogical recommendation from researchers in this area because these are the most direct ways of teaching this kind of mathematics. If math is about replicating procedures and memorizing facts, then explicit instruction seems an efficient choice.

In the 1960s, mathematics education was transformed by what was called the "cognitive revolution." The most influential aspect in mathematics education was constructivism, or the idea that we all approach new learning with some prior learning in place, learning that we build from to learn new things. The mind—and student thinking—is the main focus of this tradition. Mathematics is seen as a complicated, interconnected web of concepts and strategies. This body of research developed an argument for inquiry-based mathematics, with students taking an active role in their own learning.

While mathematics educational research moved into decades of research based on a constructivist theory of learning, special educational research has historically been actively opposed to constructivism (Woodward, 2004). Special education research has spent decades researching how explicit instruction increases the procedural skills of students with disabilities. At the same time, mathematics education has tended to leave students with disabilities out of research, which has meant much less research looking at the mathematical thinking and problem solving of students with disabilities in inquiry-based mathematics (Lambert & Tan, 2020).

So the research is different because the research fields are different, not because the kids are different. This difference in how adults approach research, not a difference in what children need or want, has created our current situation. According to the National Mathematics Advisory Panel, "It is important to note that there is no evidence supporting explicit instruction as the only mode of instruction for students [with LDs]" (2008, p. 1229).

RESEARCH ON THE TWO PEDAGOGIES

So what do we know about the efficacy of these different instructional practices? Although there is a lot of research on explicit instruction and inquiry-based instruction separately, it is hard to compare because most research does not compare one with the other.

One influential paper that compared explicit instruction with inquiry-based instruction (Alfieri et al., 2011) included two large meta-analyses of research across multiple content fields. In their first study, Alfieri et al. compared "unassisted discovery learning" with "explicit instructional practices." They defined unassisted discovery learning as teaching in which teachers give students no scaffolds or guidance, no questioning or discussion, just a problem. Not surprisingly, explicit instruction compared with problems posed with no guidance was more effective. I think we all could have predicted that.

In their second study, they created a new category that they called "guided discovery learning," which was inquiry-based problem solving but with scaffolds and support, such as feedback and teacher questioning. In this comparison, they found that guided discovery learning was more effective than explicit instruction (Alfieri et al., 2011). To avoid using the outdated term "discovery learning," I will call this category "guided inquiry."

Despite the finding that guided inquiry was more effective than explicit instruction, this paper by Alfieri et al. (2011) has been improperly cited to support the idea that explicit instruction is more effective than inquiry-based learning. Perhaps those who do so truly believe that teachers just give students math problems, and then walk away, assuming that kids will just figure out mathematics on their own. If this did work, our jobs would be so much easier! But we know that this doesn't work, and it is not what is happening in our classrooms. Kids need support and guidance in inquiry-based mathematics. In this book, I will be providing stories of teachers like Mr. Jay who purposefully use questioning, discussion, and scaffolds to support students in guided inquiry.

I want to highlight an impressive series of studies that has investigated the efficacy of guided inquiry learning for students with disabilities. In a series of rigorous studies spanning decades, Bottge and colleagues have developed and assessed a curriculum specifically designed for students with learning disabilities (LDs) to participate in inquiry mathematics, called "Enhanced Anchored Instruction" (Bottge, 1999; Bottge et al., 2002, 2007, 2010, 2014). Through the use of video-based problems, researchers immersed students with learning disabilities in contexts such as building skateboard ramps and hovercrafts to learn algebra and fractions. By removing textual barriers, their work has allowed students to engage in challenging mathematics through open-ended problem solving. Their initial studies were situated in special education resource rooms, where they found strong positive effects, particularly on student problem-solving skills (Bottge, 1999). In their first studies testing the approach in inclusive general education settings, the students with disabilities did not do as well as in their previous studies (Bottge et al., 2002). They found that the students with learning disabilities did not participate equally in small groups, and received less teacher support. They also found that the teachers needed more professional development to delve into the content they were teaching.

So these researchers redesigned their work, adding in additional professional development for teachers to make sure they not only understood the mathematics of the units but also how to engage all students in small group work. These modifications were successful, resulting in significant gains for all students, in which the students with learning disabilities had the same growth as those without a disability (Bottge et al., 2007). A second round of redesign for this team added an instructional module that focused on the procedures and concepts of fraction computation using a blended approach that included explicit instruction as well as guided inquiry (Bottge et al., 2010). This redesign again increased the achievement of students with disabilities (Bottge et al., 2014).

The work of this group of scholars demonstrates empirically that students with learning disabilities can learn complex mathematics through guided inquiry-based problem solving, to which multiple studies across different settings can attest. I respect how these researchers engaged in design research, paying careful attention to the barriers that emerged for students and redesigning their intervention before the next study. We also have evidence from other qualitative research that students with disabilities can engage and thrive in inquiry-based classrooms, but they need teachers to be flexible and responsive, providing specific scaffolds as needed by students (Lambert & Sugita, 2016).

EXPANDING BEYOND THE BINARY

What I notice about the research of Alfieri and colleagues (2011) on the efficacy of instructional approaches is that they started with the two absolute ends of a spectrum, with student-driven instruction with no teacher guidance on the one side (*unassisted discovery learning*) and teacher-driven instruction (*explicit instruction*) on the other side, but they saw the need for another category of pedagogy used across many research studies: *guided inquiry*. This approach is a scaffolded version of inquiry-based instruction, with some of the scaffolds being teacher questioning and feedback.

I want to propose another kind of pedagogy that teachers and researchers use that is somewhere on a continuum between inquiry and explicit instruction: *guided strategic development*, inspired by work from Arthur

Baroody and colleagues (2015). Baroody and colleagues compared this kind of instruction with direct instruction:

> Although a pattern, relation, or strategy is not explicitly provided or explained to a child (as in direct instruction), this type of discovery learning involves considerable scaffolding. Instruction and practice are organized to direct a child's attention to regularities or a strategy. For example, items are arranged sequentially to underscore a pattern or relation and prompt direct attention toward a regularity or strategy without explicitly stating it. Feedback provides some explanation of why a response is correct or incorrect as well as specifying whether an answer is correct or not. (Baroody et al., 2015, p. 94)

This discussion describes a critical feature of my teaching toolkit that I had not so clearly seen described before this article: carefully sequenced instruction that is highly scaffolded, yet still allows students to do the thinking. Scaffolds can include the sequence of problems designed to prompt discussion of particular strategies (as in a number string, discussed in Chapters 9 and 11) or the purposeful use of scaffolds in the Instructional Routine Connecting Representations (Chapter 13). In *guided strategic development*, students are still thinking, but the routine or practice is more heavily scaffolded.

Baroody and colleagues, for example, documented the efficacy of this kind of strategy instruction on students learning addition strategies such as doubles (Purpura et al., 2016). They found that less scaffolded approaches were equally effective for more intuitive strategies such as adding a one, but that more scaffolded instruction was effective for doubles (Baroody et al., 2015). Effective scaffolds include comparison of multiple strategies (Durkin et al., 2017), including discussing how strategies work and when one strategy is more efficient. Another effective scaffold is student self-explanation, or when students are given the opportunity to explain strategies and why they did or did not work (Rittle-Johnson et al., 2017).

Inspired by Mr. Jay's work with Araceli, I also add one more pedagogy: *strategic coaching*. This type of instruction can be focused on mathematical strategies or on metacognitive strategies. It can be whole group coaching, but it is often done through one-on-one conferencing that provides focused coaching for a student, taking into account what they know, and providing guidance for what they do not know. This just-in-time support provides as much guidance as a student needs, when the student needs it.

Now we can describe a little bit more clearly a spectrum of instructional approaches, beyond a binary.

I don't create these new categories to add something new for us all to learn. Instead, I am trying to name what great teachers (and innovative researchers) already do.

So let's return to what Mr. Jay does. I would consider his facilitation of the Visual Pattern Task as a great example of *guided inquiry*. Students are thinking, talking, sharing, and driving the problem solving. Mr. Jay has set up the structures of the class to support high levels of student engagement, through the practices of *The Thinking Classroom* (Liljedahl, 2020). At other times, he engages students in *guided strategic development*, such as when he gave students a sequence of the rules for exponents and had them find patterns. He also engages in one-on-one *strategic coaching* and *explicit instruction*.

So how can we sequence this work? Let's look again to what Mr Jay. does. He begins most topics with *guided inquiry* tasks like visual patterns, in which students are able to investigate how algebra works. It is accessible to all, multimodal, and engaging. His goal with this work is to have students feel confident as problem solvers and to understand the big ideas behind the topic he is teaching. Here he is going for innovation knowledge.

When students are at the point that they are ready for a procedure, he shifts toward goals of efficiency. When necessary, he provides *explicit instruction* in procedures like solving equations, although always short and to the point. And when necessary, as in the case of Araceli, he provides that just-in-time *strategic coaching*, specifically tailored to what the student needs. Finally, Mr. Jay provides students with lots of opportunities to practice what they have learned. Beginning with problem solving and then providing more guided instruction is a research-supported strategy (Sinha & Kapur, 2021).

Mr. Jay transitioned away from explicit instruction early in his career because he did not believe that his students were learning (and remembering what they learned) with explicit instruction alone. But he also wanted to shift their identities as mathematical learners. And this is what he sees being a critical element for his shift toward guided inquiry as the core of his practice, "I just want them not to hate math." In interviews with his students, I saw their respect for his pedagogy. They enjoyed problem solving and working in groups. They had a lot to say about the importance of being able to work together to solve challenging problems. And they also respected how Mr. Jay would review something if they needed. And not one of them said that they hated math.

REFLECTION QUESTIONS

1. What are your goals as a math teacher? How do they connect to the ideas of innovation and efficiency?

2. What have you heard about explicit and inquiry instruction, particularly for students with disabilities? What did you learn from this chapter? How would you explain it to another teacher?

3. In what ways are you explicit as a math teacher? In what ways is your teaching inquiry based? How do you combine the two?

PART 2

DEFINING UDL MATH

CHAPTER 5

WHAT IS UNIVERSAL DESIGN FOR LEARNING IN MATHEMATICS (UDL MATH)?

IN THIS CHAPTER, WE WILL . . .

- Explore the history of Universal Design and Universal Design for Learning (UDL)
- Discuss learner variability
- Determine what makes an expert learner in mathematics
- Unpack the UDL Math Design Elements with learner narratives

> If the teacher came into the classroom snarling and spouting facts in rote fashion, with no explanation of the core meanings, my disabilities flared and I failed. But in subjects such as physics, biology, and algebra, taught using multisensory methods by kind, enthusiastic teachers, I had nearly perfect grades.
>
> —Schmitt, 1994, p. 118

Abraham Schmitt, in his autobiography of growing up with a learning disability, explains that the approach of the teacher mattered to his learning, as did the way content was presented. He responded better to multisensory instruction in science and math, teaching that was focused on core meanings rather than on rote learning. He brings up how his teachers affected his engagement, including his relationship with them. He also shares how he was able to excel in science and math classes when given the right conditions. This quote illustrates the complexity of learning that is central to the framework of Universal Design for Learning (UDL) and what matters to disabled learners in math classrooms.

In this chapter, we explore Universal Design for Learning in Math (UDL Math), beginning with the roots of UDL in Universal Design. I present UDL Math as a flexible framework to help educators design more accessible and engaging mathematics classrooms. I do not see UDL as yet another framework to be applied or as a checklist of particular strategies. Instead, following authors like Jay Dolmage (2015), I see UDL as a "way to move," a way to notice what is not working for our students (barriers), and to creatively open up our classrooms so that more students can be successful.

Throughout the chapter, I will rely on quotes from insiders, those who have experienced learning mathematics in our schools with disabilities, particularly learning disabilities such as dyslexia and dyscalculia. I have gathered all the quotes from the chapter into an activity called *Barriers and Supports in Math Class From a Neurodiverse Perspective* that is in Appendix B (p. 260). One way to experience this chapter would be to stop now and read all of those quotes at once to begin your own analysis of what barriers exist in math class and how we could redesign math class with empathy.

THE HISTORY OF UNIVERSAL DESIGN

UDL was inspired by the Universal Design movement in architecture and product design. Universal Design sought to find elegant and effective ways to maximize the use of buildings and products, pioneered by Ronald Mace, a disabled architect. One of his legacies was to demonstrate that disabled perspectives on design for disability were particularly effective and innovative (Hamraie, 2017). A key idea from Universal Design is that when we design for the variability of users at the beginning, rather than retrofitting at the end, the design is both more accessible and more elegant.

A classic example of Universal Design is the OXO vegetable peeler (on the right). Take a look at these two vegetable peelers. What do you notice? Which has a wider group of people who can use it?

SOURCE: vegetable peelers by thechefsco and OXO

The OXO vegetable peeler was created by a designer who was married to a woman with arthritis and was having trouble peeling apples (Wilson, 2018). Their collaboration created a tool that met her needs (easier to hold and position), as well as easier for many others, such as children. It can be used by those with low motor tone, as well as by anyone who has peeled a million potatoes to get ready for a family event.

Another example of Universal Design is closed captions (Meyer & Rose, 2005). Deaf people initially needed to buy expensive converters to be able to use televisions, which were not designed with Deaf people in mind. Eventually, the technology was built into all televisions, so now both Deaf and hearing people can use captions. Captions also help people with processing differences.

In both of these cases, the innovation works for disabled people *and* for nondisabled people. In fact, designs get better for everyone when they are more accessible. This might seem like a back door to prioritizing the needs of nondisabled people. Instead the point is related to the complexity of people, both disabled and nondisabled. I do not have arthritis, but I love the OXO vegetable peeler because it allows me to peel more potatoes. I am not Deaf, but I love captions because they help me process language better, as well as follow the narrative while my dog is barking. When a design is simple and inclusive and supportive across human variability, it has potential to become part of our living landscape.

UNIVERSAL DESIGN FOR LEARNING

UDL was developed in the 1980s in Boston by a group of medical clinicians from the organization later called "CAST" (Meyer et al., 2014). Taking its inspiration from Universal Design, UDL is an educational framework that seeks to create inclusive schools through designing from the outset for the natural variability across learners.

UDL is radical because it situates the problem in our classrooms and schools, not the kids, aligning with the social model of disability (Waitoller & King Thorius, 2016). It is radical because it conceptualizes learners as complex—it acknowledges learner variability. It is radical because the goal of schooling is not memorization but development as an expert, strategic thinker. Although many educational frameworks focus only on content (in UDL the area of Representation), UDL has an equal focus on emotion, affect (Engagement), and strategic development (Action and Expression).

Let's unpack UDL by exploring key features:

- ▶ Understanding learner variability
- ▶ Developing expert learners
- ▶ Leveraging interconnected networks of the brain

Understanding Learner Variability

In UDL, learners are conceptualized through a lens of learner variability, which comes from the learning sciences (Rose, 2017), a concept that is broader than disability labels and applies to each and every human. Each individual has a unique brain, created through dynamic interaction between genetics and experience (Rose, 2017). Individuals vary across contexts—students may pay attention differently at home and at school. We also vary in how we see, hear, and move. We vary in how well we can remember mathematical facts, as well as in our ways of paying attention. Learners vary in their emotional response to mathematics. And we vary in how we develop strategies in mathematics.

> ### Think About It
>
> How do learners vary in your math class? Do they vary in how they pay attention? Their memory? Their enthusiasm for math? Prior knowledge? How else do they vary?

Does the prevailing approach to education reflect this fundamental fact of individual difference? Not really. Educational researchers are trained to see averages across a population, not in how people differ from those averages (Rose, 2017). A research study finds that one approach works for across the average, and it is determined to be an evidence-based practice, despite possibly wide variability in who it benefits. When we simplify and flatten individual differences, we sometimes end up describing nobody. We can also miss critical elements of HOW students learn, particularly those at the margins.

The science that has emerged to help us understand complexity across individuals and their development is called *dynamic development systems theory*, which is part of the learning sciences (Osher et al., 2020). Rose (2017) and other scientists of individual differences have documented how variable development is. A pioneer of this approach, Esther Thelen (2005), found that babies learn to crawl in different ways and on different timelines. Yet there was not an unlimited set of pathways: Babies tended to follow one of several developmental pathways. Similar findings have been found in mathematics (Siegler, 2007), reminding us of multiple developmental pathways in a learning landscape rather than a linear ladder of development. Although humans are highly variable, we can use patterns across that variability to plan for wide groups of kids. UDL asks us to design across variability, understanding development as complex.

Learner variability does not replace the concept of disability; they can exist side by side. Disability is an identity, a community, and a political movement for justice for disabled people. Learner variability applies to all, including those with disabilities. Certain aspects of human variability have been labeled as disabilities. And each person with a disability is unique, variable in more dimensions than their disability category suggests.

> **Although humans are highly variable, we can use patterns across that variability to plan for wide groups of kids.**

Think about Attention Deficit Hyperactivity Disorder (ADHD), for example. Using a neurodiversity lens, individuals with ADHD have both a set of challenges around attention and a set of related strengths. Using a social model, the problem of ADHD does not reside in the individual student but in classrooms that often seem designed specifically to penalize differences in attention. Our school system demands that students pay attention in particularly demanding and narrow ways. For instance, the ability to sustain hyper-focus on projects, typical of people with ADHD, is not allowed in school because it does not fit within the structured schedules of most schools where students have to move from class to class every 45 minutes. Thus, even though differences in attention exist, it is the narrow confines of our schooling system that create the disabling conditions of ADHD. Using a learner variability model, we can focus on the wide differences in attention across contexts for all our students. ADHD is still an identity, still a community, and an individual difference that is on a continuum across humans. Learner variability does not negate disability identity or community.

In this book, I put disability at the center of the discussion. Yet many of the popular texts on UDL rarely mention disability (Lambert, Greene, et al., 2022). I assume they avoid mentioning disability for a specific reason: They are trying to encourage general educators to see UDL as a useful framework for all kids. And it *is*! Yet UDL began with disability because these students are marginalized in our classrooms and schools. And, more than that, as I argue throughout this book, by providing access to neurodiverse students we can transform mathematics.

Learner variability can also be confused with an older idea of learning styles. A common misconception is that each student has a single dominant learning style, like a visual learner or a verbal learner. Yet none of us only learn through one modality. Yes, we all engage differently in learning (learner variability!); however, there are not static, fixed patterns in how each individual learns across all situations (Rogowsky et al., 2015).

> **A common misconception is that each student has a single dominant learning style, like a visual learner or a verbal learner. Yet none of us only learn through one modality.**

Rita, whom I met in the same classrooms as Luis in Chapter 2, took a learning styles quiz in sixth grade. She explained to me her score told her she was "not a visual learner." I visited Rita in her classroom almost 30 times during her sixth- and seventh-grade years. I saw her multiple times using this way of understanding herself ("not a visual learner") in a way that limited her learning.

In seventh grade, I sat next to her as she worked on an integer problem that was in the context of sea level. The problem asked the following: An explorer hiked up a mountain that was 5,430 feet tall. She hiked down and then dove into a lake at the bottom of the climb to negative 600 feet. What was the total vertical distance she explored that day? Rita and her group were having trouble solving this problem since they could not figure out which rules for addition and subtraction of integers to apply. They had written down positive 5,430 and negative 600, but they didn't know whether to add or subtract. I suggested to Rita that she could draw a picture of the situation. Rita leveled a pained look at me and reminded me that she was "not a visual person" and that "number lines don't work for me." I gently suggested that maybe it would help, just in this situation. She obligingly drew out the situation and instantly figured out that she needed to add the two distances. Rita's sixth-grade teachers (Mr. Pierce and Ms. Scott) would have been so sad to know that this was the result of their learning styles quiz. It was not their intention to make Rita feel that she could not understand number lines, that she was never going to learn through visuals. Rita may not prefer number lines in some situations, but in others, they work for her. Static ideas of learning styles can limit students.

Expert Learners in UDL

UDL is based in two interconnected research fields: the learning sciences and neuroscience. The learning sciences is an academic field that studies learning across multiple disciplines. A core tenet of the learning sciences is that people learn complex practices like mathematics through sustained engagement in those practices (National Academies of Sciences, Engineering and Medicine, 2018). Learning math is not just learning math content but also learning how to do math. Research in the learning sciences influenced the goal of UDL: *expert learners*. Rather than conceptualizing the goal as students learning particular content, the goal of UDL is that students become expert, strategic learners across their life spans.

> **Rather than conceptualizing the goal as students learning particular content, the goal of UDL is that students become expert, strategic learners across their life spans.**

This is a transformative difference in the purpose of schooling, particularly for students who have been marginalized by traditional math classrooms. As soon as a student is seen to be "struggling," the focus of their education tends to narrow to content and skills alone. UDL focuses our attention on engagement in what mathematicians actually do, as reflected by the Standards of Mathematical Practice (SMPs; National Governors Association Center for Best Practices & Council of Chief State School Officers, 2010). The SMPs reflect decades of research on the importance of mathematical practices—or on the ways in which mathematicians and successful math learners engage in mathematical activities such as problem solving, modeling, and proof. Access to problem solving and mathematical proof help to develop agency in mathematics, or the sense of oneself as able to solve and persist in solving complex mathematics (Boaler & Sengupta-Irving, 2016).

Think About It

What would you see or hear from students who were expert learners in mathematics?

What is an expert learner in mathematics?

Work on developing self-regulation when math class feels tough.

Makes connections to what they already know and across topics.

Knows what they do not know.

Motivated by learning math (mastery-oriented vs. performance-oriented).

Jumps into problems and solves them. Persists when stuck.

Sets goals for their own learning.

Collaborates.

Develops and shares math strategies.

Wants feedback and pays attention to it.

Strategic Sense Makers

Are students constructing identities as strategic sense makers in math?

Asks questions when they need help.

Engages in the math strategies of others.

Uses multiple tools and models to make sense of problems.

Knows how to study.

Keeps working until they reach understanding. Math questions nag at them.

Knows what supports help them. Advocates for them.

Can describe their strengths and challenges in mathematics.

Asks questions to push the group's thinking further.

For me, an expert learner in mathematics is a strategic sense-maker. In my years as both a special educator and a general educator teaching mathematics, I was most concerned for students when I saw them consistently not making sense of mathematics. Some students, when presented with a word problem, would ask me again and again what operation to use. These habits were most pronounced in students who had experienced rote, narrow mathematics teaching in previous grades. These students expected teachers to tell them what procedure to use. In special education, we have a term for this: learned helplessness. We often use it to apply to students with disabilities who are not allowed to think on their own, thus developing habits of relying on adults for guidance. In this case, the focus on replication and memorization of mathematics, rather than on developing a student's sense-making, develops habits that may not serve the student long term.

LEVERAGING INTERCONNECTED NETWORKS OF THE BRAIN

UDL researchers, including scholars in neuroscience and education, identified three interconnected networks of the brain that factor significantly in learning: engagement, representation, and strategic action (Meyer et al., 2014). These three areas of learning form the basis of the UDL guidelines. The first network, labeled here as "engagement," is affective, involved in how we process our emotions and affect. Researchers in UDL have focused significant attention on the critical role that social and emotional processes play in learning. The second network, "representation," is recognition, involved in how we recognize objects and patterns in the environment. The third network, "strategic action," is involved in how we plan and monitor our actions, including learning. These three networks work together in the complex process of learning in content areas such as mathematics. I find these three dimensions most helpful when we use them as different lenses to look at learning. Too often, we focus only on content. What are students learning, and how will we teach it? The three dimensions in UDL remind us that learning is first and foremost emotional and that developing students' self-understandings is as important as the content we teach.

Engagement

Emotion affects engagement and thus learning in profound and fundamental ways (Immordino-Yang & Damasio, 2007). All students choose whether they engage in mathematics—we either create the conditions or we don't. Students have strong emotions in math class that affect their identities as math learners and their ability and willingness to engage (Lambert, 2019). To fully engage in mathematics, students need opportunities to work with meaningful mathematics that they find relevant as well as challenging. Students also report the importance of a supportive classroom environment where they feel comfortable enough to take risks such as sharing their answers in class, as well as the importance of collaboration (Boaler & Sengupta-Irving, 2016).

Representation

How do we present information to students in mathematics? And what representations do students use to solve problems? Although the representations students make are usually included in UDL under strategic action, I move them to the category of representation. In mathematics, we think of representation as central to mathematics—both what representations we model for students and those they take up. The area of representation in math also includes how we sequence and design instruction. Another critical component is focusing on core ideas, investing in the most critical content for learners.

Strategic Action

Strategic action is the category of how we as learners plan our response to input. As we develop strategies in mathematics, or in metacognition, we become more planful in how we respond to mathematics instruction. We can develop strategies in self-regulation (being aware of and in control of our emotions) and executive functioning (planning and organization). This area also includes how we give students feedback, which is how students develop these strategies. Assessment, then, is a critical feature of this area.

UDL MATH

I have designed UDL Math to center mathematics as a human practice: teachers as designers and students as agentic problem-solvers. UDL Math provides a blueprint for creative, empathic design of math learning experiences that begins with the students in the margins. That includes students with disabilities, as well as students who have been marginalized in mathematics because of their race, culture, language, gender, or sexual preference. UDL aligns with culturally responsive pedagogy if we can truly center the experiences of students of color in our work (Waitoller & King Thorius, 2016).

> **UDL aligns with culturally responsive pedagogy**
> **if we can truly center the experiences**
> **of students of color in our work.**

Figure 5.1 • *UDL Math design elements*

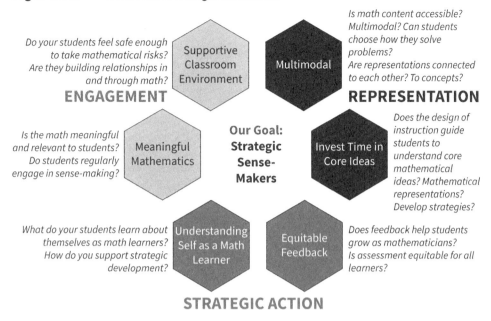

In this section, we will explore some critical elements in mathematics of three UDL networks: engagement, representation, and strategic action. Figure 5.1 describes six important elements to consider when designing accessible mathematics experiences. This is not a checklist (and should not be made into one!), but it is a way to explore various important elements in our classrooms. I designed these based on research across the learning sciences, mathematics education, and special education. I also integrated analysis of the experiences of those with disabilities, from both memoirs and interview studies. Each section begins with a quote from an adult with dyslexia or dyscalculia reflecting on their experience learning mathematics. They are the experts on their own experience after all, and I am putting them front and center to remind us all to listen to our students. In each section, we return to the three gestures in Chapter 1. We begin by understanding the barriers in our classrooms (how math class is too narrow), then how we can open up our classrooms, and finally additional strategic support we may need to offer.

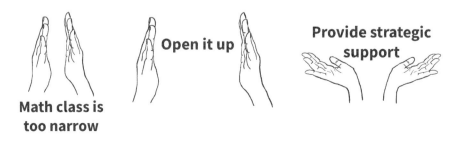

Opportunity for Meaningful Mathematical Problem Solving

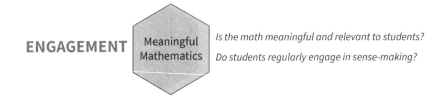

ENGAGEMENT — Meaningful Mathematics — *Is the math meaningful and relevant to students? Do students regularly engage in sense-making?*

MATH IS "HARD" because of how boring and time-consuming it is. Homework usually consists of doing the same problem 40 times in a row! Then tomorrow, we will do 40 more of the same problem, except with one extra digit of complexity thrown in. The pages march by, an endless procession of mind-numbing paperwork, a treadmill of uninteresting problems. What I fail to understand is that the "harder" classes are where math becomes far more interesting. Instead of 40 dull problems, they give you five interesting ones. Instead of pointless drills, you can begin to see how to use math as a tool. They finally give you a pile of two-by-fours and let you start nailing things together (Young, 2011, p. 119). ●

Shamus Young, an adult labeled with a learning disability reflecting on his experience in schools, described mathematics classrooms as filled with boring and repetitive work, which makes math "hard." He contrasted this with real mathematics, where he could become interested in problems and engaged in finding solutions. Not only do students need opportunities to solve meaningful, engaging problems, but they also need this consistently. We want the math classroom to be a place where students expect to be challenged and engaged.

Some barriers to student engagement in problem solving include

- Lack of engaging, relevant, interesting mathematical problems
- Instruction that does not give opportunity for students to think for themselves
- Lack of opportunity can create learned helplessness, when students don't know how to start solving a problem or what to do if they get stuck
- Lack of opportunities to collaboratively solve problems

We can open up math classrooms by

- Giving students plenty of opportunities to solve engaging, relevant, interesting, accessible mathematical problems

- ► Giving students the freedom to think through problems themselves
- ► Giving students the opportunity to collaborate with peers to solve problems

We can provide support for students by

- ► Strategic coaching them in ways to start with a challenging problem, as well as what to do when they get stuck
- ► Pairing them with other students whom they work well with to get them in the habit of solving problems
- ► Creating structures for problem solving that support engagement and collaboration

Supportive Classroom Environment

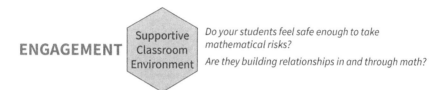

ENGAGEMENT — Supportive Classroom Environment

Do your students feel safe enough to take mathematical risks?

Are they building relationships in and through math?

SOON AFTER ENTERING fourth grade, the truth became apparent. Although I could recite the numbers and the multiplication tables that I had memorized, they were only symbols with numerical names that didn't mean anything to me. I didn't understand the concepts behind them. Faced with the daily onslaught of progressively more difficult mathematical concepts, I could no longer deny there was a problem. I started to shut down completely. I found myself unable to cope, and for the first time, I became clearly aware of the fact that I didn't get things my classmates did. I began to feel less and less comfortable at school. I felt anxious that someone would find out I couldn't understand everything. I always felt the most vulnerable during the math portion of the day. (Abeel, 2005, p. 22) ●

In her memoir about growing up with dyscalculia and math anxiety, Samantha Abeel described the transition to fourth grade when she was asked to do more than memorize. She had significant difficulty understanding the concepts and symbols of mathematics, which is one useful way to understand dyscalculia. She described how this felt viscerally—she began to feel extremely anxious, "vulnerable" during math class, and started to "shut down."

This feeling of being vulnerable in math class, of being afraid to be called on or called out for not knowing something in mathematics, is a problem that goes far beyond Samantha or dyscalculia. Students can feel unsafe when wrong in math class (Bibby, 2002). Mathematics is a deeply emotional subject, in which students can feel joy, but often report anxiety and pain. It is the only subject with its own anxiety: math anxiety. While all students, including high-achieving students, can experience math anxiety, students with disabilities have math anxiety at a higher rate than students without disabilities (Devine et al., 2018). As teachers, we want to help students feel confident enough to problem-solve and take mathematical risks. Strong relationships with teachers are especially important in math class (Battey et al., 2016).

Some barriers to student engagement include

- Students perceiving that they are not "good at math"
- Being put on the spot, or under the pressure of timed or high-stakes tests
- Feeling judged for a wrong answer

We can open up math classrooms by

- Sending students messages that math is about thinking through problems and sharing your work, not about speed or perfection—mistakes help us grow!
- De-emphasizing competition and speed in mathematics class and emphasizing collaboration and time for thinking
- Giving students opportunities to solve math problems with their peers

We can provide support for students by

- Working with students to reshape their self-understandings as math learners
- Preparing students to share their strategies by having them first share their strategies with a teacher, a paraprofessional, or a friend
- Using strategic coaching on how to manage anxiety

Multimodal Mathematics

Is math content accessible? Multimodal? Can students choose how they solve problems?

Are representations connected to each other? To concepts?

I FIRST NOTICED there was something different about my brain in primary school. Dyscalculia was not a recognized condition at the time, certainly not at any of the schools I attended. As soon as I was expected to detach visual aids from maths, it became a problem for me. I could understand maths when I could see the things to count, even my fingers. Removing this, broke my fragile relationship with maths. No one understood why I could not grasp these supposedly simple concepts. My memory of this time was there were a lot of teachers who just didn't understand why I could excel in certain subjects and fail stunningly in anything related to maths. (LozMac, 2018, para. 1) ●

Loz Mac wrote about the connection between visuals and mathematical understanding. Multiple means of representation matter for access, particularly for students with sensory disabilities. Deaf students cannot access mathematics if they are not given access to the discussions of teacher and peers through a translator. Blind students cannot access mathematics if visuals are not communicated, such as through specially designed abacuses, or tactile technologies that can model graphs in 3-D. As this quote demonstrates, visuals can be critical for mathematical sense-making for students with dyscalculia as well.

> **Multiple means of representation matter for access, particularly for students with sensory disabilities.**

UDL calls for multiple representations of content. In mathematics, these visual representations ARE the content, not simply "visuals." The number line, arrays, and equations are themselves multiple representations for mathematical content. We need to (a) provide multiple representations and (b) create connections between them. Fractions, for example, are a concept that needs to be understood through multiple representations (Lamon, 2007). Instead of just showing students area and other models of fractions, we need to scaffold their understanding of how the representations are connected, as well as help them see equivalence across representations.

This approach also connects to student choice in what representations they use as they solve problems. Students want to solve problems in ways that make sense to them (which may or may not initially make sense to us).

The students in Chapter 1 solving the 12 chairs problem were given the freedom to solve the problem using drawings, manipulatives, or numeric equations. There was no mandate for how to solve or what method to use.

Some barriers to student learning in the area of representation include

▸ Math instruction that is inaccessible because it is only one modality

▸ Assumptions that students already understand mathematical models like the number line

▸ Limits on students to solving problems using only certain methods and/or representations

We can open up math classrooms by

▸ Routinely providing multimodal access to math content and interaction in math class

▸ Using multiple representations in how we present content

▸ Allowing students to solve problems whatever way makes sense to them

We can provide support for students by

▸ Designing instruction that systematically teaches students about complex mathematical representations like the number line

▸ Guiding students to be strategic in what representations they use to solve problems

Invest Time in Core Ideas

REPRESENTATION Invest Time in Core Ideas *Does the design of instruction guide students to understand core mathematical ideas? Mathematical representations? Develop strategies?*

Learning . . . just learning real quick. It takes me time. I could tell you that it takes me a while to learn, especially in Math. It's my worst subject. It could take me weeks to learn one single thing. There's a lot of subjects I can learn then I forget it, real quick, do it again, learn again. To me, it's just learning it at that moment in an hour, and hour and a half, the class we have. It takes a couple of classes for me to get to know the subject.

—Interview with Santiago, in Connor, 2007, p. 205 ●

A fundamental barrier for neurodiverse students learning mathematics is time, as Santiago, a young man with a learning disability, pointed out; it takes some students longer to learn the same content. Students feel that math class moves at a pace that is impossible for them, they may feel rushed by timed tests, and generally feel like there is not enough time for them to learn. Students may dislike pacing guides as much as we teachers! So how do we give students the time they need?

The first step in this process is to prioritize core ideas in mathematics. Think of mathematics K–8 like a physical structure, like a house or a school building. Certain mathematical ideas are like load-bearing walls—without them, the whole structure will come tumbling down (Freitag, 2021). Other mathematical ideas are like drywall or plaster: important to completing the structure but not vital for holding up the house. What we need to do is figure out what ideas are load-bearing and invest time into these core ideas. Thus, planning carefully so that students invest their precious time in what's most important is essential.

One core idea is the idea of equivalence in fractions. Students need to understand equivalence to understand how fractions work—equivalent fractions have the same ratio of numerator to denominator. They are the same, even though they are different. And this tricky concept is necessary for operations such as adding and subtracting fractions, and for algebra.

The second step is to provide enough time for students to really learn the concepts, skills, and strategies we value. Students will need to experience topics like equivalent fractions in multiple ways across time. Once they understand it, they will need practice so that they don't forget it.

We can design sequences of tasks and activities that engage students in core ideas. Core ideas can also help us limit excessive and repetitive assignments, another barrier for students. Instead of worksheets with many problems, classroom and homework should include a smaller number of problems focused on core ideas. Core ideas also help when we need to modify instruction for students with intellectual disabilities, as these students often need more time with core ideas (Krähenmann et al., 2019). Students with memory differences will also need support to retain concepts, for example, in the form of distributed practice.

To identify core ideas, I suggest consulting the Achieve the Core one-pagers for each grade level, which include the most important standards for each grade (https://bit.ly/3rwktDw). Another source is the introductory pages of each grade level in the Common Core State

Standards (National Governors Association Center for Best Practices & Council of Chief State School Officers, 2010), which focus on the big ideas. I also try to make sure that we multitask in our teaching. When a student is learning multidigit addition and subtraction and building their understanding of the number line at the same time (Chapter 9), for example, I know their time is being well spent.

Some barriers to student learning in this area of representation include

- ▶ Math instruction that feels rushed, in which students are not given enough time to develop understanding
- ▶ Messages to students that being good at math is being fast
- ▶ Movement from topic to topic without connections between the topics

We can open up math classrooms by

- ▶ Providing time for students who need more time
- ▶ Providing practice by revisiting previous ideas through routines like number strings or games
- ▶ Reminding students that math is not just about speed, but that developing understanding takes time

We can provide support for students by

- ▶ Designing instruction that provides sufficient support for core ideas
- ▶ Using consistent teaching routines (where the content changes but structure of the routine is consistent)
- ▶ Developing our own understanding of the core ideas we teach

Equitable Feedback

STRATEGIC ACTION *Does feedback help students grow as mathematicians? Is assessment equitable for all learners?*

BY EIGHTH GRADE, I had learned the correct math procedures but still needed extra time. In that class we were doing "rapid math," which provoked terrible anxiety in me and which I would do almost anything to avoid. The task in this exercise was to complete an entire page of calculations in five minutes. I would sneak the book home the night before, answer all the questions, and then write the answers in my book lightly in pencil; in class the next day, all I had to do was copy over my answers. This was the only way I could complete the exercise in the allotted time. Though I had done the work (at home), I felt like a fraud. (Arrowsmith-Young, B., 2013, p. 21) ●

The issue of feedback and assessment is critical for all math learners, but again, it is particularly important for those who may need additional support. In this quote, Barbara Arrowsmith-Young, who has a learning disability, engaged in a critique of one very traditional assessment practice: timed tests. Nervous about the quiz in school, she found a way to give herself the extra time she needed, copying answers lightly into her book the night before.

Assessment can be a major barrier for students with disabilities as excessive and unhelpful assignments can burden those who might need extra time (Lambert, 2019). Grading elements of school such as homework and binder organization discriminate against students whose disabilities make those aspects of school particularly challenging. Assessment needs to be focused on helping both teacher and student do their jobs with the best information possible.

Some barriers to student learning in the area of feedback include

- ► Long and boring assignments
- ► Grading systems that discriminate based on disability
- ► Lack of actionable or timely feedback for students. Feedback may only come in grades or on a test, too late for students to act
- ► Individualized Education Program (IEP) goals in math that are disconnected from classroom practice

We can open up math classrooms by

- ► Using assessment to understand students and be responsive to what they need
- ► Revising our grading systems to allow students to show understanding over time in different ways
- ► Using dynamic assessment or assessment that provides scaffolding to more accurately gauge what students can do in contexts that support them

We can provide support for students by

- ► Providing strategic coaching in how students can engage in assessment that is stressful, such as high stakes testing
- ► Including students in assessment, such as self-assessment, to develop their self-understandings

Understanding Self as a Math Learner

STRATEGIC ACTION

What do your students learn about themselves as math learners?

How do you support strategic development?

AMONG THE ADVANTAGES [of LD] was a better understanding at a young age of my limitations and weaknesses. Though this might not sound like much of an advantage, one must remember that every person has their own weaknesses and limitations. I was able to realize, for example, that to get through math, I should draw out the problems. This system let me visualize what I was trying to do. (Garret Day, in Rodis et al., 2001, p. 99) ●

Critically important to our goal of helping students become strategic sense-makers is self-understanding (Desoete & De Craene, 2019). We are simply trying to make our students think about their own thinking, as well as to learn about their own learning. We want them to know themselves as math learners and to know how to advocate for what they need.

For many mathematics teachers, this dimension of learning (strategic action) will feel the most unfamiliar of the three dimensions of UDL. We may think about how to develop mathematical strategies and problem-solving strategies but not strategies around self-regulation and executive functioning. Yet these processes are central to our classrooms. We rely on students being able to handle the organizational demands of our classrooms, which requires executive functioning. Executive functioning refers to the work of the prefrontal cortex, including how we plan learning, as well as working memory and attention. We also need students to develop strategies to negotiate the emotional demands of our classrooms: self-regulation. Self-regulation refers to how students learn to manage their emotions during challenging situations. The most important step as a teacher is to recognize that these skills are teachable and that students can improve in these areas with our support. The ultimate goal is for them to understand themselves as learners and thus be able to self-advocate in the future.

Some barriers to student learning in the area of understanding self as a math learner include

▸ No opportunity to reflect or discuss what works for you as a learner

▸ Classrooms with little flexibility or choice

We can open up math classrooms by

▸ Regularly talking with our students about what works for them

▸ Sharing what we know about ourselves as math learners to model metacognition

▸ Allowing students to have choices about how they learn

We can provide support for students by

▸ Creating individual plans to support students who need more strategic coaching in understanding and managing their emotions in math class (self-regulation) or staying focused and organized in class (executive functioning)

▸ Debriefing with students when they are having difficulty in class, coaching them to reflect on what happened and what they might do next time

▸ Embedding self-assessments and self-reflection as a regular habit in the class

REFLECTION QUESTIONS

1. What was new for you in this chapter about UDL and/or UDL Math?

2. What barriers to learning mathematics resonated with your experience as a learner? As a teacher?

3. How do you develop students' self-understandings? Self-regulation skills? Executive functioning skills?

CHAPTER 6

DESIGNING WITH UDL MATH

IN THIS CHAPTER, WE WILL . . .

- Learn about relationships between UDL Math and Design Thinking
- Explore empathy interviews
- Observe two teachers as they redesign collaborative group work for neurodiverse learners

IN THE SUMMER of 2020, as teachers tried to prepare for an uncertain fall because of the coronavirus 2019 (COVID-19) pandemic, Dr. Kara Imm and I were lead designers on an online professional development program that would connect one of her passions, Design Thinking for Educators, and one of mine, Universal Design for Learning in Mathematics (UDL Math). Our intention was to help this group of math educators and special educators prepare for the uncertainty by learning how to design new forms of math learning. During the course of the summer, teams of educators designed innovative solutions to the problems that they were faced with. For example, one team wanted to design for families during distance learning. They decided that they wanted to help families better understand the importance of the mathematics of home, to value the math families were already teaching their students. They designed a social media campaign in which they shared how families taught the mathematics of their home and culture to students.

In the next year, one of our participants, whom we will call Zelda, was teaching secondary math over Zoom to special education classes. As so many of us experienced, teaching math virtually is particularly challenging. Zelda had shared an Open Middle Problem with her students (Figure 6.1). This kind of problem, designed by Robert Kaplinsky, is designed to allow students to experiment with multiple solutions to a problem. Here the students are working with equivalency that includes variables and coefficients.

**Figure 6.1 · ** *Zelda's Zoom slides*

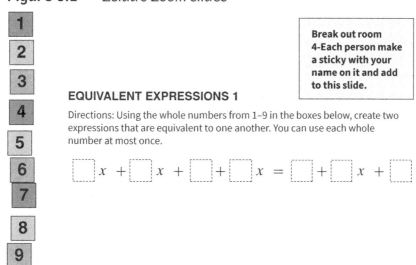

Break out room 4-Each person make a sticky with your name on it and add to this slide.

EQUIVALENT EXPRESSIONS 1

Directions: Using the whole numbers from 1–9 in the boxes below, create two expressions that are equivalent to one another. You can use each whole number at most once.

$$\square x + \square x + \square + \square x = \square + \square x + \square$$

SOURCE: Reprinted with permission from openmiddle.com.

She had the problem on a Google Jamboard, and her students were taking a long time to engage, or so she thought. In an interview a few months later, she told us how in waiting for the students to start posting answers, she started blaming herself for asking her students to do something that was too hard. She wanted to just change activities, cut her losses, and provide students with something less challenging.

In the past, Zelda reported, she would have done so. But after the work we had done with UDL and empathy interviews in the summer class, she stopped herself from assuming she knew how the students were feeling. Instead, she took a deep breath and asked the students. The students told her that they were thinking, and needed more time, but did NOT want her to take the problem away. In reflecting on that moment, Zelda called her line of thought "deficit thinking," assuming that a problem was too challenging for her students. She said:

> I can catch that thought and be like, no it's not that they can't do it, it's like—what, do we need to try again? Does it need more time? You know, and also asking them, like, "How is this going?"

She went on to give us a way to think about *how* to do UDL Math:

> Design thinking and UDL are like an active process . . . not, like, an approach . . . but it's like in those moments in a teaching moment, even in, even in your live-on-your-feet lesson, as you shift and adjust, like that is . . . UDL.

> (Lambert et al., 2023) ●

PUTTING THE DESIGN BACK IN UDL

So how do we actually "do" UDL Math? Unfortunately, UDL is often presented as a passive process. Teachers are encouraged to use UDL guidelines as a checklist to see if their lesson plans are "UDL" and, if not, apply some of the guidelines to their lessons. This passive "checklist" approach is absolutely the opposite of Universal Design, which asks that we begin with variability in mind at the beginning versus retrofitting after the fact. Even an experienced teacher like Ms. Murphy, whom you will meet in this chapter, told me that learning about UDL in the past in professional development felt overwhelming to her, focused too heavily on the UDL Guidelines.

Research on successful teachers of inclusive education that includes students with disabilities in general education classrooms has documented that these teachers share a creative problem-solving approach (Naraian, 2017). Successful teachers of neurodiverse students need to try new approaches and to figure out what works. These teachers are constantly seeking to increase access for students at the margins, including developing empathy and understanding of the perspectives of students who are marginalized. This approach can be a way to center not only disability but also race and other social positioning and identities (Indar, 2018).

The work in this chapter has been inspired by Design Thinking for Educators (IDEO, 2012) and, more specifically, by the work that Kara Imm has done to implement that process with math educators at Math for America and in our collaboration on UDL Math.[2] In this chapter, I do not present the full Design Thinking process. Instead, I present how teachers have used a simplified version of this process to identify barriers, open up their mathematics classroom, and provide strategic support. These are the three gestures that I use with teachers, which developed from discussions of this kind of design work with teachers:

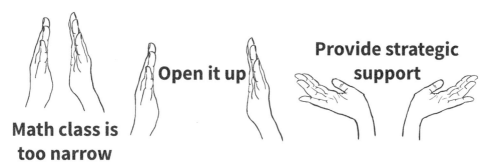

Open it up

Provide strategic support

Math class is too narrow

We will also explore a few tools from Design Thinking that are helpful in this process.

BORROWING FROM DESIGN THINKING: TOOLS FOR DESIGN

Design Thinking for Educators is a mindset (IDEO, 2012). Educators face myriad challenges in our work, including creating safe and engaging spaces for neurodiverse students. A Design Thinking mindset is (a) humanistic, seeing empathy as the root of good design; (b) optimistic, looking for the challenges we can redesign around; (c) collaborative; and (d) creative. We need this mindset to find new ways to teach mathematics that will serve all of our students. And this design goes well beyond designing lessons and units. Because the barriers for students with disabilities are also within systems, routines, interactions, and structures, we need to expand what we design (Imm et al., 2024).

The first tool from Design Thinking is the empathy interview. The design process begins with empathy for the users—those who will use what we design. Empathy is a critical tool to improve student experience. By orienting the entire process in empathy for the user, Design Thinking has the power to shift teachers' solutions from those that work for the teachers to ones that

---

[2] These data were collected and analyzed with the assistance of my colleagues Kara Imm, Avery McNiff, Rachel Schuck, Sara Zimmerman, and Sunghee Choi (Lambert et al., 2021; Lambert et al. 2023).

work for their students. Dr. Imm explains empathy interviews in depth in the sidebar box on this page. The discussion offers sample questions as a place to start; the most effective questions take into consideration exactly what you are redesigning and what you already know about the student.

The second tool is to look for pain points and pinch points. *Pinch points* are when you know as a teacher that something is not working for all your kids and you can identify what is not working (unit, idea, routine, etc.). It might be a particular assessment that is not working. It could be a single concept that you struggle to get all your kids to understand each year, like the slog through multidigit subtraction in second grade. You can engage in this process based on that pinch point, which becomes what you redesign. Another place for a redesign is a *pain point*, or aspects of math class that make students feel strong negative emotions. You may know what is a pain point for your students by observing them. Students often feel threatened when they are asked to perform under pressure, or likely to be judged for being wrong. You can also use empathy interviews to find pain points for students.

Think About It

What pain points and/or pinch points can you identify in your math classroom?

Educator Perspective: Kara Imm on Empathy Interviews

Kara Imm (Figure 6.2) explained that empathy interviews originate from the practice of Design Thinking—the first step in designing for another human (e.g., a user) is to better understand their lived experience. That is, not to assume we know how someone else thinks and feels about an event, encounter, or experience but to really find out. So, empathy interviews are one way that designers explore the questions, "Who is the user? How do they experience _____? And how do they feel about it?"

We take the position that all teachers are designers and that, typically, our students are our users. There is plenty we can learn

Figure 6.2 • *Kara Imm, researcher and teacher educator*

SOURCE: Kara Imm

about our students simply from observing, interacting, and building relationships with them. But an empathy interview achieves something different. Our goal is to uncover stories, emotions, and perspectives that might not emerge from everyday classroom interactions. It is also to expand and deepen our perspective about a student: We might "know" them in this moment as an individual student, but they are also known over many years within a peer group, classroom/school community, family, and other communities.

Despite their name, good empathy interviews sound nothing like other interviews (e.g., job interviews) and everything like a natural conversation. The focus is not to get feedback on our teaching but to "paint a portrait" of the kid you are interested in knowing. It's not necessary, or often the goal, to interview all of your students. Instead, we are often most interested in learning about kids for whom the class/instruction/experience is *not* working—the students who are marginalized, excluded, or not invested in the experience of math class. When we uncover what's not working (and perhaps why), we begin to identify a problem of practice, allowing us to redesign some aspect of teaching and learning mathematics for this student (and others like them).

Let's brainstorm possible questions for math empathy interviews:

Tell me about the math you do at home with your family.	I heard a student in another school tell me that some kids get extra help in math. Is that true at your school? What kind of help?	If you had a friend who was having trouble in math, what advice would you give them?	If there are different kinds of math learners, what kind of math learner are you? Why?
Who stands out in your math class? Why?	Do you talk in math class a lot, medium, a little, or not at all? Why?	If you had a magic wand, what one thing would you change about math class?[3]	What is your favorite memory of math, in school or out? Why?
Tell me about your math class.	Tell me about a time you didn't feel successful in math.	What languages do you speak in math class? At home when talking about math?	Tell me about a time you felt successful in math.

---

[3] I learned this question from educators at High Tech High.

DOING UDL MATH: TWO TEACHERS TACKLE COLLABORATIVE GROUP WORK IN EARLY CHILDHOOD

Ms. Murphy and Ms. Diaz are experienced early elementary teachers who have been working in grades K–3 for many years. They are both teacher leaders in mathematics who provide professional development to teachers in various ways, as well as serving as leaders in their respective schools. Through participating in countywide math professional development for many years, they have formed a close friendship. Both are general education teachers with credentials in elementary education (Figure 6.3).

Figure 6.3 • *Ms. Diaz leading a share of student work*

Both teachers were very interested in learning about UDL Math because their schools were moving toward inclusion of students with special education services into general education. Both teachers had more students in special education included in their general education classrooms that year. Ms. Diaz had previously had two to three students with Individualized

Education Programs (IEPs) in her classroom each year. But this year, she had been asked to include 10 students with IEPs in her classroom of 22 second-grade students. Both teachers supported inclusion wholeheartedly. Yet it seemed to be creating new challenges for them.

Identify the Barriers Part 1: How Do Teachers See the Math Class as Narrow?

In our session, I started by putting my hands together, to make a narrow space between them, and said, "Math class is too narrow." Several teachers nodded right away. I asked the group to share how they saw math class as too narrow. They responded as follows:

- ▸ Students are told to solve problems one way.
- ▸ Students are only allowed certain ways to explain their thinking.
- ▸ Students are tightly controlled, asked to sit for long periods of time.
- ▸ Listening is the main modality of learning.
- ▸ Math class can be a space of either right or wrong, with little space in between.

I then asked the teachers to start thinking about places in which their own math classrooms felt narrow to them, or might feel narrow for students.

PURPOSE
Know your
goals

At their table, Ms. Diaz and Ms. Murphy jumped immediately into a discussion of the challenges of collaborative problem solving for their younger students. Ms. Diaz and Ms. Murphy felt very strongly that collaboration in problem solving was the most critical practice in their mathematics classroom, even for kids in Grades 1 and 2 (their current classrooms). In a reflection, they wrote:

> We want all our students to be able to interact with the math in dynamic ways. Looking at different approaches to solving problems and communicating their ideas. We want our classroom to help support these students to interact with others in cooperative groups and communicate their ideas with others. We do not want math time to be solitary.

This year, they each had students who seemed to either not want to work in groups or needed more support doing so. Ms. Murphy had an autistic student whom we will call Anthony who was well above grade level in his math skills. He seemed to prefer to work alone rather than with other students. To Ms. Murphy, it seemed as if Anthony did not enjoy working with students who did not have his level of expertise.

Ms. Diaz also had multiple students who seemed to have either a lack of inclination or a lack of skills to engage in collaborative math work. For example, she had a student who was dyslexic who would get upset if presented with any text, including in math. Yet she was mainly concerned about Tomás, a second grader with autism. He recently had learned to count consistently with one-to-one correspondence and was counting by ones for all addition and subtraction problems. He would stand back during partner work, looking at the problem but not talking. It was unclear whether he was listening to the others in his group. At other times, he would jump in and interrupt the students in order to share immediately.

Ms. Diaz and Ms. Murphy discussed how their collaborative process was too narrow. What wasn't working for all of their students? What could they tweak to help all students engage in the collaborative work? They talked about how for both of them, the student whom they really wanted to engage in collaborative work was autistic, and yet the two students were so dissimilar. One was labeled as "gifted" in math, whereas the other needed support in early mathematics. One dominated small-group conversation, and the other rarely spoke. This is an important reminder of the variability within disability!

The teachers wrote in their reflection:

> The need to work in cooperative groups requires our students to use social skills that cause challenges to be able to do the math. We want to change the structure of cooperative grouping that would allow these students to positively participate.

I notice and appreciate that these teachers do not see the students as the problem to be fixed but see the problem as "the structure of cooperative grouping." So often, students with disabilities are considered to be the problem. The focus would be on fixing Tomás and Anthony. However, these teachers understood that the most important change has to come from within their structures and routines.

Identify the Barriers Part 2: How Do Students See the Math Class?

I asked Ms. Diaz and Ms. Murphy whether the students would see this problem of practice in the same way they did. We had discussed empathy interviews already, and the teachers got excited about designing an empathy interview that would work to help them better understand how their students felt about collaborative groups. Ms. Murphy and Ms. Diaz decided to interview two students each: one of their autistic students who did not seem to like groups (Anthony and Tomás) *and* a student who was not autistic and frequently worked with those students. What I like about their design is that it purposefully gathered data from students with different experiences. Whenever we design a solution that works across student variability, we are designing more effectively. Here are the empathy interview questions they designed for their young learners:

- Imagine it is a day when we work in groups for math class. How do you feel? Why?
- Who do you like to work with in groups? Why? What makes them a good partner?
- Are there times another student is hard to work with? Why? What do you do then?
- What do you enjoy most about math class?

Making a Plan to Provide Strategic Support

After doing these interviews, Ms. Diaz and Ms. Murphy met to discuss what they learned. In general, students expressed their enjoyment of group work in math class. Three out of the four students interviewed said that they liked working in partners in math class, that it was more "fun," and that "working together is more fun than alone." The one exception was Tomás in Ms. Diaz's classroom. He did report liking games and working on the whiteboards, just not group work. Most students reported that they learned more when with a partner. Both students with autism noted that it was particularly important to be friends with math partners. Both students in Ms. Diaz's class discussed working on whiteboards as their favorite time in math.

Ms. Murphy was particularly interested in Anthony's perspective, whom she believed did not like group work. During group work, he would argue with other students about the math problems. But in his interview, he said, "I like working with partners, they help me with strategies" and "I like doing problems. It gives my brain a workout." He also said that his favorite time of math was working on problems with partners. This shook Ms. Murphy, who had assumed the opposite.

Tomás was the only interviewed child who was ambivalent about group work. His hesitations were connected to when he had to work with another child whom he did not consider a "friend." He told a story about a negative interaction between him and another child at recess and about how he did not want to work with that child in math.

The other student in Ms. Diaz's class really liked working in groups, and when asked whether another student was "hard" to work with, they said that "sometimes people try to do it by themselves even though we were partners."

In this case, they saw that almost all students reported both enjoying partner time *and* learning from it, including the most enthusiasm from a student with autism whom Ms. Murphy thought did not like working in groups. The other student with autism, who was in Ms. Diaz's class, only disliked group work when paired with a student he disliked. It felt like the pinch points for the students were working with someone they did not like or someone who did not problem solve together. Making group work better seemed to be connected to helping students work better together.

So how do we help all students to communicate, share, and engage more in math partner work? And what do we do about assigning partners?

Both Ms. Murphy and Ms. Diaz had long used high-quality inquiry mathematics curricula such as *Contexts for Learning Mathematics* by Fosnot. Working together, they had already been experimenting with group problem-solving practices for a year after they read the book *Building Thinking Classrooms in Mathematics, Grades K–12: 14 Teaching Practices for Enhancing Learning* (Liljedahl, 2020). The book provides a set of teaching practices for classrooms in which students are actively thinking and problem solving (see the Teaching Practice Guide online for more). Both teachers had already taken up the practices of visible nonrandom grouping (putting students into random groups) and using vertical nonpermanent surfaces (whiteboard easels that they placed on student tables). They employed these practices to deepen engagement of students in inquiry mathematics, an example of *guided inquiry.*

Online Teaching Practice Guide

qrs.ly/l7f7rwq

So what were the barriers for their students? It seemed that they had already opened up the classroom. They had shifted into more choice and flexibility in student problem solving, which seemed to increase engagement of some but not all students. So they decided to focus on the third element of UDL Math: Provide strategic supports.

They decided to add a few more supports that would improve group work and communication for all students and specifically support students like Tomás who needed support to engage:

- Build in opportunities to reflect on collaboration
- Provide multimodal tools/manipulatives to support collaboration
- Form strategic groups

Build in opportunities to reflect on collaboration

The first element they added was making the norms of group work more explicit and asking students to reflect on their work in the partnership each day, which is an example of whole group *strategic coaching.* They created a structure for discussion at the end of the problem for students to reflect on their problem solving and their partner work. Ms. Diaz asked her students:

- What did you learn as a math learner?
- What did you learn as a problem solver?
- What did you learn about yourself?

Provide multimodal tools/manipulatives to support collaboration

They looked for specific tools that would help all students participate, such as a ten-frame or a ruler. They would hand that tool to the student who did not participate as easily, giving that student an important tool that would help the group. In other cases, they added additional multimodal tools so that all kids could engage nonverbally. This was an important support for Tomás, who worked well with tools like the hundreds chart.

Form strategic groups

This final element was something Ms. Diaz tried but not Ms. Murphy. Ms. Diaz decided to support Tomás by making sure he was always in a group of three. She conjectured that this approach would help the group get started with the problem and not put another student in the position of working alone while Tomás had enough thinking time.

SEEING THE PLAN IN ACTION: VISITING MS. DIAZ'S SECOND-GRADE CLASS

Try it out

I visited Ms. Diaz's second-grade classroom one day as she was working on this problem of practice. Her class had 19 students, 7 of whom had IEPs. Three additional students with IEPs were mainstreamed into the class for part of the day. Most students were Latino/a, and a large percentage were multilingual learners. During the math period, a special education co-teacher also worked with Ms. Diaz, as well as two paraprofessionals.

As the class began, Ms. Diaz gathered the students on the rug. I noticed all the students on the rug were in different stages of restlessness, from some students sitting perfectly still to others moving constantly while still sitting "criss cross apple sauce."

Ms. Diaz started by launching the problem the students would do that day. Their task was to figure out how the outside of the shape could be filled in with the lengths provided, the "Miles of Tiles" task designed by Inside Mathematics.

Ms. Diaz adapted the problem by cutting out the linear blocks into paper strips made of cardstock for each small group. This task was multimodal, had multiple solution paths, and included a visual/concrete aspect that made it particularly accessible to these students. As she launched the task, she read all the text and modeled using the paper strips.

"Miles of Tiles" task

https://bit.ly/41sldal

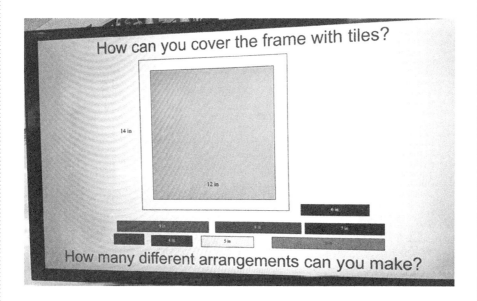

> ## Try It
>
> Try to solve the problem.
>
> *How can you cover the frame with tiles? How many different arrangements can you make? (Blocks have lengths of 3 in., 4 in., 5 in., 6 in., 7 in., 8 in., 9 in., and 10 in.)*
>
> What do you notice about this problem? What mathematics will students be exploring?
>
> What strategies might they use?

Before she sent the students out to work, Ms. Diaz reminded them of their collective agreements for problem solving. This poster was part of a discussion in which students reflected on what makes a good partner:

When We Problem Solve:
- never give up
- every mistake gets you closer to the answer
- every problem is a fun treasure hunt
- everyone has good ideas worth listening to!

Ms. Diaz then walked around with a basket with pattern blocks in it, each block with a group number written on it. She gave each student a shape. In our debriefing, I learned that she purposefully made sure that Tomás was in a group of three by assigning the last student to whatever group Tomás had been placed in.

Ms. Diaz asked the students to move to the tables. Each table had been outfitted with an easel and one whiteboard marker. A piece of paper with the problem was clipped to the table with a plastic sleeve so that students could draw right on the paper with their whiteboard markers. Also at the tables were the paper strips that the students could use to try to see what fit.

I started at Tomás's table with three students. Besides himself, his group included a very shy girl named Shauna and a slightly less shy girl named Briana who held the pen for much of their work. Using another practice from *The Thinking Classroom* (Liljedahl, 2020), Ms. Diaz had given each group only one whiteboard marker so that they needed to communicate. As I watched them, before any teacher drew near, they started by talking about Patrick from SpongeBob. Briana did a quick drawing of Patrick and erased it quickly as the teacher walked by. All three children smiled at each other and then started with the problem. I wondered if perhaps these kids needed to establish a little solidarity before they took mathematical risks together.

Figure 6.4 • *Tomás's group at its whiteboard*

Figure 6.4 shows their group at work. They were using both the paper strips, which they placed on the square, as well as rewrote the measurements with the whiteboard marker. I noticed in all the groups that the multiple tools allowed multiple students to be actively involved at the same time. In this little moment, all three students were holding pieces or writing, showing how the problem got all students engaged. Tomás, on the left, engaged quietly at first by holding, and then placing, the paper strips.

Initially just Briana and Shauna talked about the problem. Tomás gravitated to the paper strips, putting them together, touching them to the sides of the paper. The girls decided that the top would be 14, the sides 13, and the bottom 12. At one point, they needed to figure out how to make one side total 13. Shauna counted on her fingers, starting with a 7 and then adding on 6. She then whispered to me "13" and then jumped up and down, extremely excited.

Briana, holding the pen, wrote out a break-it-up strategy on the board, breaking up 6 into 3 and 3 and giving one 3 to the 7, before adding the leftover 3.

Tomás watched the students as they solved this computational problem perhaps not sure how to engage or simply thinking about his own strategy. The special education teacher, who had been observing their group, then asked Tomás in a quiet voice, "Do you want a number line or a hundreds chart?" Tomás smiled and then sprinted over to where there was a blank hundreds chart in a dry erase folder, started counting while touching spaces with his finger, and shouted out, "6 plus 7" as well. He then explained to the girls how he solved it, reenacting his strategy on the tool (counting by ones and then counting all). I felt that this group was working together splendidly, both making progress on the mathematics and in making all members of the group an integral part of their community. Both the multimodal tool and the group of three seemed to be working for Tomás.

Ms. Diaz led a short share, where one group discussed how they solved it as two 14s and two 12s. Another group tried to do four 12s, with a corner, but had trouble making the paper strips work with their plan. The share was brief and used the visuals that students created. Ms. Diaz used the word "equivalence" as she made brief connections across student work. She asked a question using this same word to end the share, paying attention to developing the mathematical vocabulary of her students. Across the room, I saw so much excellent mathematical thinking and strong collaboration. These second graders worked collaboratively on a single complex math problem for more than 30 minutes, an impressive feat for second graders. Every group ended up with a solution. ●

REFLECTING ON THE DESIGN

I met with Ms. Murphy and Ms. Diaz a month later as they reflected on what worked in their respective classrooms. Both agreed that their redesign of group work was in general a success. They felt that their autistic students were more included and felt more positive about collaborative work in math class.

Ms. Murphy reflected on the importance of the empathy interviews to her work. For her, the most important part of this process was learning what Anthony, whom she thought did not like group work, actually did. Through the empathy interview, Ms. Murphy learned that not only did he like group work, but he also appreciated how it helped him grow mathematically. This insight created a shift in how she saw her student. That shift made a difference in how she engaged with him and in how she interpreted his actions during group work.

Ms. Murphy tried the first two strategies they agreed on but believed that the biggest impact was from shifting to visibly random grouping from *The Thinking Classroom* (Liljedahl, 2020). She reported that once she made it clear to her students that groups were completely random, and that you would get a new partner the very next day, students just stopped complaining about their partners. And, according to Ms. Murphy, it made both partners in each group work a little harder to understand each other.

Their work together to implement UDL in math class was creative and collaborative. Making math class more accessible is not work that is ever finished. There is no perfect UDL classroom that would be accessible to any child who walked or rolled in. But we can have a mindset of creative problem solving to help kids, which Ms. Murphy and Ms. Diaz certainly did!

As I watched Ms. Murphy and Ms. Diaz discuss their work and what they might try next year (both want to do empathy interviews with all students at the beginning of the year), I was struck by how lucky they were to have each other. The work of redesigning, of making mathematics accessible, of opening up our classrooms, this work is hard and it is easier in community.

REFLECTION QUESTIONS

1. What is your feeling about empathy interviews? How might you use them in your work?

2. As you read the chapter, what kinds of redesign did you imagine? What did you think about redesigning (curriculum, units, lessons, spaces, interactions, routines)? Who might you design with?

3. Have you had students who had difficulty solving problems in groups? What have you tried?

PART 3

DESIGN IN ACTION: CLASSROOM STORIES

CHAPTER 7

INVESTING IN CORE IDEAS

IN THIS CHAPTER, WE WILL . . .

- Visit a K–1 special education class as it focuses on core ideas about place value and number sense through Choral Counting and Counting Collections
- Explore the concept of core ideas as worth the investment of time
- Explore core ideas as a way to adapt instruction for students with intellectual disabilities

Figure 7.1 • *Hannah, K–1 special education teacher, working with a student*

HANNAH BENAVIDEZ'S K–1 classroom (Figure 7.1) is a self-contained space for about 10 Latino/a students with significant support needs, most of whom have autism. Her small group is diverse in how they think, feel, and engage in the world. Her students' support needs are varied, with some students needing augmentative and alternative communication (AAC) devices to communicate and others who love to talk verbally. The children also have varied mathematical skill levels. For example, one student could add and subtract multidigit numbers, while others in the class were learning how to count to five. Some, but not all, of her students have intellectual disabilities. Hannah is an exceptional teacher who combines both a kind demeanor and high expectations, always expecting that her students have important ideas that should be heard.

One morning I observed the class with a group of special educators from around her district. Hannah's students were doing Choral Counting and Counting Collections (Franke et al., 2018; for more, see the Teaching Practice Guides on Counting Collections and Choral Counting online).

Online Teaching Practice Guide

qrs.ly/l7f7rwq

The class began with Hannah's students sitting at desks in a semicircle, facing a piece of chart paper. Hannah stood at the head of the class with her own chart paper and began by explaining that they would be counting on from 100 by ones (Figure 7.2).

As Hannah charted, she spoke the next numbers in a loud voice, "100, 101, 102, 103." She was joined by about half of the students, while others looked on, and some looked away. She and her students counted all the way to 125, and then Hannah asked the students whether they saw any patterns. A student noticed that the numbers at the beginning (the 100 place) stayed the same, while the last number changed. Hannah used color to show the patterns that students described.

Figure 7.2 • *Hannah leading the Choral Count*

Hannah asked whether students could find 105. One child walked up with a paraprofessional, who guided his hand as he circled the correct number. I wondered whether the child knew the number or whether the aide directed his hand. Next to me, also observing, was a teacher who worked with this child the previous year in kindergarten. She gasped and whispered to me that this was the first time she had seen this child stand up in a class meeting and do any kind of a share, in any subject. This reminded me that, just as for all children, there are different kinds of goals and different kinds of growth for kids, not just mathematical but social. While I was worrying that this child did not recognize the number, the teacher beside me was overcome to see the child so confident in front of their class.

One student, George, asked, "Does this still work in the 900s?" Hannah added that count to the bottom of the chart paper, counting "900, 901, 902". In this Choral Counting activity, students were investigating how the number system worked, extending what they knew about counting by ones to bigger numbers. Hannah's manner was quiet and supportive, while also gently pushing every one of her students to take mathematical risks.

Hannah then transitioned her class to Counting Collections, pointing out the table covered in sets of materials to count, each in its own bag. She reminded them of the tools that they could use to count their collections

(10 frames, cups, plates, rubber bands). Some students went to get their own collections and choose their own tools, while others were assisted by Hannah or paraprofessionals. The students then got down to business counting collections. Some students were working in pairs, some alone, and some with instructional aides. As the students worked, Hannah observed and supported their counting, including their one-to-one correspondence, cardinality, and knowledge of the number sequence.

A girl we will call Noemi was counting a set of round plastic circle counters, some blue and some purple. Hannah had specifically asked her to count this set and had asked her to figure out how many purple and how many blue, as well as the total. Noemi looked up at Hannah, nodded, and started counting. When Noemi miscounted in the teens, Hannah stopped her, reminded her of the sequence of numbers in the teens, and listened as Noemi counted again. When Noemi finished counting, Noemi recorded her count using a digital recording tool. Usually in Counting Collections, the students are advised to use paper to record their counts, but Hannah had found that her students talked and produced more records of their counts using a tablet. Noemi took a picture of her items and then annotated it in color.

One boy in the corner, Juan, was counting with a paraprofessional, repeatedly placing soft puff balls into a container with a soft top, made for holding snacks. For each object he put in, he would touch the button on his AAC device for each number, which would then speak out loud the count for him. He seemed happy, delighted even, with his counting. When he finished the count, he did it again immediately, repeating the count multiple times. Hannah said that he loved that container and putting things into it, so she was integrating it into Counting Collections. The paraprofessional provided feedback for Juan, who was just becoming fluent with the number sequence in the teens. When he pressed the wrong number, she simply pressed the correct one and he copied her. The aide provided this support so quietly and gently that I never heard her speaking to Juan.

George was given a much bigger count than the other students, who were mostly counting sets below 30. Hannah gave George a collection that included both a stack of six boxes of paper clips that were marked 100 on the side and a pile of loose paperclips. Hannah told him she needed 735 paper clips and then asked whether she needs to order more and, if so, how many. George went right to work, skip counting by 100s, and keeping track on a piece of paper.

Hannah moved around the classroom, asking questions and adding challenges to students' counts. Some students recorded audio in their tablets, as well as images. When students finished with one count, they were able to pick their next counting collection from a large variety of options Hannah had gathered over time.

Hannah finished the class session with a share, which was the most challenging part of math class for this group of young children. Hannah supported one student to share their physical count in the middle of the rug, with students gathered around. The child showed how they grouped items into tens, while Hannah narrated the strategy. During the share, I saw Noemi sneak away, turn away from the group, and begin to silently count something, tagging with her finger, and moving her lips as if she was recounting some set. I wondered what she was imagining or recounting. Her engagement, as a 6-year-old with autism, was different than other students. While she did not stay at the meeting area, it was clear that she was engaged in counting.

I want to call attention to how skillful special education teachers like Hannah move between more explicit and more inquiry-based teaching as they work with their students. Using *guided inquiry*, she designs her class so that it is meaningful to her students. She allows for choice in what students count— allowing Juan to count an item that matters to him. She asks students to share their strategies, always letting them lead the way with their own thinking. Other aspects of her practice are far more explicit, providing support for students. She also reminds the students of the order of the numbers with immediate feedback, encourages them to grab a hundreds chart if they need a reminder, and uses repetition of numbers and routines to help students. In other words, she uses multiple tools to support her students, including *strategic coaching* or 1:1 assistance to students. I never saw a whole class *explicit instruction* lesson, perhaps because her students have such a range of prior knowledges that such a targeted lesson could hardly work for most, certainly not all, of her class. I see this flexibility between inquiry-based approaches and more explicit guidance all the time in experienced special educators.

During the debrief with me after the lesson, Hannah shared Juan's journey in counting. Initially, Juan did not engage in Counting Collections. When he did count, he would not seem to care if he got a different number counting the same set. So Hannah worked to make the counting more meaningful to him. Once she found an object that he really loved to count, he did so, and when he counted the same set and got 16 one time and 17 another, he recognized this as a problem that he needed to solve. As we debriefed, we discussed how students like Juan were often given tasks that were repetitive and did not make sense. Hannah did not assume that Juan could not do the task but that she needed to change the way she structured the task.

Hannah noted during our debrief that she was unsure whether the whole-group debrief is a useful tool for her class. She was committed to developing her students' ability to reflect on their own problem solving and engaging them in the problem solving of their peers, but she did not need her class to look exactly like others, ending with a lengthy share. We ended by brainstorming new ways she could hold a share, possibly moving toward pair-shares of collections to end each class. ●

CORE IDEAS: INVESTING IN NUMBER SENSE AND PLACE VALUE

Students need a *lot* of experience with numbers to develop number sense, as well as with place value, an important component of number sense. Critical to understanding place value is *unitizing*—understanding and working with groups. The important idea is unitizing by 10s and 100s or seeing how numbers are created through multiples of ten. To understand this, students need to have experience both counting by tens (and hundreds and so on) and breaking up big numbers into tens (and hundreds and so on).

Place value is built into our number system—a multiplicative base-ten system. Each digit symbolizes a number ten times bigger than the one to the left; multiplication is embedded in the notation system itself. Place value is often taught using place value charts, but kids can easily learn to fill those out without understanding the multiplicative groups behind the numbers. Place value is so much more than filling out a chart. Students need to understand place value to understand counting money as well as decimals.

Counting Collections and Choral Counts are a meaningful way to provide *lots* of practice for kids with this load-bearing wall of mathematics. During a count, students are encouraged as they make groups that work for them, often starting with 2s, then 5s, then 10s. And after enough counting, they break numbers into 100s. When a student makes groups of 10 and uses them to count a large set, they are building their unitizing skills. Counting Collections begin with counting real objects so that students ground this conceptual work in concrete objects. I have seen teachers rush unitizing, just telling students that now this stick represents a ten, or using base-ten blocks before a student really understands that the stick is both one ten and ten ones. Counting Collections makes the student make those groups of ten, and then break them back into ones, composing and decomposing numbers into the units that make up bigger numbers.

Hannah started her year with the routine of Counting Collections, and then she would return to the routine for a few days in between new math units. In this way, Hannah was working on the core principles of counting, number sense, and place value with her students with a repeated routine that allowed sufficient time for students to develop new skills in counting. Some children were working on one-to-one correspondence and cardinality of the sets that they counted, like Juan. Others were working on grouping their sets into groups of ten, something that Hannah highlighted in the share. Grouping into tens is a way to understand the complex concept of place value as our number system is a base-ten system. George, who was in a self-contained classroom because of behavior differences, was working on grouping into 100s. The routine of Counting Collections allowed the students to repeatedly engage in these core ideas. It is also naturally differentiated: The routine stays the same, but Hannah provides a big set of objects for George and one below 20 for Noemi. Every day Noemi's number set was larger, pushing her toward bigger and bigger numbers.

Similar core ideas about numbers emerged in the Choral Count, when Hannah asked students to count from 100, and a student asked whether the same pattern emerged after 900. If it went 100 and then 101, did it go 900 and then 901? These are very important ideas for K–1 students.

Understanding the logic of the number system, or place value, is a core idea. Number sense and place value are definitely load-bearing walls for the rest of mathematics—in other words, these ideas about numbers and the number system are core mathematical ideas that are worthy of significant investment.

> **Number sense and place value are definitely load-bearing walls for the rest of mathematics—in other words, these ideas about numbers and the number system are core mathematical ideas that are worthy of significant investment.**

EXTENDING COUNTING COLLECTIONS

Counting Collections can be transitioned to other, related, counting activities, such as school stores. When I was a resource room teacher in Los Angeles, I had a school store in the corner of my room—just a shelf with various items that I knew kids liked. I had sticky notes with prices that I would change based on the students coming into my room, as I taught small groups in kindergarten through sixth grade. Some kids needed decimals, whereas others did not. One of these students, Asia, was 8 and had Down syndrome. She *loved* playing store. I was also able to teach her to use a calculator with a play register machine. She was challenging for her general education inclusion teacher because she refused to do the math worksheets her classroom teacher gave her in her class. But in my room, with the store, as long as we "played," she engaged deeply in the math.

When I was a fifth- and sixth-grade teacher in New York City, I did something similar: I took students to the neighborhood bodega and pet store frequently. We would use these real-life situations to count money, make change, and estimate costs. Connecting math to their real-world goals such as buying items with cash at a store is an important part of math instruction for students with disabilities.

Special educator Suzanne Huerta uses Counting Collections in her special education, self-contained classroom of fifth graders. Her students had already been doing Counting Collections when some students wondered how many Legos were in the classroom altogether. They began counting the Legos, eventually deciding to make groups of ten in little paper cups. Here are the Legos stacked in cups of ten, in plates of 100.

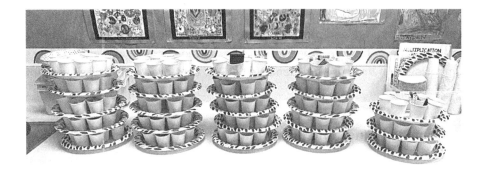

SOURCE: Reprinted with permission from Suzanne Huerta.

Ms. Huerta then guided the students to think about numbers using the count.

Thousands	Hundreds	Tens	Ones	Our Class Counting Collection of Legos
			1	$1 \times 1 = 1$
		1	0	$1 \times 10 = 10$
	1	0	0	$10 \times 10 = 100$
1,	0	0	0	$10 \times (10 \times 10) = 1{,}000$
2,	3	1	3	$2{,}000 + 300 + 10 + 3 = 2{,}313$

SOURCE: Reprinted with permission from Suzanne Huerta.

We can see the power here of using place value charts *after* students have counted and organized this giant set. Now the place value chart has meaning!

Counting Collections and/or store contexts can help students understand the next step in place value: decimals. Counting money itself provides important practice in unitizing. I sometimes see students counting three dimes and a penny as "10, 20, 30, 40." To understand coins, students have to unitize. Students need to understand that one dime is the same as 10 cents (or 10 pennies). This concept is complex but well worth taking the time to let students learn it.

> **Students need to understand that one dime is the same as 10 cents (or 10 pennies). This concept is complex but well worth taking the time to let students learn it.**

APPLYING CORE IDEAS TO SUPPORT STUDENTS WHO NEED MORE TIME

One of my fifth-grade students, Tami, who had Williams syndrome, was an engaging and funny girl who loved her identity as Puerto Rican and loved music. Tami was absolutely capable of learning new things, but she did not generally learn at the same pace as the other students in the class. So as I planned each unit in math, I made sure to identify what the core idea was in the unit—that would be my main goal with Tami.

Tami, like all other students, had a unique set of strengths and challenges in math. She had come from a traditional school and had learned procedures for addition, subtraction, and multiplication. She could mostly do these operations accurately, yet might have difficulty with matching an array to 3×4 or thinking about why 2 groups of 6 was 12. Because of a combination of visual and fine motor issues, she could not always count objects successfully. She was not used to using visuals or talking about why a procedure worked. I felt Tami needed more experiences with making sense of what she was doing, particularly connecting visuals and manipulatives with numeric symbols.

For example, one day we engaged in a problem on finding volume while redesigning the fish tanks in our room.

I AM THINKING about getting a fish for the classroom. The person at the pet store told me that this fish needs 60 cubic inches of space in their fish tank. I am wondering what dimensions are possible for this amount of space. Can we figure out all the possibilities? You could also start by playing with 12 cubic inches. ●

Try It

How many possibilities can you find? With whole numbers? With fractions? How would you solve it if you had connecting cubes?

The core idea for this problem was the relationship between volume and the associative property of multiplication (is a $2 \times 3 \times 2$ box the same as a $2 \times 2 \times 3$ box?). I was pretty sure that starting with the number 60 would be overwhelming for Tami and that she might not get to the core ideas about volume and the associative property. So I gave a choice to the class to start with 12 if they preferred, and I dumped tons of connecting cubes on every table. Tami was sitting with a group of her friends, who were all working with 60. Tami chose to start with 12 instead. I saw her peers check in with her and talk to her about her arrangement of the 12. Tami needed lots of cubes as she preferred making each combination and keeping it physically in front of her rather than dissembling it. She came up with four different ways to make the tank, and I was able to encourage her to systematically make sure she had made them all and record them using parenthesis, meeting my goals for her around understanding and representing the associate property.

My work with Tami was premised on this concept of core ideas. What was the most important idea in this lesson? And what possibilities does it hold for engaging in earlier core ideas? I was able to both engage Tami in the grade-level objective, which was problem solving with the associative problem and finding volume, and give her more opportunities to work on a core idea: connecting multiplication to visual models.

I present this story not because I think it was perfect practice but because it was a workable, equitable solution. Tami was able to engage in a grade-level lesson, but I needed to modify some aspects of the task—she needed a choice for smaller numbers, and she needed the manipulatives to keep the different boxes in her memory. But those were not special accommodations for Tami. I offered the same accommodations to all students. Other students chose to start with 12, including some students with more familiarity with multiplication. Also, by integrating choice, I reminded Tami that she is in control of her education, that she can make choices about her learning that work for her.

REFLECTION QUESTIONS

1. How can Counting Collections as an instructional activity support students to work on core ideas of counting, number sense, and place value? Would you say that Counting Collections is differentiated? How?

2. What core ideas do you invest in with your students?

3. How can core ideas support students with intellectual disabilities in inclusion settings?

UDL Math Connections

Engagement	Representation	Strategic action
Hannah chooses a routine to engage students and to support their behavior because they know the expectations. She works to support her students to do group activities in math, such as Choral Counting, to develop mathematical community.	Hannah designs around two core ideas that students will engage with during counting collections: counting and place value. The routine itself is multimodal as students count concrete objects and then represent them on paper or a tablet.	Hannah works to help her students be more strategic in their counting, to use strategies like tagging, and to begin to group their objects in groups of 10.

Unpacking a Core Idea: The Development of Counting

How do students learn how to count? There are a few important principles to learning to count (Franke et al., 2018).

Counting Sequence

Number names follow an ordered sequence, the same every time. There are patterns in our counting system (except in the tricky teens).

One-to-One Correspondence

Each object you are counting corresponds to exactly one number. We can see this in how kids tag objects while they say numbers.

Cardinality

Understanding that counting results in the size of the set. In other words, the last number you get to in a count is the total amount. One way to assess this is to ask a student who has just finished counting a set, "How many?" See more on assessment of these understandings in the "Three Counting Tasks" sidebar in Chapter 3 on p. 48.

Another important development in early numeracy is subitizing or recognizing instantly a small quantity, like 2 or 3.

Students learn the rules of counting by counting with feedback, whether at home with their families or at school with peers and teachers. Students need plenty of opportunities to count to develop these ideas and become practiced in using them, particularly some neurodivergent students who may have strengths in one area of counting while still developing in others.

CHAPTER 8

DESIGNING TO SUPPORT LANGUAGE VARIABILITY

IN THIS CHAPTER, WE WILL . . .

- Visit a K–3 special education class as the students solve story problems about addition
- Explore how to support problem solving for students who need additional support in their processing of language
- Explore how to support multilingual learners with disabilities through mathematical agency

THE MOMENT I realized the magic in Kayla Martinez's (Figure 8.1) K–3 special education classroom was when the students left the meeting area, right after she had introduced a story problem about marshmallows and hot chocolate. Students, quite young students, moved about the room in a purposeful way. Some grabbed paper and connecting cubes. Others went for rekenreks (also called "math racks"), ten-frames, or base-ten blocks. Some students started to work alone, others stayed back to ask Kayla a question, and others sat next to a friend. One child got materials and then went right to sit by a paraprofessional. What I saw were students experienced in not only solving problems but also in making choices about how they solved problems.

Figure 8.1 •
Kayla, K–3 special education teacher

Kayla's classroom included students from kindergarten to Grade 3, which is a wide grade span for any classroom. Not only were students at different levels of prior knowledge of numbers and addition, but they also presented a range of language processing differences. All of Kayla's students had Individualized

Education Programs (IEPs). Most of her students had learning disabilities, which can include difficulty in both expressive language (what children can say) and receptive language (what they can understand). All of her students this year received speech and language services. In addition, she had students who were also multilingual learners. Kayla's problem of practice was making sure that challenges in processing and understanding language did not affect her students' access to inquiry-based mathematics.

As I pulled up a chair to observe the class, Kayla launched her story problem for the day. The problem was as follows:

> Mr. C (the art teacher) loves marshmallows in his hot chocolate. First, he added ____ marshmallows. Then he added ____ more marshmallows. Last he added ____ more marshmallows for good luck. How many marshmallows did he add to his hot chocolate?
>
> Choose your number set:
> (4, 5, 9), (6, 7, 19) (173, 36, 86).

SOURCE: Reprinted from istock.com/baibaz.

> **Try It**
>
> Solve the problem with each of the different number sets. What do you notice about this problem? What strategies would students use? Would the strategies used be different for different number sets?

Kayla started her launch of this problem by making sure all her students understood the context of making hot chocolate. Using a microphone to support students with hearing impairments, she asked the students what they knew about hot chocolate. A short discussion ensued about whether marshmallows are a good addition to hot chocolate (apparently, yes!). Kayla then discussed how she makes hot chocolate and showed a short video of someone making hot chocolate, including adding marshmallows at the end.

Next Kayla revealed the problem on a chart paper without any numbers, sometimes called a "numberless problem" (Bushart, https://numberlesswp .com/). Using a numberless problem is a great way to get students to start with meaning and not rush to computation. It can help students avoid making what I call "number salad" (when students just grab numbers and toss them). Students learn to do this when they are not given sufficient opportunities to make sense of problems for themselves. Without the numbers, students can focus on understanding the action in the problem first.

> **Using a numberless problem is a great way to get students to start with meaning and not rush to computation.**

Kayla read the problem out loud while pointing at the text to support comprehension. Kayla reported that she always makes sure not just to unpack unfamiliar nouns but particularly verbs, which can be tricky for her students. To support learning of verbs in this context, she pantomimed "adding" marshmallows while both saying and pointing to the word. Finally, Kayla again asked students comprehension questions to make sure that they understood the language and the context. Throughout, she had students turn and talk, not only to restate the problems in their own words but also with specific comprehension questions tailored to the context.

Only then did Kayla show the students the number sets. Her students ranged from kindergarten to third grade and were at all different levels in mathematics. Here the number choices were

$$(4, 5, 9), (6, 7, 19) \ (173, 36, 86)$$

Allowing students to choose a number set is a great example of how choice can develop strategic thinking in students. Instead of passing out different worksheets with different levels of number sets, Kayla asks students to choose for themselves. The availability of the next number set gives an automatic extension task for students who finish the first number set they try. If students consistently pick numbers that don't work for them, we can do some *strategic coaching* and ask them why they picked a particular set.

As students began to work on the problem, different options for engagement were available. Students spoke in both English and Spanish as they worked. Students were working in pairs, independently, or with a paraprofessional. It was clear that students knew where the manipulatives were and felt trusted to make their own choices about what to use. Again, allowing students choice means that they are learning what tools work for them, thus developing their own strategic self-understanding.

Kayla moved from child to child, asking two simple questions: "How many marshmallows?" and "How do you know?" She asked follow-up questions about the details of their strategies and encouraged students to talk to each other. I watched her as she spoke to one child, Hugo, who had grabbed base-ten blocks and was using the largest possible number set (173, 36, 86). We could see three piles of base-ten blocks in front of him, one pile for each number. When Kayla asked, "How many, " he started with the first pile and counted by ones, using the individual squares on each base-ten block to count rather than the entire amount. Soon, he lost track of his count and started again. Kayla watched him quietly. When he finished, she asked Hugo to represent his thinking on paper.

Kayla told me later that she thought that rewriting the amounts would help him develop his understanding of these bigger numbers and, in particular, encourage him to work with larger number units than one. His representation (Figure 8.2) did just that as he represented the 100 block as a unit of 100 (instead of counting by ones), and the 10 blocks as one unit of 10. He then counted with units of 100 and 10, starting with the 100, skip counting by tens, and then the ones.

Figure 8.2 · *Hugo's written work for 173 + 36 + 86*

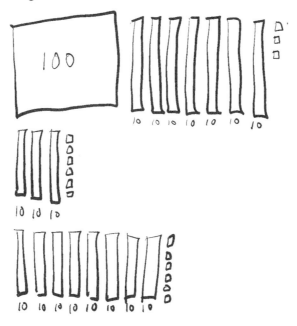

Just as in Counting Collections (Chapter 7), representation of thinking on paper (or digitally) pushes students to move from the concrete to the more abstract, and it can help students unitize, which is critical in developing understanding of place value. Place value, in turn, underlies multiple strategies for addition with multidigit numbers. By asking Hugo to re-represent his strategy in another modality, Kayla pushes him to reflect on his strategy. Each iteration of a student strategy comes with a bit of refinement, some additional clarity for the learner.

Across the room, most students were using direct modeling for this problem (drawing or counting each item), with some students counting on from the largest number. By the end of the class, every student had solved this addition story problem using at least one number set.

When students finished, Kayla asked them to record their strategies in an app on their tablets. Each student snapped a picture of their work, both their recording sheet and their manipulatives, if they used them. Students then recorded a short audio file explaining their strategy. Most students seemed comfortable with this process and recorded their strategies on their own.

I saw one student, Diego, instead walk up to a paraprofessional and describe his strategy. He began hesitantly and seemed to gain confidence as he spoke. After he finished, the paraprofessional asked him to record his strategy. Having students engage in sharing their strategies one on one before sharing in the whole group is called a "rehearsal." Rehearsals can be particularly useful to support students who are shy or need extra time to plan their verbal response.

The next step was the share. Kayla gathered her students in the front of the class on the rug. Each student who shared held a microphone to amplify their voice, just as Kayla did. In the share, Kayla asked two students to share their direct modeling strategies. The first child stood up and showed how she used a ten-frame to solve 4 + 5 + 9. The second student showed how he used a rekenrek for the same problem. The final student was Hugo, the one who had used base-ten blocks for 173 + 36 + 86. He shared how he had to count multiple times to find an accurate answer and how he changed his answer. He also shared how the base-ten blocks helped him solve such a big problem. As the students came up to share, Kayla represented their thinking on chart paper. The students used this representation of their thinking as they shared, for example, Hugo, counting onto the representations Kayla made of his base-ten blocks (Figure 8.3).

Figure 8.3 · *Hugo shares, supported by Kayla*

SUPPORTING LANGUAGE DURING CONTEXTUAL MATH PROBLEMS

As a teacher trained in student mathematical thinking through cognitively guided instruction (CGI), Kayla used story problems in sequences to develop particular mathematical concepts and strategies (see "Unpacking a Core Idea: Early Addition and Subtraction With Story Problems" on p. 138). Her work is based on research that students can develop both strong number sense and understanding of the operations by working in real-life contexts (Carpenter et al., 2015). She is using *guided inquiry* with her students.

One critique of inquiry-based mathematics is that because the mathematics is embedded in language, the cognitive load of the math plus the language can become overwhelming. Cognitive load refers to the amount of information our working memory can process at one time. I understand that cognitive load can be a problem for understanding. I personally cannot attend to a conversation when a TV is on in the background—I can't seem to make sense of either if they are going at the same time. If students, particularly those who may take longer to process language, are asked to process unfamiliar contexts *and* start a complex math problem at the same time, they can't do both at once without support.

This difficulty may be real, but it should never function as a reason to exclude children from solving complex math problems. I have heard that single phrase, "cognitive load," used as a way to discourage teachers from including students with disabilities in inquiry-based problem solving. This problem is not insurmountable, as Kayla shows us. As long as students understand the context of the problem, and the action occurring, they can solve it using whatever languages and manipulatives make sense to them. Simply by making the problem familiar, you reduce cognitive load. In fact, using authentic contexts is recommended for both students with learning disabilities and multilingual learners (Kelemanik et al., 2016).

> Simply by making the problem familiar,
> you reduce cognitive load.

Another argument I have heard about using inquiry mathematics is that students should not solve problems without sufficient prior knowledge. Some would say that you cannot give students this problem until they can already do addition. But clearly, all these students with a range of prior knowledges were able to solve this as long as they were able to solve it in a way that made sense to them. Is the necessary prior knowledge the abstract, symbolic procedure of 4 + 5 + 9 = 18? Or is the necessary prior knowledge that the student understands the story about the marshmallows, knows how to count, and understands that the action of the problem is combining different amounts together? With that knowledge, students can represent and solve the problem. In a way, the most important prior knowledge is that these students believe they *can* solve a problem without being told exactly how to solve it. These students did not wait to be given a strategy. They started right away, making choices about what manipulatives to use and what strategy to use. I could see how comfortable they were solving problems without being told what procedure to use. That confidence comes with lots of opportunities to solve problems.

> The most important prior knowledge is that
> these students believe they *can* solve a problem
> without being told exactly how to solve it.

In the end, students in this self-contained special education class were successfully solving a multi-addend word problem using their own strategies.

I recognize Kayla's success facilitating a class at multiple skill levels. We all know it can be challenging to plan mathematics when students are at different levels. Kayla has an exceptionally wide range of student skills in her class as the students are in four grades (K–3), as well as having disabilities that can affect mathematical development. As we noted in Chapter 3, students with neurodiversities may have interesting paths through mathematical trajectories. Their development can take more time, or less, through certain topics. Some of her students are working to understand number and beginning to count. Other students are working with multidigit addition in the hundreds. Kayla's strategy to address learner variability is to offer choice.

SUPPORTING MULTILINGUAL LEARNERS

Choice is also a key element for how Kayla supports her multilingual students. First, it is important to reject deficit thinking about multilingual students. Being bilingual brings social and cognitive benefits (Marian & Shook, 2012). Bilingualism is a gift. However, when schools treat multilingual learners as if they are a problem, we create problems for these students. Using the social model, we can see the problem is not a child with the opportunity to learn two languages, but a school system that is inflexible about which language a child learns in. Language is a barrier if we make it so. So we must begin instead with an asset-based lens.

> **Language is a barrier if we make it so. So we must begin instead with an asset-based lens.**

We should not remove or simplify language but instead provide access to it (Moschkovich, 2012). We want multilingual students to have access to rich language environments that provide lots of opportunities to listen and talk. Students learning a second language need opportunities to practice their newer language, as well as to return to their first language if it provides access for them. Access can be supported by multimodal instruction, as Kayla demonstrated, using visuals, videos, and gestures. Best practices in supporting multilingual learners in mathematics include revoicing student strategies, asking clarifying questions, and using gestures to communicate mathematical ideas (Moschkovich, 1999).

As I think about Kayla's work, I turn to the research of Dr. Juanita Silva, an expert in meaningful mathematics for multilingual learners with learning disabilities. Her research documents how students can make sense of challenging problems when both languages are seen as resources, when students are given access to multiple languages, and when students are encouraged to make sense of the math using what they know. In one study, Dr. Silva described her work with a group of three students solving CGI story problems (Silva, 2021). Dr. Silva, who is bilingual, moved back and forth between Spanish and English as she taught, responding to what language the students used, and whether they seemed to need an idea or question in another language. Students made sense of the problems through both Spanish and English. This example uses multiple modalities to support student strengths, here offering (and valuing) both languages and allowing students to take the lead on which helps them more at any particular instance. This kind of responsive teaching is a gift that bilingual educators can offer students.

Dr. Silva found that these students demonstrated mathematical agency when given choice as they worked. She found students responded well to choice in

1. Language spoken
2. Which math strategies to use
3. Whether to work individually or with others
4. How to participate in discussions

She further supported these students by creating many opportunities for them to participate in mathematical discussion, including teacher questioning about the details of what they did mathematically. I also see these elements of choice in Kayla's classroom. Because her students need additional support processing language, Kayla gives them lots of choice in how they engage, as well as chances to revise their language and their mathematics.

In the work of Dr. Silva and Kayla, we can see how supporting students in the language of mathematics is, first, a matter of trust. We need to assume that these students have mathematical ideas and can solve complex problems. Next, we need to provide access to complex problems through multimodal, language-rich instruction. Another critical feature is choice, so that students can develop as strategic sense-makers and learn to trust their own thinking.

REFLECTION QUESTIONS

1. What do you know about language processing differences? How has difficulty understanding and producing language affected students in your math classroom? How have you supported these students?

2. Reflecting on the teacher moves of both Kayla and Dr. Silva, how would you respond to your multilingual students with specific learning disabilities in mathematics?

3. If you were told that students with learning disabilities and/or language processing differences could not "handle" inquiry-based mathematics, what might you say?

UDL Math Connections

Engagement	Representation	Strategic action
Kayla opens up the classroom by using a central story problem. While her students are working at different math goals and have different support needs, she creates community and collective purpose by having one central problem, with multiple problem sets, multiple tools available (rekenrek or tens frame), and different ways of engaging (work alone, with a partner, or with a paraprofessional). Choice is central to her classroom.	Kayla supports through multimodality. She starts the launch with visual storytelling, along with gestures. She supports students to read the text of the problem through read-aloud, gesture, and comprehension checks. Students have choice in what representations they use to solve the problem.	As they solve, she questions them about their strategies, developing their self-understandings as a learner. Students rehearse for the share by practicing their strategy share. Choice develops self-understanding as students need to think about what works best for them.

Table 9.1 • *A rekenrek number string*

What Dina showed on the rekenrek	Selected student strategies	What she wrote on the board
	"I saw 5 reds and 1 white, so 6, and again, so 6 plus 6" "I saw a 10 of red beads, and then 2, so 12"	5 + 1 = 6, 5 + 1 = 6 6 + 6 = 12 10 + 2 = 12
	"I saw 10 on the top, then 2" "Same as the last one, but the 10 is different"	10 + 2 = 12
	"I saw 5 and 2 which is 7, two times. I know my doubles, so 7 + 7 = 14" "I saw a 10 in reds and a 4 in whites"	5 + 2 = 7 7 + 7 = 14 10 + 4 = 14
	"Same as last one, but 1 bead less" "I thought of 6 + 6 but 1 more"	(7 + 7) – 1 = 13 (6 + 6) + 1 = 13
	"I saw that there was almost a 10 on the bottom, so I took a bead from the top and gave it to the bottom. That made 17" "I saw 8 + 8, and added 1" "I thought of 9 + 9 and took away 1"	8 + 9 = 7 + 10 = 17 (8 + 8) + 1 = 17 (9 + 9) – 1 = 17

Think About It

What mathematical strategies is this number string designed to support kids to try?

For this number string, Dina had a few goals related to their ongoing work on addition and subtraction below 20. Her number choices encouraged students to think about doubles, which are particularly interesting on the rekenrek since they are so visual. She was also working to get them to see, and work flexibly with, groups of five and ten. That last problem is a beautiful chance to use doubles plus or minus one, or to make a 10 by moving one bead from the 8 to the 9.

After the rekenrek number string, Dina gathered her second graders at the rug and told them all about a problem she needed help with. Dina was starting a new math unit that built from *Measuring for the Art Show (2007)*, designed by Cathy Fosnot in her New Perspectives for Learning series (2020). Dina first called the students' attention to what she called a "sad bulletin board" in the back of the classroom, totally empty. A few students had been telling her that she really needed to put up some student work. She told them that she had been given colored papers in different sizes that she wanted to use for a display of their artwork but did not know exactly how long the pieces of paper were and how many would fit. She asked for their help measuring the papers. She pulled out a stack of papers, with each color of paper having different measurements. The blue papers were exactly the length of 10 connecting cubes by 14 connecting cubes. Another paper, purple, was the length of 30 by 44 connecting cubes. The class was enthusiastic about helping, and they soon got to work across the room in partnerships. Dina had given each pair of students a resealable bag with two colors of connecting cubes.

As Dina and I walked around the room, we watched students as they measured. We wanted to make sure that they understood where to start their measurements, holding their stick to the edge. One of her mathematical goals was to develop students' spatial understanding of the number line, and thus she paid careful attention to where they positioned zero. If she saw students not being careful about lining up the edge, Dina sat down with the pair and engaged with them until she was sure they were not only able to measure but also understood exactly why the measurement depended on it.

So why didn't she give them a ruler? Because what Dina wanted was for her students to create their own rulers. At first, students just made random use of the colors in the measuring sticks. However, 15 minutes in, one pair of students made a measuring stick that was color coded by 2s. Dina stopped the class and highlighted this measuring stick, which happened to be made by a student with dyslexia, whom we will call Kamir. She asked Kamir to share why they made

Figure 9.2 • *Kamir and partner measuring the purple paper*

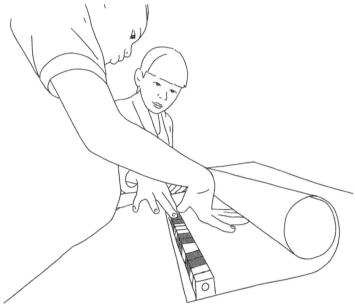

their measuring stick with this repeated pattern (see Figure 9.2). Kamir told the class groups of two made the counting easier. Dina wondered aloud if any other numbers would be helpful.

As the students got back to work, I watched another partnership of a boy and a girl start planning to make a measuring stick with fives (Figure 9.3). Others started using tens. By the end of the first session, all of the groups had remade their measuring sticks with groups of 2, 5, or 10. Dina ended the first day by showing these different configurations and holding a conversation about the lengths students found.

She asked the following questions: What was the length of the blue paper? Did we all find the same amount? Even if our measuring sticks were different? The conversation focused on equivalence and on making sure everyone was measuring the same way.

The next day, students finished measuring all the papers and had checked their measurements with other students. Dina ended this day by calling the students together. She called their attention to the connecting cubes she had affixed to the whiteboard, using groups of 5 (Figure 9.4).

Figure 9.3 • *Students measuring in groups of 5*

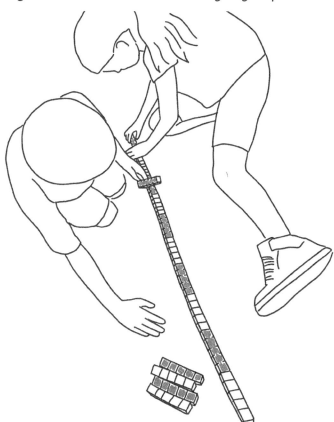

Figure 9.4 • *Dina connects measurements to the line of connecting cubes*

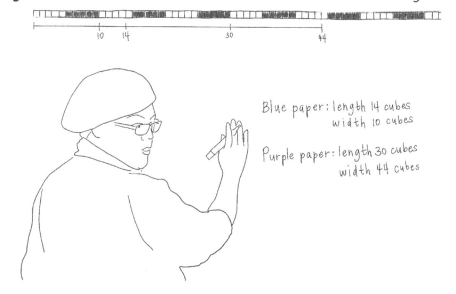

Blue paper: length 14 cubes
width 10 cubes

Purple paper: length 30 cubes
width 44 cubes

As students shared their findings for each piece of paper they measured, Dina marked the whiteboard with each measurement (Figure 9.4). Dina slowed down the discussion whenever there was a disagreement about the measure of a paper and had the students who disagreed remeasure using their connecting cubes in front of the whole class. Dina was carefully creating a mapping for students between the connecting cubes number line and what is called an "open number line," where not every unit is marked. The open number line is the mathematical model that her sequence of lessons was designed to develop for students. At this point, Dina had now co-created a number line with her students, one that carefully mapped space to magnitude.

Thus far we felt confident with the students. They seemed to have developed in 2 days an understanding of the number line as linear space. Our next lessons were designed to further develop student understanding of number lines through a game. We took a game from the unit (the Jump Jump Game) in which students hop a plastic frog in jumps of ten and one around a number line. We modified the game to be a long number line of 100 since we were particularly interested in students' conception of the number line. We laminated the boards and gave the students whiteboard markers so they could mark up the board. We hoped that would make their thinking about where numbers were more visible. Our work in this part of the sequence was to decontextualize the number line away from the specific context of measuring.

The next day, Dina did another number string with her students, but this time using a number line. The sequence of problems in the string was designed to connect to the numbers the students had measured in the colored papers and mapped onto the whiteboard. Her intention was to help students connect their developing understanding of a number line to strategies for addition. Her number string was as follows:

> Number string:
>
> 26 + 10
>
> 26 + 12
>
> 26 + 22
>
> 44 + 30

> **Try It**
>
> Before you learn how the students solved these problems, think about how you or your students might solve them using mental math.

She gathered the students on the rug, no paper and pencil to be seen, and reminded them of the expectations of the number string: (a) Raise your thumb when you have an answer and (b) do not stop others' thinking by shouting out. Dina wrote the first problem on the board, read it out loud, and then waited. Students let her know they were ready with an answer with a quiet thumbs-up. When all students had their thumbs up, she called on a student who added 10, who said that she just knew that 10 more for 26 would be 36. Dina represented that with a big jump of 10 on a number line right below her connecting cubes line. Figure 9.5 shows the whiteboard when Dina finished the string.

Figure 9.5 · *Dina's completed number string*

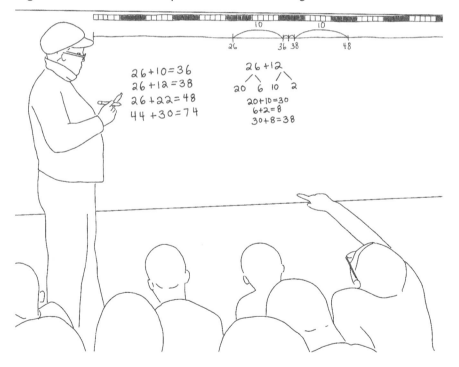

Dina posed the next problem, 26 + 12, and again waited until she could see most of the students with their thumb raised, ready to share. The first student to share had used a decomposition by place value strategy, breaking up 26 into

20 and 6, and 12 into 10 and 2. The student then added the tens in her head, then the ones, and then combined them.

Then Dina asked if anyone had solved it using the number line and pointed at the connecting cubes line at the top of the whiteboard. One student shared that he had just added two more to 36. Dina added that to the previous problem. Another student commented that this was a nice strategy, easier than breaking the number apart. Other students nodded. Dina noted that she loved when they used patterns in the problems to find shortcuts.

The next problem was 26 + 22. Students seemed excited to use the number line again for this one. "It's just another ten," a student burst out, and Dina smiled, calling on the student. The student wanted to use the open number line at the top of the board, adding just one more ten, since the problem added just one more ten. Dina again carefully represented that strategy at the top of the board, making sure to align her open number line with the connecting cubes above. Another student shared a decomposition strategy, which Dina also represented.

The final problem was 44 + 30. This problem was not connected to the previous string of problems, which all started with the number 26. Instead, this final problem pushes students to generalize a strategy to a new set of numbers. Dina posed the problem and gave additional time for the student to think. Feeling the bubbling intensity of the students who wanted to share, Dina had them first turn to a partner and share their strategy. Across the room, noise broke out as the pairs started talking about their strategies, fingers pointed up at the board. Dina walked around the meeting area, listening in to student strategies and making choices about what strategies she wanted to represent.

For this final problem, Dina called on a student, Luisa, who had used the number line. The student said that she "started at 44, and then I made one jump of 10." Dina immediately started drawing a new number line under the problems, starting at 44 and then with a jump of 10. Dina prompted, "And where were you then?" The girl replied, "54." Dina marked 54 on the number line. Luisa talked Dina through the rest of her strategy, including naming each jump of ten. Clearly, Luisa had been using the number line as a mental tool as she thought about the problem. Another student shared a splitting strategy for the same problem, and they briefly discussed the connections between the strategies. Dina and I exchanged an excited look: Luisa's thinking was exactly what Dina had been designing for. She wanted her students to not just understand the number line but also to use it as a tool for thinking mathematically! ●

DEVELOPING THE MATHEMATICAL MODEL OF THE OPEN NUMBER LINE

Both Dina and I were exposed through the work of Math in the City to realistic mathematics education (RME), a tradition of mathematics educational research and curricular design that began with Hans Freudenthal's (1991) work as a mathematician in the Netherlands. One critical element of RME is that students should all have experience "mathematizing their lived worlds" (Freudenthal, 1991). Every child has a right to make sense of math and to use math to make sense of their worlds. Dina believed this with a passion. Dina was a strong advocate for increasing the opportunities for Black and Latino/a students to engage in meaningful mathematics. Our collaboration came from our desire to better support students of color with disabilities to mathematize their worlds.

> **Every child has a right to make sense of math and to use math to make sense of their worlds.**

A second key idea from RME is how to design learning sequences that help students deeply understand mathematical models (Van Den Heuvel-Panhuizen, 2003). The term *mathematical model* is reserved for a few critical visual models that matter a lot in mathematics: number lines, arrays, and ratio tables, for example. The sequence to develop a model begins with the learner engaging with the model informally in a context. In this case, the students start by using connecting cubes to measure paper, a real-life context. The teacher explicitly connects the informal model to the formal model. In this case, the informal model was the connecting cubes measuring stick. The formal model was the number line Dina drew on the board. Lastly, while provided with the mathematical model, students were asked to think about mathematical problems that could be solved with it. Here Dina asked students to solve addition problems in their minds, while keeping up the connecting cubes to suggest its use. Dina purposefully used the number line to represent student strategies, and we could see a progression within the number string of students using the number line to think. RME, then, gives a specific and well-documented view of how to help students understand the most important mathematical representations (Table 9.2).

Table 9.2 · *Stages of model development*

Students engage with a model in a real-life context, creating an informal model.	The teacher makes connections between the informal model and the formal model.	Students begin to solve problems using the model as a "tool for thinking."
Students were asked to measure papers using measuring sticks made of connecting cubes, which they fashioned into number lines. They designed their own number lines, based on whatever number helped them count.	Dina recreated a measuring stick and attached it to the whiteboard. She then started drawing number lines that mapped onto the quantities of the measuring stick. She began to use the formal model (the open number line) to represent student strategies.	After this investigation, games, and number strings, students began thinking with the open number line. They used it mentally in number strings and used it as a model for solving problems in written work.

DEVELOPING THE NUMBER LINE

The number line is a critical mathematical model that students use from kindergarten all the way to calculus. Many students are simply given number lines to use without much introduction of how they serve as models. But number lines can be confusing, particularly for some students with disabilities (Geary et al., 2008). Some number lines, particularly in the early elementary grades look like this:

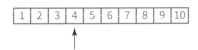

If you ask a student where 4 is on this number line, they will point to the entire 4, which makes sense.

But what about this number line, where only the numbers are marked. Where is 4 now?

Do you see where this might confuse a child? Four is now the whole measurement, the entire space from the mark of zero to the mark of 4. Number line #2 is a closed number line, in which all the iterations are marked. RME also has another kind of number line, one in which only the numbers you use are marked, an *open number line*:

USING THE NUMBER LINE AS A TOOL FOR THINKING

The ultimate goal for Dina is not just to develop understanding of the number line but also to leverage that understanding into student strategies for addition and subtraction. The open number line is a powerful model for strategies such as making jumps of ten and multiples of ten, useful for both addition and subtraction.

If students are given plenty of opportunities to make sense of situations (story problems or tasks) that require addition and subtraction, and are given experiences so that they can understand place value and number sense with bigger and bigger numbers, students will develop strategies, sometimes called "invented algorithms," for multidigit addition and subtraction. We have lots of evidence of students developing these strategies without being taught (Carpenter et al., 2015), including students with disabilities. Students with disabilities can develop these strategies, just as other students do. For example, students with mathematical difficulties used the adding to subtract strategy when the numbers made sense to do so, a finding across multiple research projects even when the students (a) had low achievement in mathematics and (b) had not been directly taught this strategy (Peters et al., 2014; Van Der Auwera et al., 2022).

Dina's students were at that moment inventing multiple strategies for addition. Just because kids naturally invent all of these strategies (and I have seen all of them in my work as a teacher) does *not* mean that every student in your class needs to know how to do every one of these strategies. This is how some textbooks seem to have interpreted the research behind the common core. Some approaches force students to use all of these strategies, teaching each strategy directly and asking students to practice it. This is not a good idea, particularly for students who need more time to make sense of a strategy and/or may forget it. Students should be exposed to multiple strategies (but do not need to be exposed to all of them) *if* students in the room are using them. Your goal, particularly for students who need more time to construct and remember strategies, is to support all students to develop some strategies and to make sure they become proficient at the ones that work for them. Let your students do what makes sense to them! Don't force it! (For more, see "Unpacking a Core Idea: Strategies for Multidigit Addition and Subtraction" on p. 156.)

> **Your goal, particularly for students who need more time to construct and remember strategies, is to support all students in developing some strategies and to make sure they become proficient at the ones that work for them.**

SUPPORTING THE DEVELOPMENT OF EARLY ADDITION AND SUBTRACTION

I want to return to another way in which this lesson supported Dina's students. Dina typically began her class with a number sense routine, like the rekenrek number string. Rekenreks were created in the Netherlands in the 1990s as a modification of an abacus to support students working flexibly with groups of 5s and 10. A study using randomized groups found that using a rekenrek was significantly more effective than the same instruction using a ten-frame for students with learning disabilities (Tournaki et al., 2008). Why is the rekenrek so supportive? The rekenrek is helpful to develop the strategies of doubling, as well as to help students visualize *compensation*, the concept behind making tens. For the problem 8 + 9, for example, students might think of it as a double (8 + 8) plus one more, or make a ten by giving one from the 8 to the 9. That strategy of making tens is made concrete for students when you slide the beads. For more on student strategies, see "Unpacking a Core Idea: Fluency With Addition and Subtraction Below 20" on p. 155.

Dina saw the rekenrek as an important model for early addition and subtraction but also as a way to support linear conceptions of number. These groups of 5 and 10 were a precursor to her longer measuring stick made of connecting cubes, another way to support understanding of numbers as linear space.

MATHEMATICAL MODELS THAT MATTER

The number line is not the only mathematical model that matters for students. Another particularly useful model is the array, which is powerful for developing the conceptual understanding of multiplication. Arrays also help students understand area, which extends to concepts in algebra and geometry. You can follow this same design trajectory by first having students explore arrays in the real world, using arrays to represent their thinking, and then eventually students may think with arrays as a mental tool. Other useful models are the ratio table and the double number line, which can represent proportions and variables, which we explore in Chapter 13.

Dina's teaching was designed to develop important mathematical models. She used a variety of mathematical pedagogies to support this development. The work designing measuring sticks through an investigation was *guided inquiry.* She also provided *strategic coaching* with individual students to support them, being particularly explicit about how to measure. As the unit progressed, Dina used number strings, an example of *guided strategic development.* Number strings are carefully scaffolded to support student development, but they always allow students to take the lead in sharing their own strategies.

REFLECTION QUESTIONS

1. What is the role of carefully sequenced instruction in math such as how Dina sequences instruction on the number line? How does that support student learning?

2. What did you notice and wonder about Dina's classroom? What more would you want to know about her work and her students?

3. The design in this chapter all works toward students using a number line as they think. Have you seen students who struggle with a number line? Students who use it as a tool to think with? What has worked in your experience to help students understand this critical tool?

UDL Math Connections

Engagement	Representation	Strategic action
Dina created a mathematical community of problem solvers in this second-grade classroom. She did so through a combination of high expectations and warmth.	Dina's lesson sequence is about developing a number line, which is much more than a visual. It can become a tool for thinking if students can internalize it. This unit is designed to do that, a specifically mathematical kind of multimodality.	Dina provided students with specific feedback on their measuring. We made sure that all students were able to use the tool correctly, and then we checked to make sure they were generalizing to the number line.

Unpacking a Core Idea: Fluency With Addition and Subtraction Below 20

As students move away from direct modeling, they begin to develop strategies for addition and subtraction. Students develop fact fluency with addition and subtraction problems through three phases (Bay-Williams & Kling, 2019).

- ► Phase 1. Counting (counts with objects or mentally)
- ► Phase 2. Deriving (using reasoning strategies based on known facts)
- ► Phase 3. Mastery (efficiently produces answers)

Students do not learn all the facts at the same speed. Instead, some facts (like the doubles) typically will be learned to mastery well before others. Bay-Williams and Kling (2019) called these the "foundational facts." Next, students learn the facts that are a little more tricky, those called "derived facts." Table 9.3 gives examples of foundational and derived facts.

Table 9.3 · *Foundational and derived facts in addition and subtraction*

Foundational facts	Derived fact strategies
• Plus and minus 0, 1, and 2 (5 + 0, 5 + 1, 5 + 2, etc.) • Doubles (5 + 5, 6 + 6, etc.) • Combinations to 10 (3 + 7, 8 + 2, etc.) • Adding a one-digit number to ten (10 + 2, 10 + 7, etc.)	• Near doubles (using a double to solve a problem that is close, like using 6 + 6 to solve 6 + 7) • Making 10 (making a friendlier problem using 10, like changing 9 + 5 to 10 + 4 by moving a one) • Pretend a 10 (turning 8 + 5 into 10 + 5, then taking away the extra 2)

We can support students to develop the number sense necessary for these strategies through Story Problems and other activities that develop their number sense and counting, like Counting Collections. We also support them by guiding them toward strategies for the derived facts. Once students begin to use some deriving strategies, we support their development by giving them lots of opportunities to develop strategies, hear other students' strategies, and talk about their own strategies. Rekenrek number strings and games are great ways to do this!

A frequent mistake is to rush students through Phase 2: Deriving. Not only does it take time for students to develop and practice these strategies, it is also where students develop the thinking about operations and equivalence necessary for future mathematics, especially algebra. Students using a Making 10 strategy who think deeply about why 9 + 5 = 10 + 4 are thinking about algebraic equivalence. These strategies also matter as they begin to develop strategies for multidigit addition, such as using compensation to solve 99 + 50.

Unpacking a Core Idea: Strategies for Multidigit Addition and Subtraction

Research has documented that students develop multiple strategies for multidigit addition and subtraction (Carpenter et al., 2015). I recommend giving students lots of opportunities to develop and discuss these strategies. We should ensure that every child has strategies that work for them; children should not be forced to use strategies that do not make sense to them. Table 9.4 illustrates some of the most common strategies. See also Table 9.5.

Table 9.4 · *Student strategies for multidigit addition*

Strategy description	Example
Decomposition by place value/ splitting Students break up numbers into place value units and then combine the units together. They usually work with the biggest chunks first.	$47 + 25$ 5 40 7 20 $40 + 20 = 60$ $7 + 5 = 12$ $60 + 12 = 72$
Keeping one number whole and adding on Students start with one number and then add on chunks that make sense to them, usually 10s and multiple of 10s, then 1s. The number line is a great model for this strategy.	10 10 47 57 67 5 to 72 Start here
Compensation Students play with the addends to make addition easier. As long as they don't lose or add quantity, this works!	$47 + 25$ $+3$ $50 + 22 = 72$ take 3 from the 25 and give it to the 47

Try It

Try to work out these strategies for 39 + 42

Table 9.5 · *Student strategies for multidigit subtraction*

Strategy description	Example
Keeping the subtrahend whole and removing The subtrahend is the number you are subtracting from. Students keep that number whole and remove chunks of numbers, usually tens and multiples of tens first.	$81-27$ *start here* 7 20 54 61 81
Adding to subtract Students often prefer to do addition rather than subtraction. In this strategy, students usually add on until they get to the difference.	50 3 1 27 30 80 *start here and add until you get to 81* $3+50+1=54$
Decomposition by place value Students break up numbers into place value units, and then subtract the units from the units of the same size, and combine the answers. If you get a negative number, keep at it. It works out (wonderful question to puzzle out why).	$81-27$ $80-20=60$ $1-7=\,^-6$ $60-6=54$

Constant difference
 	
This is another strategy where you try to make the problem a little easier. If we can change the problem so that the number we are subtracting is a multiple of ten, we add or subtract the same amount so that the difference stays the same, and then solve.
	27 81
	   3 3
	   30 84
	
	$84-30=54$

> **Try It**
>
> Try to work out these strategies for 64 – 39

Again, all students do not need to learn all these strategies. Help students develop some strategies, and make sure they become proficient at the ones that work for them.

Learn More:

Carpenter, T. P., Fennema, E., Franke, M. L., Levi, L., & Empson, S. B. (2015). *Children's mathematics: Cognitively guided instruction* (2nd ed.). Heinemann.

Fosnot, C. T., & Dolk, M. (2001). *Young mathematicians at work: Constructing number sense, addition, and subtraction.* Heinemann.

CHAPTER 10

DESIGNING FOR FACT FLUENCY

IN THIS CHAPTER, WE WILL...

- Visit with me as I teach a small-group intervention in multiplication
- Discuss the development of multiplication and the role of fluency
- Explore using math games to support fluency in addition and subtraction

SHORTLY AFTER STUDENTS were able to return to school in person in California in 2021, after some of the restrictions of the coronavirus 2019 (COVID-19) pandemic were lifted, I began working with an elementary school to design intervention for students returning with unfinished learning. We decided that an important need for intervention was a group of fourth and fifth graders who needed more support with multiplication. The school I was working In was majority Latino/a, with more than half of the students multilingual. Almost all the students came from families below the poverty line. The students in these grades had a wide range of experiences with schooling during the pandemic. Some students had a lot of support and attended every online class. Other students could not attend, or had a lot of difficulty learning online, connecting to lessons through the screen.

Our team decided to do an afterschool math club for students who needed more support in multiplication. Of the 18 students we included in the program, several did not successfully answer any questions (or only one) on our initial assessment of early multiplication. In our first session, I noticed that two of these students also did not participate. I wanted to learn more about these students so that I could support them. While most of the teaching in this program was done by undergraduates, I decided to teach these two students in my own small group.

Before our first meeting, I pored over what I knew about these two students. Franco was a fifth grader, Latino, multilingual in Spanish and English, and had an Individualized Education Program (IEP) for autism. His teachers described him as inconsistent in math. I soon learned that Franco had a wry sense of humor. He had attended Zoom classes the previous year, but his teachers noticed that he was much less successful learning through the screen. I also wondered about Franco and language. I had the impression that he did not completely understand some of the questions that were posed to him, and so I speculated that he might know quite a bit more than we knew.

Jeremy was a fourth grader, Latino, multilingual, and had an IEP for a learning disability in reading: dyslexia. He was a playful, engaging kid who loved games and playing at recess. Jeremy had attended less than half the Zoom classes the previous year, and now he seemed to be much more in need of intervention in math than before the school shutdown from the COVID-19 pandemic, when his work in special education was focused on literacy. I noticed that Jeremy seemed to be counting under his breath but not using his fingers. He also did not want to draw, as many students did when stuck. I thought that I could perhaps give him blocks as a manipulative instead.

I decided that both Franco and Jeremy might benefit from hands-on work with multiplication. I designed an intervention based on studies of constructivist small-group intervention in multiplicative thinking using towers of blocks to engage students in early multiplicative thinking (Tzur et al., 2020). In this kind of small group intervention, we begin with understanding what the students know, building through purposeful tasks designed specifically for these students (Hunt & Ainsle, 2021).

In our first session, I piled connecting cubes on the table and asked them, "Can you make me one tower of 3 cubes?" I immediately wrote the words on the whiteboard as I asked: "1 tower of 3 cubes." My somewhat odd request was immediately taken up by both students, with Jeremy first making a stack of 4 and then correcting. I drew a representation of the tower of 3 cubes they had made. I then asked how many cubes, and they both said "three." I wrote "3" and said, "one group of 3 is three" before writing the words. I then wrote 1 × 3 = 3, saying the multiplication equation out loud as I wrote. This careful documentation of what we doing was important to connect what we were doing to the symbolic and linguistic demands of the task.

Next, I asked, "Can you make me 2 towers of 3?" I again wrote on the whiteboard. Franco made them, and so did Jeremy, but then stacked them on top of each other. I asked what tower he had made, and Jeremy looked at me, puzzled. Franco replied, "one tower of 6." Jeremy looked quizzical, then counted, and then nodded. I asked how many blocks in 2 towers of 3, and they both agreed 6. I wrote an equation and read it out loud.

Our last problem doubled the previous one, asking them to make four towers of 3 blocks. Jeremy made the towers, then solved for the total by doubling the previous answer, since "3 plus 3 is 6, so 6 doubled is 12, or 3 plus 3 plus 3 plus 3." As he explained his thinking, Jeremy used the blocks to model his thinking, moving them as he explained his thinking (Figure 10.1). I could see that with these towers in his hands, he had access to strategic thinking about multiplication. The towers supported his mathematical reasoning and his ability to share it in words.

Figure 10.1 ·
Jeremy showing his strategy for four towers of three blocks

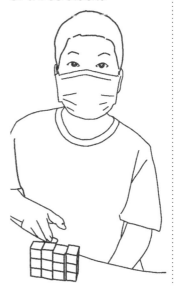

In one of the next sessions, we did the following sequence of tower building:

- ▸ 2 towers of 5
- ▸ 4 towers of 5
- ▸ 6 towers of 5

Figure 10.2 • *Whiteboard showing Franco and Jeremy's strategies for multiplication*

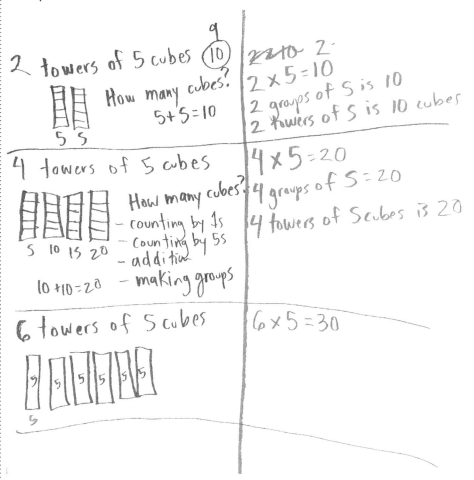

Figure 10.2 shows the board after we had finished. This sequence provoked both students to skip count rather than counting the objects (because of my choice of 5, great for skip counting). They also started a conversation about the relationship between 5s and 10s, and Franco started working with 10s, doubling the towers for 4×5. I also asked them to predict the multiplication problem before I wrote it. Both were able to do so.

Throughout, I wrote the language that I used out loud. I paired the language with visuals of the towers and the equations. I also wrote out the strategies they were using for multiplication, "Counting by 1s, counting by 5s, addition, making groups." We noticed and named the strategies they used each time.

Both boys became quite skilled at creating and naming towers. Both students moved from *direct modeling*, or counting each object, to skip counting and doubling. I felt that Jeremy really learned when building these towers for himself. He wasn't really a kid who was into drawing, but he was a builder who loved making things. And for Franco, the solidity of the blocks along with the careful documentation of the language allowed him to feel confident with the words that were being used. I saw much more understanding when he held the towers in his hand than in any other context. I could see him carefully paying attention as I wrote out phrases like "4 groups of 5."

After this session, I moved both Franco and Jeremy out of my group into one of a group led by an undergraduate researcher. I felt they had the foundation necessary to now engage in the work of the other students. We were using the Building Fact Fluency curriculum for Multiplication and Division (Fletcher & Zager, 2021), a wonderful resource that systematically moves through the multiplication factors through a sequence of 3-Act Tasks, number strings (called "number talks"), games, and story problems. Similar to the work from realistic mathematics education (RME) developing the number line in Chapter 9, these lessons have purposeful use of visuals that both support and stretch students' mathematical strategies in multiplication.

Both Jeremy and Franco thrived in their understanding of multiplication.[1] Jeremy used the idea of towers in his new small group, sharing for example that he solved a problem with tens by thinking of towers. By the end of the year, after 15 total sessions, Jeremy was using a combination of skip counting and derived fact strategies, building on to facts he knew. He still used his fingers or blocks for skip counting if the factor was challenging, like skip counting by fours. Franco progressed even further, showing understanding of multidigit multiplication. By the spring, Franco began to consistently use a known fact and build on it, for example, solving 6×6 by knowing 5×6, and then adding one more group of 6.

---

[1] These data were analyzed with the assistance of my colleague Tomy Nguyen.

They also developed more sophisticated understandings of the array model over time, as we started with a block array and moved to a closed array. By the spring, both students were using open arrays (Table 10.1).

Table 10.1 · *Transitions of the array*

Block array	Closed array	Open array
Students can start with arrays by building them with blocks or by looking at photos of arrays in real life. This image is of Jeremy's blocks.	In a closed array, every box is shown, allowing students to count if necessary.	Interior lines are no longer necessary, useful for bigger numbers.

MATH FACT FLUENCY DEVELOPS THROUGH MULTIPLICATIVE THINKING

We chose multiplication for this post–COVID-19 pandemic intervention group because multiplication is a core idea in mathematics. Underlying multiplication and division is *multiplicative thinking*, the rather powerful concept of thinking in and with groups. Understanding of multiplication is much more than memorizing the multiplication facts. As these students had entered fourth and fifth grades without being able to solve bare multiplication problems, they really needed supportive extra instruction to develop their understanding and fluency with multiplication and division.

It is odd that we often discuss multiplication fact fluency as if it is fundamentally different than students learning multiplication. Really, it is just the end of a process, one goal (Figure 10.3). The underlying idea in multiplication is the idea of *unitizing*, to work with groups like we work with ones. Unitizing helps us understand that ten ones make one ten, that 6 groups of 5 is 30, and that $3x$ means 3 groups of x. Our base-ten number system is based on groups of ten getting ten times bigger as we move along the places, a multiplicative system.

Figure 10.3 • *Landscape for multiplication and division*

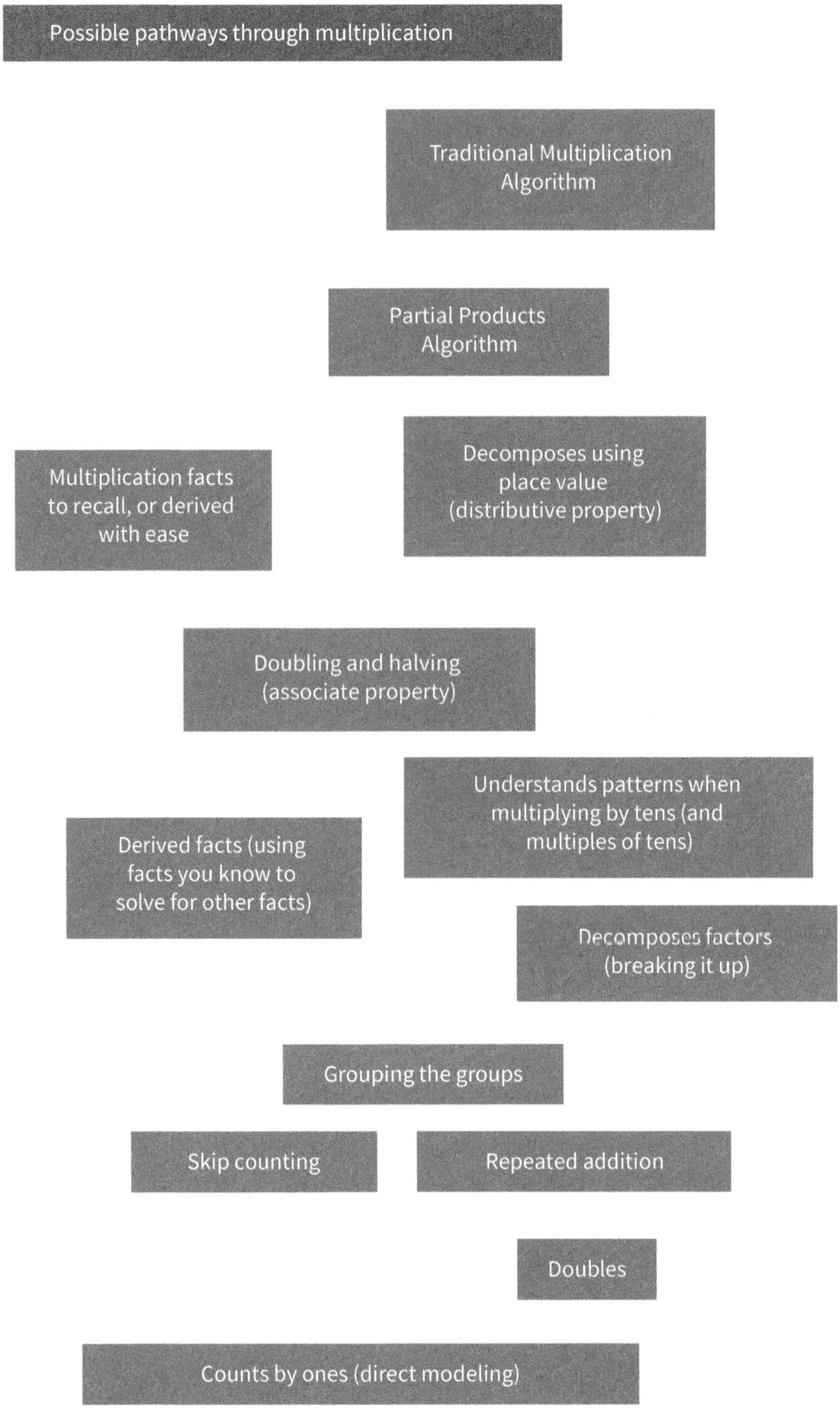

Possible pathways through multiplication

Traditional Multiplication
Algorithm

Partial Products
Algorithm

Multiplication facts
to recall, or derived
with ease

Decomposes using
place value
(distributive property)

Doubling and halving
(associate property)

Understands patterns when
multiplying by tens (and
multiples of tens)

Derived facts (using
facts you know to
solve for other facts)

Decomposes factors
(breaking it up)

Grouping the groups

Skip counting

Repeated addition

Doubles

Counts by ones (direct modeling)

To understand unitizing, students need to develop multiplicative thinking. Additive thinking is putting things together (and apart), whereas multiplicative thinking is putting groups of things together (and apart). One tricky thing is that there is always a ratio, two quantities that you have to understand in relationship.

Students learn multiplication first through direct modeling situations that call for multiplication and division (see "Unpacking a Core Idea: Early Multiplication and Division With Story Problems" on p. 174). Using direct modeling (representing/counting each item), very young students can solve these kinds of problems. The next step is to solve problems with more efficient strategies, like skip counting by one group. Certain factors are much easier for most students to skip count by and thus easier to work with (2s, 5s, and 10s). You can see that I made sure that our early work was in groups of 2, 5, or 10, what Bay-Williams and Kling (2019) called the "foundational facts" (for more, see "Unpacking a Core Idea: Fact Fluency With Multiplication" on p. 176). It helps students to have foundational facts efficiently in their minds to be able to use derived facts. A student needs to know the 10s to be able to think about the 9s using a subtracting one group from 10 strategy. However, in working with neurodiverse students, I never assume that one thing will *always* come first.

Students then begin to develop additional strategies, also called "derived facts." When Jeremy solved 4×3 by doubling 2×3, he was using a doubling strategy. When Franco solved 6×6 by using a fact he knew (6×5) and adding another group of 6, he was using a strategy I have heard students call "breaking it up." A frequent mistake is to rush students through this phase.

When I was planning my lessons for Franco and Jeremy, I was not designing for fluency alone. I was laying the groundwork for fluency by developing their conceptual (understanding the underlying core ideas) *and* procedural (understanding how to solve problems) knowledge simultaneously. Sometimes I hear educators separate conceptual and procedural knowledge in mathematics as if the two were completely separate. They seem separate when we define procedural knowledge as only knowledge of a small set of standardized procedures, like the multiplication algorithm. But procedural knowledge in the research literature is simply knowing how to solve a problem efficiently, not doing it in one particular way.

In these multiplication lessons, Franco and Jeremy were exploring concepts and strategies simultaneously. This idea is supported in research that has found the two kinds of knowledge develop at the same time (Rittle-Johnson, Schneider, & Star, 2015). When students were given carefully sequenced practice problems in arithmetic (similar to my sequences with the towers, or in number strings), students developed both conceptual and procedural (strategic) knowledge compared with when using a control condition (Canobi, 2009). Particularly when we are teaching mathematical operations, when students develop strategies, they are also strengthening their conceptual understanding. Jeremy learned how to skip count using the towers (strategy) as he learned to think multiplicatively with groups (concept). It is actually weird to think of teaching them separately! In this intervention, I was using *guided strategic development* to support students to develop new strategies in multiplication, as well as games to provide practice.

Critical to this kind of intervention is to notice and name student strategies. When Jeremy doubled to solve the problem, I named the strategy and wrote it on the board. When Franco used a known fact to figure out another fact, I called attention to that strategy, and we decided on a name for it. Figure 10.4 shows a chart paper of when I led a group discussion in the afterschool program about strategies we used for multiplication. This chart stayed up during our sessions as a way to encourage everyone to name and notice strategies.

Figure 10.4 · *Rachel's chart of student strategics*

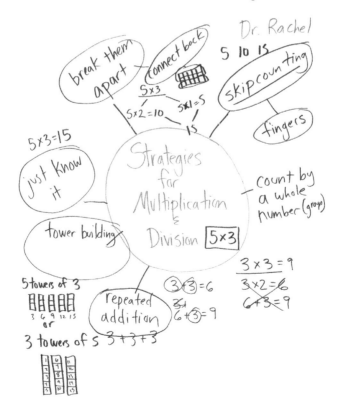

One little detail on this chart illuminates an important aspect of representing student thinking. To make the chart, I asked students how they would solve 5×3. Students gave me different strategies, and I represented them on the chart, much like a single-problem number talk. One student used 3×3 instead to explain a breaking-it-up strategy, telling me that they used two threes and then added one more three. I first represented it as 2×3 and then 6 + 3. The student was bothered by the way I represented it (I could tell by their quizzical expression). I asked the student how to write it, and they told me to write 3 + 3 = 6 and then 6 + 3 = 9. The student was thinking using repeated addition, and I changed their strategy into multiplication before they were ready. This is why I often ask, "Does this look right?" or "Did I represent your thinking?" I want the students to see their thinking represented on the paper in a way that they understand, so that they come to understand symbolic representations of their thinking.

> **I want the students to see their thinking represented on the paper in a way that they understand, so that they come to understand symbolic representations of their thinking.**

NEURODIVERSITY AND MULTIPLICATION FACT FLUENCY

When we are working with neurodiverse students on their multiplication fact fluency, we need to keep several things in mind. First, we need to make sure that math fact fluency does not interrupt grade-level instruction in mathematics. I have seen students pulled out of middle school math because they did not have their multiplication facts memorized. Multiplication is incredibly important, but any intervention must be simultaneous and not replace a student's engagement in the math of their grade level.

Second, the idea of memorization as the singular goal can discriminate against neurodiverse students, who may have particular difficulty memorizing (rather than reconstructing) math facts. We use different parts of our brain when we derive math problems using reasoning strategies and when we recall from memorization. Those verbal areas of the brain can be impaired in individuals with dyslexia, making it part of the disability to have difficulty with fact recall. It is critical to remember that there are multiple developmental pathways for dyslexia, and so not all students with dyslexia will have these phonological deficits (De Clercq-Quaegebeur et al., 2018). Use of reasoning strategies in multiplication facts rather than just recall was associated with higher math achievement and higher scores on computation for dyslexic students (Erenberg, 1995). I recommend making sure that students understand the reasoning strategies necessary for derived facts and moving toward fluency with games and other low-stakes practice. In this afterschool program, I also introduced flashcards that the students made. For some students, the flashcards made a difference in their recall. For others, the strategy was less effective.

> I recommend making sure that students understand the reasoning strategies necessary for derived facts and moving toward fluency with games and other low-stakes practice.

And third, memorization of math facts carries emotional weight for students who have experienced failure in this area. In the same classroom as Luis, I met a boy named Elijah. Elijah also had a learning disability, but he had a lot more difficulty with language processing, taking time to understand what was said to him, and needing to plan his responses (Lambert, 2017). Like so many seventh-grade teachers, Ms. Marquez got frustrated that so many of her students were counting on their fingers and decided to use some class time for students to quiz each other on multiplication facts. I was walking by Elijah and his partner Bobby when I saw Elijah clearly upset. Elijah was using scratch paper, keeping track of a derived fact strategy. Bobby had told Elijah that it didn't count if he didn't recall the fact quickly without using scratch paper. Elijah defended himself, telling Bobby, "I know them all, just pressure." His hand went up and down his body, suggesting that he was feeling pressure throughout his body. When I asked him months later about this moment, Elijah told me that he knew his multiplication facts, but when rushed or stressed, he could not recall them. I love how Elijah defended himself against unjust mathematical pressure! And how he knew himself in this way, showing strong self-understanding. This came from *strategic coaching* with his sixth-grade special education teacher, Ms. Scott, about his disability.

I do not recommend timed tests for students on recall of facts because I have heard many, many adults and children tell me about the fear and anxiety that come with timed activities. Considering how negative most people's relationship with math is, I don't see why we would use timed tests when there are many other ways to help students develop fluency (not memorization, but efficiently producing answers). I do use timed activities in some of my research since I need to accurately measure growth, but I use 1:1 interviews that I audio record so I can see what strategies they used and how long it took. If I do a written test, I have used a two-pen assessment: Students work within a particular time frame for a certain amount of time, and then they switch to another pen color. They then have unlimited time using that pen. This way you can collect data about what they did under two different time conditions.

> I do not recommend timed tests for students on recall of facts because I have heard many, many adults and children tell me about the fear and anxiety that come with timed activities.

MEANINGFUL PRACTICE THROUGH GAMES

Students will also need substantial practice to be able to recall facts. Franco and Jeremy needed support with fluency for their addition and subtraction facts, as well. I decided to add some game play that would support their strategy development and fluency in addition and subtraction. I chose Shut the Box (Figure 10.5), which was originally a pub game in England. In this game, students throw two dice and add up the pips (dots on the dice). They roll in the game box, with nine levers that are originally placed up, each with a different digit 1–9 written on it.

Players take the number they roll and can put down the lever for that number. So if they roll a 3 and a 5, they can put down the lever for 8. But they could also choose to put down the lever for 1 and 7; or 2 and 6; or 1, 2, and 5 (which means they are not only doing sums but also practicing decomposition of numbers; see Figure 10.5). In our version of the game, players took turns rolling until one person shut their box!

Figure 10.5 • *Students playing Shut the Box*

As I gathered the boys together to start one of our lessons, I told them we would begin with a game and showed the box. Franco and Jeremy smiled enthusiastically, excited to be playing a real game. Kids love when games have "real" pieces and boards! Franco rolled a 6 and a 3. I could see him counting, moving his lips looking at the pips on the dice, counting first the 6 and the 3, and then all together. I asked him what was his strategy, and he told me "fingers." Jeremy rolled a 5 and a 4. His strategy was different. He started with the bigger number (5), counting on using his fingers to keep track, "6, 7, 8, 9." I asked Jeremy what his strategy was, and he called it "add on." They went back and forth playing for a few rounds. Both continued to consistently use the same strategy, until round 5.

On his last play, Franco rolled a 5 and a 2, and he started with 5, and used his fingers to keep track as he added on, "6, 7." Franco smiled widely and told me, "I tried his strategy!" Not only had Franco tried Jeremy's strategy, but he had also strategically chosen the larger number to add on to! I was so delighted. It also demonstrates how the most important move when students are playing games is to get them to notice and name their strategies, and then how this facilitates other students to take up new strategies. For more on how addition fact fluency develops, see "Unpacking a Core Idea: Fluency With Addition and Subtraction Below 20" (p. 155). Our research team is currently investigating a push-in intervention program where we play nondigital math games with students to address unfinished learning. We have started, using our observations and interviews with teachers and students, to begin naming features of great math games, which include the following:

- ▸ Engages students in core ideas in mathematics (including mathematical talk)
- ▸ Includes mathematical models and/or visuals (the dots on the dice)
- ▸ Includes a strategic element (not just a worksheet disguised as a game!)
- ▸ Allows for students at different skill levels to play together

One of the most popular games in our work is Multi (Joyful Mathematics, https://bit.ly/3rux7mt). This game is tic tac toe on both nine small boards (each of which has a factor of the digits 1–9) and one big tic-tac-toe board. Students chose factors to make multiplication problems, allowing them to work strategically to win boards or block opponents. The board includes arrays, which some students use to support their thinking. We have noticed that students love playing in pairs against another pair; we have found that students engage in a lot of mathematical and strategic talk to plan moves together (for more on games, see the online Teaching Practice Guide).

Online Teaching Practice Guide

qrs.ly/l7f7rwq

REFLECTION QUESTIONS

1. Have you seen math fact fluency be a barrier for students? How?

2. What did you notice and wonder about my work in this chapter? What more would you want to know about my teaching, or our intervention programs?

3. How have you used games in your classroom? How might they support students' math fact fluency?

UDL Math Connections

Engagement	Representation	Strategic action
I worked to create a small-group environment in which Franco and Jeremy felt safe. Intervention is designed around engagement in mathematical problem solving, including games.	Multimodality is at the heart of this intervention, where I am working to help them connect the concrete manipulatives to the symbolism of an equation and to the visual of an array. There is a purposeful sequence to instruction.	I notice and name students' strategies to help them learn new strategies. I support them using multiple modalities to express what they know.

Unpacking a Core Idea: Early Multiplication and Division With Story Problems

Just as in addition and subtraction, we build on a student's natural intuition about number by using simple story problems with specific mathematical structures (Carpenter et al., 2015). Three basic schemas exist (Table 10.2).

Students see these two kinds of division as quite different initially as they directly model the action in the station. Over time, they see both as division, and use other more number-based strategies like skip counting, repeated subtraction, or repeated addition.

Table 10.2 · *Multiplication and division problem types*

Problem type	How students interpret the action with direct modeling
Multiplication *Rachel has three packs of pens. Each pack has 6 pens. How many pens does she have all together?*	A multiplication problem is when we know the size of the group and the number of groups. Students who are direct modeling might count out cubes in groups, or draw it out.
Division through equal sharing (also known as "partitive division") *Rachel has cookies to share with her class. She has 24 cookies, and 8 students. How many cookies will each student get if she shares them equally?*	This is a problem in which we know the number of groups but not how many in each group. Students who are direct modeling might deal out blocks to eight piles or make a drawing. The action is dealing out, like you deal out cards because you know how many groups, but not how much in a group.

Problem type	How students interpret the action with direct modeling
Division through measurement (also known as "quotative division") *Rachel has 36 apples. She puts 3 in a bag. How many bags does she need?*	This is a problem in which we know the size of each group but not how many groups. Using direct modeling, students tend to measure out 3 blocks, then 3 more, then 3 more, and so on, until they get to 36. Then they count how many sets of 3 they measured out.

Learn More:

Carpenter, T. P., Fennema, E., Franke, M. L., Levi, L., & Empson, S. B. (2015). *Children's mathematics: Cognitively guided instruction* (2nd ed.). Heinemann.

The students in the group were mostly using skip counting. Yola wanted to use an array to help students see taking away one group, how $3 \times 9 = (3 \times 10) - (3 \times 1)$, one way the distributive property can be useful in multiplication. She was trying to help the students move from skip counting to partial products/derived facts using 10s (see "Unpacking a Core Idea: Strategies for Multidigit Multiplication and Division" on p. 190).

Yola posed each problem one at a time, writing it on the left side of the board. After writing each problem, she asked students to show with a raised thumb when they were ready to share a strategy. She represented student strategies both with equations and using a pink card stock array she made for each problem. Figure 11.1 shows Yola's chart paper after the number string, and Figure 11.2 shows her number string annotated.

> ### Think About It
>
> Take a moment and see if you can find evidence of student strategies. What were students thinking about as they solved these problems?

Figure 11.1 · *Yola's number string*

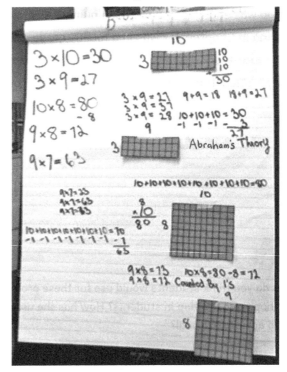

During this number string, students were excitedly discussing Abraham's strategy. Abraham, solving 3×9, first did repeated addition with 10s and then "minus 1, minus 1, minus 1 from 30." Yola had him explain his thinking, writing this on the board. Then she asked him some follow-up questions, which prompted him to make his strategy a little more efficient, "It is just minus 3 because 3 times." Yola also modeled the strategy on the array so that students could see where the "minus 1, minus 1, minus 1" was, as well as the "minus 3." Abraham uses this strategy again for 9×7. You can see how Abraham is beginning to understand the distributive property through his own unique pathway.

As I observed this number string, I noticed a student we will call Inez because, unlike the rest of the students in her fourth-grade math group, she wasn't using her fingers to keep track of her skip count. I was pretty sure Inez was skip counting because I saw her mouth move, but she held her hands under the table, almost as if to make sure she didn't use them. When students were having a pair share about a problem, I quietly knelt by Inez and asked her if maybe her fingers would help, mentioning how helpful I thought fingers could be. She treated me to a dismissive look and told me she didn't "need to use her fingers." I also noticed that Inez also did not share any answers with the group or with her partner during turn and talks.

Figure 11.2 · *Yola's number string annotated*

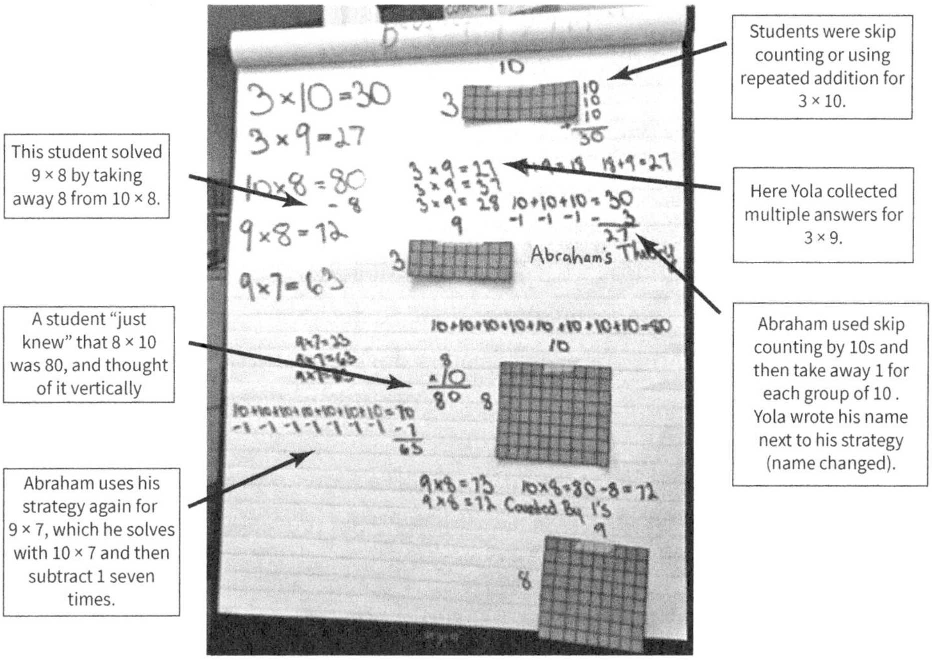

Students were skip counting or using repeated addition for 3×10.

This student solved 9×8 by taking away 8 from 10×8.

Here Yola collected multiple answers for 3×9.

A student "just knew" that 8×10 was 80, and thought of it vertically

Abraham used skip counting by 10s and then take away 1 for each group of 10. Yola wrote his name next to his strategy (name changed).

Abraham uses his strategy again for 9×7, which he solves with 10×7 and then subtract 1 seven times.

I have worked with many students who preserved their mathematical dignity by eschewing certain tools, fingers being the most common (despite how helpful fingers are mathematically; Moeller et al., 2012). In my experience, that usually means that the child has been shamed for using the tool, whether it is fingers or a hundreds chart. I know that when I am dealing with a child who has previously been shamed in math class, that child needs special attention and urging to take risks in mathematics.

Inez is Latina and multilingual and in fourth grade at the time of the study.[1] She was a friendly, kind, interested participant in the social world of the classroom. Inez did not have an Individualized Education Program (IEP) but was undergoing a second referral to special education. We focus on Inez as an example of a student who may or may not have a disability but does need more support in math.

Yola told me after the session that she too was concerned about Inez—more than anyone else in the small intervention group. Yola noticed Inez was always attentive, always had her eyes on the board, yet she did not answer any of the problems or engage in pair discussions about the problems. Yola decided that she needed to shift the learning conditions so that Inez could participate in the number string, which would then hopefully lead to new mathematical understandings about multiplication. But engagement needed to come first. This became Yola's focus in the next number string—how could she help Inez take risks and share in this small group?

Here's a little background about our intervention program (Lambert, Nguyen, et al., 2022). This project was designed to (a) provide opportunities for students to exercise mathematical agency through sharing ideas in mathematics and (b) increase student strategies in multidigit multiplication. We used an assessment and teacher recommendations to decide which students to invite. Undergraduates taught the small groups during math time in a local school using number strings (Fosnot & Uittenbogaard, 2007).

We checked in with the classroom teacher to learn a little more about Inez. Inez's fourth-grade teacher told me that Inez did not participate very often in

---

[1] These data were analyzed with the assistance of my colleagues Tomy Nguyen, Monica Mendoza, and Avery McNiff (Lambert, Nguyen, et al., 2022).

math class, and when she did, she often had strategies in math that she (the teacher) struggled to understand. We noticed on Inez's written assessment that she had little written work, besides a "buggy algorithm" for multidigit multiplication. She solved 10×7 as 17, multiplying the 7 times the 1 (Figure 11.3).

Figure 11.3 · *Inez's written assessment preintervention*

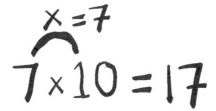

A buggy algorithm is when a student learns only part of a standard algorithm like multiplication. This can happen when students are taught to follow rules that they don't understand, such as here when Inez seems to understand something about multiplying numbers but has not connected it to the place value of the answer.

Yola started by focusing on shifting Inez's engagement. She decided to move Inez right next to her at the front of the table to see whether they could have conversations that could spark her engagement. Yola also decided that Inez might benefit from her own personal copy of the card stock arrays. So Yola moved Inez right to the front of the small group and began each problem by handing Inez her own copy of each array. With this support, Inez did start sharing her thinking. Yola and Inez chatted quietly during turn and talks. Inez seemed particularly pleased with having her own array, which she used for every problem.

Now that Inez was sharing her strategies, Yola became concerned that she did not know how to respond to some of Inez's strategies. In a number string soon after these changes, Yola posed the question 9 × 4. Inez gave an answer of 50 and said that her strategy was to skip count by 5s. Yola represented her skip counting next to an array of 9 × 4, making connections between the two models. Inez stared at the array and the skip counting represented next to it and said, "What the heck?"

Yola was not sure what to do next. She moved on but paid close attention to how Inez was using the card stock arrays. Yola noticed that she was counting each box of the array as a 2 or a 5 and would often lose track of her answer. Yola resolved to support Inez if this happened again rather than just moving on.

In the next number string, Yola posed the problem of 6 × 5. Yola asked Inez what she got for the problem:

Inez: 62.

Yola: Do you want to tell me how you got 62?

Inez: Yeah I counted the array by 2s.

Yola: You counted the whole array by 2s. Did you give each square 2? Did you go 2, 4, 6, 8, 10? [points to one square at a time while counting by 2s]. . . . Okay you counted by 2's. That's a lot of 2s to write so I'm just going to write "counted by 2s."

Counted by 2's

Notice how Yola does not give any indication that Inez is incorrect. She makes sure that she understands the strategy and re-represents it using gestures and words without judgment. But that doesn't mean that Yola is not offering feedback—the most important feedback here is the representation. By listening and then re-representing a student's strategy, we allow them to see it with fresh eyes.

Yola: So let's look at it on the array again so we can double check our answers. So how many does each column have in it?

Inez: 5.

Yola: 5, right. And they're all equal right? [gestures across the array] So they all have five on them. So if I go like this and I make two columns [covers the array so that only 2 columns are showing], how many do we have?

Inez: 10.

Yola: 10, right. And we can keep doing that so we can use it to skip count, right? Just like we did before. 5, 10, 15, 20, 25, 30. (Other students join her in counting out loud, Yola modeling on the array each number.) Inez, does that make

> any sense? How can we use it to count like that? I know you're really good at counting by 5s.
>
> **Inez:** (Inez takes her copy of the array and silently counts on it; the class waits for her) Yeah, I went really, really far (smiling).
>
> **Yola:** (laughing with Inez) Yeah you went really, really far; that's okay
>
> (Lambert, Nguyen, et al., 2022, p. 92).

Yola noted the counting by 2s strategy but decided in the moment to build on Inez's strengths in multiplying by 5s, drawing attention to the columns of 5. This is the second time that Yola worked to provoke Inez into reconsidering her thinking using a visual model, guiding Inez toward a strategy that she can use (since she knows Inez can count by 5s). Yola waited while Inez recounted using 5s. Inez appeared to move into disequilibrium by this exchange, saying, "I went really, really far." This comment appears to link her strategy to the much higher number it resulted in.

Disequilibrium is the constructivist term for that moment in which an old strategy no longer works. Connecting visual and numerical representations of her own strategy appeared to make Inez's own thinking visible to her, thus allowing her to understand her own thinking. I love also how playful this moment is between Inez and Yola as both end the exchange smiling. Inez has shifted from being the child who refused to count on her fingers to recounting on an array in front of the whole group while they watch, and then to realize herself (with the help of the representation) that she "went really, really far," a comment that links her new understanding to concepts of magnitude on an array.

In the next number string, Inez twice counts an array by ones, successfully for 6 × 6 and one number off for 9 × 6. Through discussion of her strategies in the small group, including the tutor making her strategies visible through modeling them on arrays, Inez began to develop her understanding of the spatial structure for the array. By the follow-up assessment, Inez was able to draw arrays and count them to successfully solve a variety of problems, something she was not able to do in previous assessments.

Our analysis of assessments demonstrated conceptual and procedural growth for Inez during the sessions as she moved from inaccurate algorithms that did not work and inaccurate skip counting to accurate use of array representations and repeated addition. Inez developed considerably as a strategic sense-maker but only after Yola shifted the intervention to help Inez engage and created opportunities for Inez to reflect on her own thinking. ●

INTERVENTION IN PARTICIPATION

A member of our research team, Tomy Nguyen, did a close video analysis of Inez's participation. Before these shifts, Inez did not participate verbally in 82% of problems. After the changes, Inez verbally participated in 87% of problems.

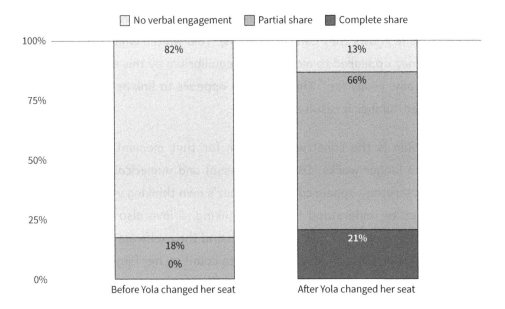

Before Yola made these changes, Inez rarely shared a partial strategy (an incomplete or inaccurate share) 18% of the time and never a complete strategy (defined as both accurate and detailed). But after these small design shifts, Inez shared a partial strategy 66% of the time and a complete strategy 21% of the time. We can see that 1) changing her seat, 2) talking to her during turn and talks, and 3) providing an array transformed Inez's engagement in the number string.

Students who are having difficulty in mathematics may need an intervention in engagement, rather than or in combination with intervention in content. Engagement in mathematical discussion matters in mathematical learning The detail in children's strategy shares predicts mathematics achievement

(Webb et al., 2014). Explaining one's own ideas clearly and engagement with the mathematical ideas of other students is correlated with student learning outcomes (Ing et al., 2015). I love how Yola started with engagement first, making sure that Inez was comfortable sharing her strategies.

> **Think About It**
>
> Have you ever done an intervention in engagement with a student whom you wanted to more deeply engage in mathematics? What strategies did you use?

WHAT IS A NUMBER STRING?

Number strings are my absolute favorite math routines. I have been teaching them since 1999 when I learned about them from Willem Uittenbogaard, a Dutch math educator who was working with New York City teachers like me for the summer at Math in the City, a professional development center founded by Cathy Fosnot. I have seen number strings called "mini lessons," "number talks," and "problem strings," but I stick to what they were called when they first were brought to the United States by Dutch math educators like Willem. I am so obsessed that I co-founded a website called numberstrings.com with Dr. Kara Imm; please check it out! You can also find out more about number strings from the Online Teaching Practice Guide.

Online Teaching Practice Guide

qrs.ly/l7f7rwq

As we saw with Dina in Chapter 9, the basic structure of a number string is a series of problems designed to help students explore particular concepts and/or develop useful strategies in computation. I get the students together on the rug or in the meeting area and give the first problem, reminding the students to use their thumbs to show me they have an answer. Problems are given one at a time to the students. I give lots of wait time, using the thumbs to give me a sense of how many of the students are ready. If they seem stuck, I ask them to turn and talk to a neighbor. After I call on a student to explain their strategy, I represent it on the whiteboard (or chart paper). I write equations to represent students' strategies, writing their names next to their thinking on the board. I also represent student thinking using a mathematical model, one I particularly want to use during that number string. You can watch me teach a number string to an inclusive class of fourth graders here: https://bit.ly/3ZzkLpN.

NUMBER STRINGS AS INTERVENTION ROUTINES

This careful attention to the development of strategies is particularly important for students with challenges in math. Students who are having difficulty in math often use the same kinds of strategies as other students, but these students don't shift to new strategies as easily (e.g., Geary, 2004). So for multiplication, we might see students who begin by using repeated addition continue to use that strategy, while their peers may have moved to thinking about partial groups.

> **Students who are having difficulty in math often use the same kinds of strategies as other students, but these students don't shift to new strategies as easily (e.g., Geary, 2004).**

This is a great opportunity to use number strings, an example of *guided strategic development*, which will more explicitly support students to develop new strategies. During a number string, we don't force a student to use a particular strategy, but the structure of the string makes certain strategies naturally emerge as objects for discussion. In a number string, student strategies are noticed and named. The teacher carefully represents the strategies of students. Students explain their strategies.

One of the many reasons that I love number strings is that students create the strategies. I think that we do need to expose students to strategies that they might not have thought of themselves, but why does it have to be a teacher's ideas? I find it much more effective when students come up with the strategies. It adds extra power when we name the strategies, such as when Yola called it "Abraham's Theory."

SUPPORTING STRATEGIC DEVELOPMENT WITH NUMBER STRINGS: PERCENTAGES

Strategic development was a core feature of my classroom work. I learned over time that while students would come up with very cool strategies during discussions, I had multiple students who would not remember those strategies from day to day. I think this is a major weakness in how teachers interpret inquiry learning—we tend to assume that once a student uses a strategy, they own it. Not true. And particularly for kids with memory challenges, they need support to remember even the most beautiful strategies they have invented themselves.

For one of my fifth-grade students, Emmanuel, math made sense when it was meaningful. Big ideas came easily to him, but remembering steps or disconnected facts seemed almost impossible. Emmanuel could use a cool strategy during a number string, and then forget it the next day.

So, for Emmanuel and multiple other students, I worked to notice and name their strategies to make them more memorable. When a student came up with a strategy, we would make that strategy an object of discussion. I taught Emmanuel many moons ago, but I still remember his delight during this number string, in which I used a double number line representation (see Table 11.1).

Table 11.1 · *Rachel's number string for calculating percentages*

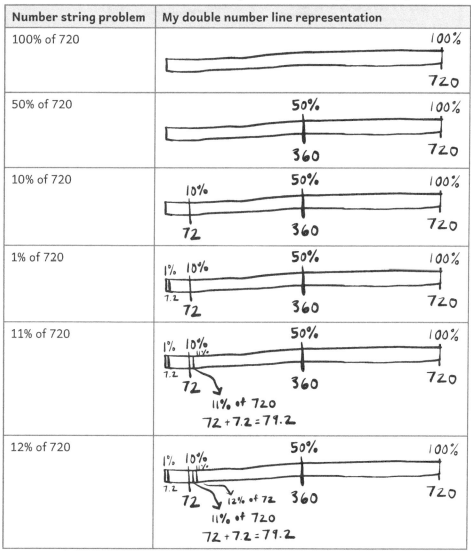

Number string problem	My double number line representation
100% of 720	
50% of 720	
10% of 720	
1% of 720	
11% of 720	
12% of 720	

The action really started on the sixth problem, when I asked the students to find 11% of 720. Emmanuel's hand shot up when he realized he could combine 10% of a number and 1% of a number together to make 11% of a number. Students asked questions about this strategy, definitely interested.

In my final problem, 12% of 720, other students tried Emmanuel's strategy, giving him credit for the idea. Before we ended the string, we wrote together a description of the strategy and made a sign:

> ## Emmanuel's Strategy
> Build a percentage by finding chunks you know (like 50% or 10% or 1%) and then combine.

In addition to these signs, which I kept up for our daily number strings, I also had students keep individual strategy charts in the first page of their math notebooks. I would use these in conferences with students, reminding them of the strategies they knew how to use and of those they were working on. Individual strategy charts can be a way to communicate with multiple teachers (paraprofessionals and co-teachers) about what strategies the student is using.

REFLECTION QUESTIONS

1. What do you notice and wonder about Yola and Inez's story?

2. Yola starts by working to increase Inez's engagement in the small-group intervention. What strategies did she use? What strategies do you use when you see that a student is not engaged enough in mathematics?

3. While Yola was teaching a small group, my story about Emmanuel comes from my own classroom in a whole class number string. How might number strings change in these different contexts?

UDL Math Connections

Engagement	Representation	Strategic action
Before Yola works to shift Inez's math, she works to shift her engagement. This reminds us that engagement comes first.	Yola is working here to help students connect multiplication strategies to the array. Using the array representations was critical to help Inez realize what she was doing.	Yola is not telling Inez what to do, she is coaching her to develop her own strategies, and using feedback to help her realize not only that she made a mistake, but why it did not work.

Unpacking a Core Idea: Strategies for Multidigit Multiplication and Division

Students develop strategies for multidigit multiplication and division through solving many problems about multiplication and division (Carpenter et al., 2015). I recommend giving students lots of opportunities to develop and discuss these strategies. We should ensure that every child has strategies that work for them, but children should not be forced to use strategies that do not make sense to them. Table 11.2 illustrates some of the most common strategies. One important underlying idea for many of these strategies is the place value patterns that happen when multiplying by tens. Students often learn that 7×10 is 70 because you "just add a zero." But that is not *why* 7×10 is 70. It is because seven groups of 10 is 70 because $(7 \times 1) \times 10 = 70$. The "trick" works because that is how our number system works—when a number gets ten times bigger, it moves to the next digit place. Number strings are great ways to help students explore these patterns, particularly if we ask students to explain why (see Tables 11.2 and 11.3).

Table 11.2 · *Student strategies for multidigit multiplication*

Strategy description	Example (5×12 and 14×25)
"Breaking it up" (partial products) Students often start to use the distributive property to break numbers apart into chunks that they multiply and then add back together. This strategy can be modeled with an open array (an array without every interior box drawn in). For a two-digit by a two-digit number (or bigger), students have more chunks they need to consider. For 25×14, students need to think about 20×10, 20×4, 10×5, and 5×4. Arrays can model these chunks and can set students up to understand how the standard algorithm works.	

Strategy description	Example (5×12 and 14×25)
Doubling and halving (or other uses of the associative property) Some students play with making an equivalent problem through redistributing factors. So for 12×5, a student might change the problem to 6×10 by halving the 12 and doubling the 5.	$\div 2 \left(\begin{array}{c} 12 \times 5 \\ 6 \times 10 = 60 \end{array} \right) \times 2$
Partial products transitional algorithm Once students have developed a partial products strategy, you can introduce them to this transitional algorithm. Students think of all the different chunks that need to be multiplied together, starting with the biggest ones. This can be used as a bridge to the standard algorithm (or replace it).	$\begin{array}{r} 12 \\ \times\ 5 \\ \hline 50 \\ +10 \\ \hline 60 \end{array}$ (10×5) (2×5) $\begin{array}{r} 25 \\ \times 14 \\ \hline 200 \\ 80 \\ 50 \\ + 20 \\ \hline 350 \end{array}$ (20×10) (20×4) (10×5) (5×4)

Table 11.3 · *Student strategies for multidigit division*

Strategy description	Example ($60 \div 12$)
Repeated subtraction Students working with division with big numbers tend to start by using repeated subtraction or by using repeated addition or skip counting until they reach the answer. So if they are trying to solve 60 divided by 12, they might add 12 until they get there. The example to the right shows how a student could repeatedly subtract 12 from 60 to find how many fit inside.	$\begin{array}{l} 60 - 12 = 48 \\ 48 - 12 = 36 \\ 36 - 12 = 24 \\ 24 - 12 = 12 \\ 12 - 12 = 0 \end{array}$ $\Big\}$ 5 groups of 12

(Continued)

Table 11.3 · (continued)

Strategy description	Example (60 ÷ 12)
Multiply to divide The most common strategy for division is to multiply until you reach the dividend using partial products. So a student might then begin to multiply 12 by different numbers until they reach 60.	$12 \times 2 = 24$ $12 \times 4 = 48$ $12 \times 5 = 60$ so $60 \div 12 = 5$
Partial quotients Students can divide by taking out chunks of the divisor.	$60 \div 12$ / | \\ ← how many chunks of 12 can I find in 60? 24 24 12 2 2 1
Ratio strategies Some division problems can be more easily solved by thinking of the problem as a fraction (fractions are just division after all!). So a student might think of 60 divided by 12 as 60/12. They can then simplify that fraction to 30/6 and then find the answer of 5.	$\dfrac{60}{12} = \dfrac{30}{6} = \dfrac{15}{3} = 5$
Partial quotients transitional algorithm Once students understand a partial quotient strategy, you can introduce them to this transitional algorithm. Students ask themselves the question: "What chunks of 12 can I pull out of this number, keeping track of what is left, and how many groups have they found?" This can be used as a bridge to the standard algorithm (or replace it).	$12 \overline{)60}$ 24 $12 \times 2 = 24$ 36 -36 $12 \times 3 = 36$ 0 $2 + 3 = 5$

Transitional Algorithms

Many readers are probably wondering where the standard algorithms for addition, subtraction, multiplication, and division fit in. Standard algorithms were developed hundreds of years ago in most cases and have been quite useful in doing lengthy computations, particularly before calculators were invented. Their usefulness is debated now as we can use calculators to do onerous calculations. Algorithms can be useful, but they can also be confusing, hard to remember, and disconnected from meaning-making in mathematics. For that reason, I worry more about whether my students can add, subtract, multiply, and divide than if they can use algorithms to do so. Algorithms are very useful, but they are not for every student.

One way to differentiate different procedures for multidigit operations is *number-based* methods and *digit-based* methods (Hickendorff et al., 2019). Number-based methods keep the value of the numbers whole. Students naturally invent strategies like partial products, in which they break up numbers based on their place value. Digit-based methods separate numbers into digits, so that students are thinking about a "5" that is really a 50, but they are thinking about it as a 5. This can be very confusing. When students are using number-based strategies, they tend to work with the biggest numbers first, just as we tend to count the biggest bills first when counting money. In contrast, digit-based strategies make students start with the smallest place values first, which can be confusing. Carrying (or "borrowing") is often confusing for students, not just conceptually, but visually keeping track.

Recommendations for teaching algorithms now delay introduction until students (a) understand the core idea of the operation and (b) have some number-based strategies that they can use. For multiplication and division, students need to understand place value and be able to use it in a partial products strategy to be able to understand how the digit-based multiplication algorithm works. For 34 × 27, students would need to be able to break the numbers up into place values and recombine so that they multiply all the partial products together. An array is useful to help them see all the chunks they need to combine. Some students like to draw the array to keep track of the parts as they work.

Once students understand this place-value based strategies, there is an intermediate step before teaching the multiplication standard algorithm: the partial products algorithm. In this algorithm, students think of the actual numbers rather than just the digits. One can guide students to stack the answers vertically. To solve 34 times 27, students would ask themselves a series of questions to find the product:

- ▸ What is 30 times 20?
- ▸ What is 30 times 7?

- ▸ What is 20 times 4?

- ▸ What is 4 times 7?

And then combine to find the answer.

When teaching a standard algorithm, it makes sense to use *explicit instruction*. Students don't need to invent these very specialized procedures; we can teach them. Carefully designed step-by-step instruction with teacher modeling and student practice is effective for teaching procedures like algorithms. I particularly recommend using a concrete, representational, then abstract (CRA) sequence in this kind of explicit instruction. Research by Flores and colleagues shows how to use explicit instruction to teach the partial products algorithm to students who are ready for it, using manipulatives to make sure students make connections to place value (Flores & Milton, 2020).

Learn More:

Carpenter, T. P., Fennema, E., Franke, M. L., Levi, L., & Empson, S. B. (2015). *Children's mathematics: Cognitively guided instruction* (2nd ed.). Heinemann.

Flores, M. M., & Milton, J. H. (2020). Teaching the partial products algorithm using the concrete-representational-abstract sequence. *Exceptionality, 28*(2), 142–160. https://doi.org/10.1080/09362835.2020.1772070

CHAPTER 12

SUPPORTING RELATIONSHIPS AND COMMUNITY IN MATH CLASS

IN THIS CHAPTER, WE WILL . . .

- Visit an inclusive fifth-grade classroom as students solve story problems with fractions
- Develop relational thinking with fractional story problems
- Learn how students describe what matters in a mathematical community
- Follow along as a teacher develops relationships with neurodiverse students

WHEN I FIRST visited Ms. Rey's fifth-grade classroom, I walked in, breathed in, and felt immediate relief. The vibe was calm, thoughtful, and kind. Kids were listening to the teacher, and to each other, with particular care. The focus of the class was clearly students' mathematical thinking.

Ms. Rey had a class of 28 students, 5 of whom had Individualized Education Programs (IEPs). Her school was not particularly inclusive for students with disabilities as most students with disabilities were in separate, self-contained classrooms, but she fought to get kids with disabilities into her room. This year, Ms. Rey had two students with autism (Oscar and Ash) full-time in her class, students who had not been fully included in general education before. Her school was a Title I school, with most students qualifying for free lunch. Almost all students in her class were Latino/a, with more than half classified as multilingual. This chapter is based on a collaborative research project on inclusive mathematics teaching (Lambert et al., 2020).[2]

In the fall of their fifth-grade year, Ms. Rey was working with her students on developing fractional number sense. One day she began by telling a story about a situation in her class the previous year, in which 4 students were trying to figure out how to share 13 brownies. Ms. Rey acted out the problem and asked some comprehension questions to make sure the students understood the context. Only then did she reveal the chart paper with the story problem written up and read it aloud, twice.

Try It

Take a minute and solve this problem.

> 4 children share 13 brownies equally. How much of a brownie does each child get?

How do you think fifth graders would solve it? What about students who were just beginning to learn about fractions?

Next, a few students passed out blank pieces of paper to each child, and they all began solving the problem (Figure 12.1). The classroom was generally quiet for the first 5 to 10 minutes in Ms. Rey's class as most students started individually. As they felt ready, students would discuss their strategies with the others sitting at their table. A few students would move around the room to discuss strategies with peers at other tables as well. I noticed that one student, Tony, always got up to discuss strategies with students at other tables. On this day, he finished the problem early and moved over to Daniel's table to talk about the problem. Daniel is a boy with dyslexia who was also a multilingual learner, one who told me in interviews that talking to a friend about the problems helped him get started. Also at Daniel's table were Ash and Kelani. Ms. Rey would circulate around the classroom, conferencing with

---

[2] These data were collected and analyzed with the assistance of my colleagues Shayne Brophy, Trisha Sugita, Cathery Yeh, and Jessica Hunt (Lambert et al., 2020).

students. She did not tell students how to solve problems, but she asked them questions about their strategy to make sure she understood.

Figure 12.1 · *Kelani, Oscar, Daniel, and Toby work on the brownies problem*

Think About It

Take a moment to look at the different strategies these students used (e.g., see Figures 12.2–12.4). How did each student solve the problem? If you were the teacher, what part of each strategy might you ask a student more about?

Figure 12.2 · *Ash's strategy for the brownies problem*

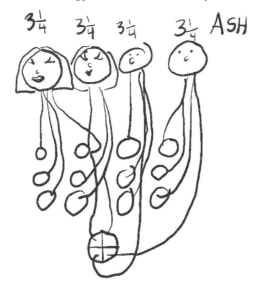

Figure 12.3 • *Daniel's strategy for the brownies problem*

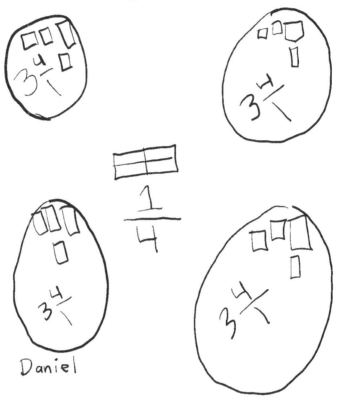

Figure 12.4 • *Kelani's strategy for the brownies problem*

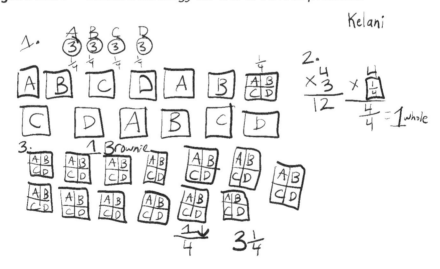

Most students solved it like Ash (Figure 12.2) using *direct modeling*—by drawing a representation of the 4 students, then drawing the 13 brownies, and finally distributing the brownies. First Ash gave out whole brownies until one brownie was left, and then she split the last one into fourths, getting an answer of 3 and $\frac{1}{4}$th.

Daniel (Figure 12.3) started by dividing 12 by 4 to find 3 for the number of whole brownies. He then split the last brownie (in the middle of his paper) into fourths and gave one out to each person. You can see that he appears to know the last part is $\frac{1}{4}$th from the image in the middle, but he flips (or transposes) the fraction when he writes it in the circles as $\frac{4}{1}$. People with dyslexia and or dyscalculia often report flipping or miswriting digits; Edmund in Chapter 3 told me that this happened frequently when he gives mathematical lectures.

Kelani's work (Figure 12.4) includes (and labels) three separate strategies (1–3). Her first strategy is similar to that of Ash and Daniel, where she first gives out whole brownies. Her second strategy is mysterious to me—I wonder what 4 and what 3 she is thinking about when she multiplies 4 times 3? Her third strategy adds something new—she splits each brownie into fourths and distributes the fourths. Although this is not on her paper, she started talking to her classmates about how the answer could be $\frac{13}{4}$ths.

After about 25 minutes, Ms. Rey led a share beginning with Daniel. He talked the class through his strategy, while Ms. Rey redrew his strategy step by step on the board. Multiple times, she stopped and asked students to turn and talk, asking them if what they did was similar or different to what Daniel had done, or to restate his strategy.

Ms. Rey pressed Daniel, as she did all her students, to explain his thinking, not just give an answer. For example, she asked students follow-up questions such as "What do you mean by one more?" and "Tell me about your thinking . . . how did you know that?" After Daniel, Kelani shared. The discussion then focused on whether 3 and $\frac{1}{4}$th was equivalent to $\frac{13}{4}$ths.

As the year progressed, Ms. Rey gave her students many opportunities to develop their knowledge of fractions by giving them increasingly more complex sharing situations (Empson & Levi, 2011). A few months later I returned to the classroom to see the students solve the problem "One can of paint paints $\frac{3}{4}$ths of a chair. If I have 12 cans of paint, how many chairs can I paint?" (you may remember this problem from Chapter 1; it's the same Sussan gave to her students, without $\frac{1}{4}$th as a number choice).

These problems both met and exceeded grade-level expectations for fractions, yet because they were in contexts the students understood, most days all students solved them successfully, and our analysis of student strategy development found that the students grew substantially in their understanding of fractions across the year, including students with disabilities (Lambert et al., 2020).

As I looked around the room, I saw students who were listening to each other, speaking carefully yet passionately about mathematical ideas. I saw disagreements being aired and being thoughtfully responded to. From my point of view as an observer, this classroom seemed to have an exceptionally strong mathematical community. As a researcher, however, I needed to also know if the students agreed. I did 12 interviews with students in that classroom to learn their perspectives. In those interviews, I asked students if and how this classroom was different than their previous classrooms in math. All the students said that it was different than previous math classrooms.

When I asked how it was different, multiple students told me that they participated much more in Ms. Rey's class, particularly in whole group. Students told me that because Ms. Rey didn't care if you made a mistake, they talked more in math class. When I asked one child why he had not participated in previous classes, he said, "Because I thought about how I would get the problem wrong or right and I thought I was kinda like in trouble or something when I was getting the problems wrong." Another said, "She makes us feel comfortable, more comfortable in class, like she helps us get our confidence, to be able to talk "cause some people like, when they mess up, they laugh at them." Students also commented that Ms. Rey lets you solve the problems "any way you want." ●

TIME AND SPACE FOR MATHEMATICAL THINKING

Let's spend some time thinking about what these students are saying. This doesn't seem that revolutionary, perhaps, that their teacher was accepting of mistakes. But it is important to know that the teachers before Ms. Rey were also good teachers. They were more traditional, certainly, in how they taught math. But this was a kind school with wonderful educators. I do not think those other teachers felt angry or upset when a student had a wrong answer. So why were the kids convinced that those previous teachers disapproved of their wrong answers? What did Ms. Rey do differently?

Based on our research team's observations and interviews, here are three critical actions Ms. Rey took (Lambert et al., 2020). She

- ▸ Gave students time and space to do mathematical thinking
- ▸ Sent messages to help them reframe mathematics away from rigid ideas of fast/slow and right/wrong
- ▸ Communicated that they were a mathematical community, working together and making sense together

First, she set up the conditions so all students could do mathematical thinking. Classroom activities were focused on sense-making, day after day. After a number sense warm-up, most days she would give the students a story problem to solve. By focusing work on actual problem solving, Ms. Rey created the conditions for students to think for themselves. She also communicated her trust in their thinking by giving them freedom to solve the problems in ways that made sense to them, rather than imposing her own thinking onto them.

Reframe Mathematics

Second, she sent strong messages about what doing mathematics is to her students. She particularly focused on two things:

- ▸ Mistakes are how we learn.
- ▸ Math may take more time

For the first message, Ms. Rey had a particular way to respond when a student "revised their thinking." One of her students, Oscar, made a mistake during a story problem on fractions, miscounting a fractional part. Ms. Rey came over and saw that he did so, and she asked if he would share "your change in thinking." The students who were called on to share were often those who had made an interesting mistake. Talking through mistakes, making sure we understood them, was important. Ms. Rey even would ask the students at the end of class what was their "favorite mistake of the day," the one that helped them learn something new. After a student would identify this partial understanding, Ms. Rey would draw a heart next to it.

One reason her strategy worked so well was that high-status students embraced this approach to math. One day in class, Toby, a Black student who had the highest math test scores in the class, engaged in an argument with his peers about the answer to a fraction division problem. He was wrong, and when they convinced him, he smiled and admitted as much. "I changed my thinking," he said, and got a laugh out of the class. The fact that Toby, well respected for his mathematical thinking, was able to admit mistakes seemed particularly important for his peers.

Ms. Rey also sent messages that mathematics takes time. One day students were not ready to share their thinking by the end of the period. She sent them to recess, telling them that "mathematicians do not hurry, instead they are thoughtful." She sent the message that good mathematics takes time, connecting it to the work of actual mathematicians.

These messages got through to her students. For the students I interviewed, these two messages were interconnected. Being worried about wrong answers was connected (for them) with being asked to answer quickly. Time meant a chance to think through a problem completely.

Does it matter how our students feel about math? In our work as teachers, we know that students generally work harder in the subjects they care about. There is evidence from longitudinal studies that achievement can be predicted not only by prior achievement but also by attitudes toward mathematics (Hemmings et al., 2011). A recent study using brain imaging found that, when given math facts to compute mentally while receiving an MRI scan, students who had lower math skills AND a positive attitude toward math showed more engagement with the brain area responsible for calculating math facts than did students with lower math skills and a negative attitude toward math (Demir-Lira et al., 2019). The researchers summarized this study as providing evidence that kids think harder when they like math than when they don't. I am glad that neuroscientists have data to confirm this idea, but I think we already knew this. It matters if we care about math. Kids think harder when they care! We all do.

Understanding of the emotional and relationship aspects of learning are critical because emotions regulate all learning; we learn when the emotional conditions are right (Immordino-Yang & Damasio, 2007). Although we should consider the social and emotional needs of all students, students with disabilities have a higher rate of emotional disabilities such as anxiety than does the general population. For example, students with learning disabilities (LD) with goals in mathematics have math anxiety at twice the rate of the general student population (Devine et al., 2018). A critical component of safe mathematics classrooms is a positive relationship with teachers. A study at a preschool found that students with LD and Attention Deficit Hyperactivity Disorder (ADHD) had more distant relationships with their teachers, with more conflict (Demirkaya & Bakkaloglu, 2015).

> Although we should consider the social and emotional needs of all students, students with disabilities have a higher rate of emotional disabilities such as anxiety than does the general population.

Develop a Sense of Mathematical Community

Ms. Rey always let students work in a way that worked for them. She let them problem solve with peers, or alone, based on their own preferences. She did not control whom they spoke to either; Toby moved around the classroom to work with different students. He did not ask Ms. Rey for permission to do so; it seemed clear that she encouraged them to decide for themselves who they were going to talk to. It strikes me that I have rarely seen this take place in math classrooms. Most days only a few students would move around to talk to other tables. On one day I observed, there was so much disagreement about the answer that by the time of the share, more than half of the students were sitting somewhere different, engaged in intense conversations about the answer. Ms. Rey communicated that she trusted them to be thinking, and so she trusted them to find the thinking partner they needed. She communicated that they were interdependent in their learning, not alone.

She also communicated that these conversations were critical to their own learning. One day she asked students to talk at their tables during a whole-group share. She prompted Oscar, who spoke very quietly when he spoke at all, to share. She walked away, and when she walked back, she saw that not all the students could hear Oscar. Instead of asking Oscar to speak louder, she asked Kelani, "Can you hear Oscar?" When Kelani shook her head no, Ms. Rey asked her, "So what can you do about it?" Kelani stood up and knelt next to Oscar. Other students at the table leaned forward. Oscar began speaking again, a little louder. In these moments, and others, Ms. Rey sent the message that her students were there to listen to each other.

DEVELOPING RELATIONAL THINKING WITH FRACTIONS

Not only is this a story about mathematical community, it also allows us to discuss one of the most challenging areas of teaching mathematics K–8: fractions! This is an equal share problem, which works wonderfully to help students think through the complex concepts at the heart of fractions.

Figure 12.5 •
Typical introductory image for fractions

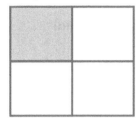

Why are fractions so challenging? One reason is how we introduce them. Often, students are given static visuals that lead them to think of a fraction in only one way, as a part of a visual whole (Empson & Levi, 2011). Students need to also understand that a fraction is a relationship between the numerator and the denominator, a ratio, and a division problem. When students only understand fractions as static images (Figure 12.5), they have trouble as their fractional work becomes more complex and more relational. Students need to see the equivalence across different visual and symbolic representations (Lamon, 2007). Students need to develop relational thinking about fractions, which is very necessary for thinking flexibly enough about fractions to understand all these different ways (Empson & Levi, 2011).

> When students only understand fractions as static images, they have trouble as their fractional work becomes more complex and more relational.

Student understanding of fractions benefits from opportunities to solve problems like the brownie problem through *guided inquiry*, given both choice in how to solve the problem and supports such as teacher questioning and discussion. Students who engage in sustained guided inquiry with equal sharing tasks like this brownie problem develop strong relational understandings of fractions, including ratio and the relationship between division and fractions (Empson & Levi, 2011). Students with learning disabilities who engage in equal sharing work develop understandings of the underlying concepts of fractions, the relational thinking about fractions necessary for understanding (Hunt & Empson, 2014; Hunt et al., 2016; Hunt et al., 2019). More about this kind of problem at the end of the chapter (for more, see "Unpacking a Core Idea: Developing Fractional Understanding Through Story Problems" on p. 210).

HOW WE USE EXPERIENCES TO FORM MATHEMATICAL IDENTITY

So how does this kind of mathematical community affect student identities in mathematics? Mathematical identity is a complicated concept. It can be oversimplified into either a positive or a negative mathematical identity, but it is more than that. I am sure that you yourself have a more complicated relationship with math than either positive or negative. It probably depends on context for you as it does for most people. Researchers tend to think of mathematical identity as a process through which we all make sense of our experiences in math. It is partly created by our experiences in math and partly by how we make sense of those experiences (Berry, 2008; Horn, 2008). Our experiences include how we feel in math class. It also includes how we make sense of experiences in which we learn if we are seen as good (or not) at math. These are all part of our experiences in math class (see Figure 12.6).

Figure 12.6 · *The process of mathematical identity*

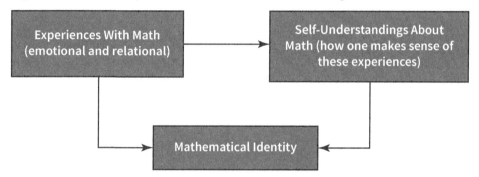

The second part is really important too—how we make sense of these experiences. We as teachers send messages about what it means to be good at math. Ms. Rey explicitly countered some of the most damaging messages, such as being good at math is being fast. We found in interviews that students took up those messages and used them to make sense of themselves. I found the same thing in the studies of students in Luis's classrooms (Chapter 2); they listened to what their teachers said about who could be good at mathematics and about what being good was.

Particularly damaging are stereotypes about mathematics around gender, race, disability, and language (Nasir et al., 2013). Negative stereotypes about mathematics circulate in our culture, sending messages to kids about who can be good at math. These messages exist, and kids differ in how they take up or reject this kind of messaging. For example, one could hear that girls are not good at math but totally reject that idea. One could also sort of reject that negative stereotype but also sort of believe it. In my work with Ms. Marquez, I found that both boys and girls took up her empowering language about gender and mathematics since she explicitly countered negative stereotypes about girls and math.

We also send messages to students about who we think is "good" at math through nonverbal cues. Students pay attention to how we group them, as well as to who has access to which tasks. In the spring in Ms. Marquez's seventh-grade classroom, she put students into three leveled groups that were never explained to students. Despite her A in math class, Rita was placed in what kids called the "middle" group. At the end of the year I asked Rita, "If there are certain kinds of math learners, which kind are you?" She responded, "I'm a middle." She used the informal name of the group to infer that she was somehow "in the middle" of math learners, not at the top, not at the bottom. Kids are always paying attention! This should remind us to never name students with ideas of their group or status in math, such as "low kids" or "high kids."

> We also send messages to students about who we think is "good" at math through nonverbal cues.

WELCOMING NEURODIVERSITY

In the year of our study, Ms. Rey had asked that two students with autism, Oscar and Ash, be placed into her class full time even though they had been in separate special education classes. In interviews with Ms. Rey, I asked how she approached working with students like Ash and Oscar. Her answer was immediate—get to know them. Before Oscar, a Latino, entered her class, Ms. Rey talked to his special education teachers to find out what he was interested in—space travel. She pulled him aside the first day of fifth grade and shared with him some books about space. Oscar then started bringing in books to show Ms. Rey (Figure 12.7). Their relationship bloomed from that moment.

Figure 12.7 • *Ms. Rey talking with Oscar*

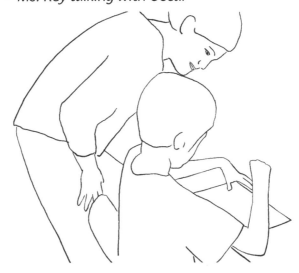

Oscar had not previously spoken very much at school. In his fourth-grade class in which he had spent some time being mainstreamed (when a child in a separate special education class spends some time in general education), he did not speak to the teacher even one on one for months. His IEP described him as "nonverbal." When Ms. Rey described Oscar to me, she used the word "shy" instead.

Oscar was very hard-working in math class. Based on analysis of videos of his class, Oscar was usually the first to start working on every problem and the last to stop. He was most often able to make sense of the fraction problems using direct modeling, drawing out problems. For the first half of the year, our close analysis of student participation found that he would rarely speak to other students during small groups, and he did not share in the whole group.

Ash, a girl in the class with autism who was Asian American and white, seemed the opposite of Oscar. While he was quiet, she was loud. Ash interrupted class on a daily basis, sometimes with her answers to the math problems, or sometimes singing Disney songs. She was not hesitant to interrupt the class if she felt there was a problem, such as when she felt a seatmate was being "mean."

While Oscar sat down throughout the entire class, Ash might get up at any point if she got curious about something. More than once, she got up to investigate the cameras we were using to record the class. Mathematically, Ash had significant skills that she seemed to enjoy showing off in math class. Her computational skills were above grade level, as was her understanding of conceptual topics. For example, she used ratio tables to solve fraction problems well before any of her peers. Figure 12.8 shows Ash and Oscar at their table during math class.

Figure 12.8 • *Ash, in the middle, and Oscar, on the right, during a lesson*

Ms. Rey also used special interests to develop her relationship with Ash. Ash was particularly interested in Pokémon, and so Ms. Rey made sure to discuss the topic with her. Ash also loved cats, and so Ms. Rey (who had several cats) would use them in story problems, which seemed to delight Ash. I once saw Kelani, who sat next to Ash, rewrite a story problem to be about cats so that Ash would engage. It worked. This was perhaps my favorite moment in the study—when I saw that kids also learned how to accommodate their neurodiverse friends!

Ms. Rey made sure to recognize Ash for what she knew and could share. She called on her frequently, which kept Ash engaged in the mathematical discussion. When Ash needed some guidance in her behavior, Ms. Rey used multiple strategies. Ms. Rey might walk closer to Ash, using proximity as a reminder. Sometimes she ignored behavior that she could safely ignore, a special education strategy I love called "planned ignoring." Ms. Rey never spoke sharply to Ash and made sure other adults also treated Ash with respect.

Ms. Rey had a way of learning about her students that went far beyond stereotypes about autism. She learned about both Ash and Oscar as individual, unique, and interesting children. She understood that they needed different things from her to thrive in her class.

To be sure, Ms. Rey used relationships to engage all of her students. She saw mathematics as relational and mathematical thinking as needing emotional space. She shared with me during a final interview in the project that while thinking about how she accommodates students with disabilities, she thought back to her own history as a learner in schools. She had been taken out of class for speech therapy and had such powerful memories of the shame of being pulled out. For her, including all kids and making sure they did not feel that shame was so central to her practice, in all subjects. For her, this emotional, relational way to teaching seemed particularly important in math, perhaps the most relational, emotional subject there is.

REFLECTION QUESTIONS

1. If you have taught fractions, what do you think is tricky for students? How do you support students to think flexibly about fractions?

2. Do you have memories of math classrooms in which you felt more or less comfortable sharing your thinking? What do you think mattered?

3. Do you have experience developing relationships with students who need more support like Ash and Oscar? What has worked for you? What might you try from this chapter?

UDL Math Connections

Engagement	Representation	Strategic action
This chapter focuses on how Ms. Rey built a safe mathematical community for all students, including how she prioritized relationships. She worked to make students feel safe taking mathematical risks.	Students had the freedom to make sense of fractions in a way that made sense to them. Ms. Rey then shared multiple student strategies to engage all students in multiple representations.	Ms. Rey led a discussion about equivalence in which students (Daniel and Kelani) compared their strategies. This is an example of purposeful development of strategic thinking in math. Ms. Rey also developed student strategic thinking through purposeful questions.

Unpacking a Core Idea: Developing Fractional Understanding Through Story Problems

Empson and Levi identified three kinds of equal sharing tasks in their 2011 book on cognitively guided instruction and fractions. Before you read Table 12.1, try to solve all three example problems using drawings to see how you solve them differently. What equation would you write for each type?

Table 12.1 • *Fraction problem types*

Problem type	Example problem	Student thinking with direct modeling
Equal sharing problem (partitive division)	*Dr. Lambert has 10 blocks of clay. She needs to split up the clay between 4 students. How many blocks of clay will each student get?*	$2\frac{1}{2}$ block of clay $10 \div 4 = 2\frac{1}{2}$
Multiple groups problem (multiplication)	*Dr. Lambert has 4 students. She wants to give each student $2\frac{1}{2}$ blocks of clay. How many blocks of clay does she need?*	$2\frac{1}{2} + 2\frac{1}{2}$ $2\frac{1}{2} + 2\frac{1}{2}$ 5 5 $5 + 5 = 10$ blocks of clay

Problem type	Example problem	Student thinking with direct modeling
Multiple groups problem (measurement division)	Dr. Lambert has 10 blocks of clay. She wants to give each student $2\frac{1}{2}$ of a block of clay. How many students can she provide with clay?	

Students generally begin with each problem type by direct modeling it. Each time a level of complexity is introduced, students may return to direct modeling to make sense of it. Direct modeling is critical to making sure everyone (including adults) has access to the complex ideas in fractions. Students eventually begin breaking the shared object into the number of shares, as Kelani did. Finally, students develop strategies that use relational thinking and/or ratio to solve. Using story problems will expose students to operations with fractions as well, such as in the 12 chairs problem (Chapter 1), which was division of a whole number by a fraction (12 divided by $\frac{3}{4}$ths).

Learn More:

Empson, S. B., & Levi, L. (2011). *Extending children's mathematics: Fractions & decimals: Innovations in cognitively guided instruction.* Heinemann.

CHAPTER 13

CONNECTING MULTIPLE REPRESENTATIONS

IN THIS CHAPTER, WE WILL . . .

- Observe a sixth-grade classroom doing the Connecting Representations Instructional Routine
- Learn about the features of Instructional Routines, designed for students with learning disabilities (LD) and multilingual students
- Explore the importance of connecting representations
- Learn from students' reflections about Instructional Routines

KIT GOLAN (Figure 13.1) is a lively and dynamic middle school math teacher. Not unusually, as a middle school math teacher, Kit noticed that they[3] often dominated the conversation in class. They wanted their students to talk more but found the same students sharing over and over again. As an educator with Attention Deficit Hyperactivity Disorder (ADHD), Kit is passionate about creating classrooms that work for all learners by designing from the margins. So they sought ways to structure student discussion to equalize participation.

Figure 13.1 • *Kit Golan, sixth-grade mathematics teacher*

SOURCE: Kit Golan

Kit also reasoned that when they, as the teacher, dominated the talk, they were doing the thinking rather than the students. Kit wanted to develop structures so that the students would be doing the cognitive work rather than

---

[3] Kit uses both he/him and they/their pronouns. I will use they/their in this chapter.

the teacher. Kit wanted to make sure that the structures they put in place would support all students. That's when Instructional Routines (Kelemanik et al., 2016) fell into Kit's life. When Kit found Instructional Routines, they felt able to provide structure to support both engagement and thinking using a consistent, repeated structure.

So let's enter Kit's classroom to see the Instructional Routine of Connecting Representations in action. Their sixth-grade class in New York City was primarily Asian and white, with a smaller percentage of Latino/a and Black students. Several students had Individualized Education Programs (IEPs). The class also had several multilingual learners, mostly students whose first language was Chinese. Most students needed more support to engage in mathematics, a not-uncommon problem in middle school! Kit called the class to attention, announcing that the class was going to be doing the Connecting Representations Instructional Routine (Kelemanik et al., 2016).

Kit started the routine by giving the students a math practice goal. Kit told the sixth graders, "Today, we will be connecting double number lines to equations so that we can think like mathematicians do, and use mathematical structure to connect two things that look different."

They then briefly reminded the class of the steps in the Instructional Routine. Throughout this routine, Kit used a Microsoft PowerPoint presentation. Similar presentations are available for free on the website Fostering Math Practices, which also includes math tasks to use in the routines (https://www.fosteringmathpractices.com/). You can also find out more at the Online Teaching Practice Guide.

Online Teaching Practice Guide
qrs.ly/l7f7rwq

Next, Kit posed the task that the students would be working on.

> **Try It**
>
> Which number lines representations (1 & 2) go with which equations (A, B, & C)?
> How do you know?
>
> 1)
>
>
> A) $3x = 6$
> B) $6x = 12$
> C) $6x + 3 = 15$
>
> 2)
>
>
> Which equation (A, B, or C) doesn't have a matching number line representation?
> Can you try to draw a double number line to match that equation?

Kit revealed two posters, one at a time: first one with the double number lines (1 & 2), and then one with the equations (A, B, & C). They posed the following questions to the students:

- "Ask yourself: 'How are the number lines similar/different?'"
- "What are the CHUNKS of these number lines?"
- "What are the CHUNKS of these equations?"

Kit then gave the students individual think time and after a minute or so asked them to turn and talk. As the students talked, they displayed the following sentence starters on a slide:

- "I noticed . . . so I connected"
- ". . . matches . . . because . . ."

As students talked in partners, Kit circulated, listening to what the students were saying. As they listened to students talk, they selected two different pairs of students to share. They quietly prepared those students to practice for sharing in front of the class, to allow them to plan and rehearse what they would say and do.

After a few minutes, Kit called the class together and asked the first pair to share their thinking. The first pair focused on the relationship between $6x$ and the 6 equivalent jumps on both number lines. The students then connected C with

1 because of the additional 3 jumps, equivalent to 3. The second pair started a different way, looking carefully at A and 1, the first equation and the first number line. Although the first number line had jumps of 3, the groups of 6 did not make sense on that number line because it was added on, not shown as equivalent.

As each pair shared, one student talked and the other used a pointer to show the other students what they were talking about. After each pair shared, Kit asked the students in the class to restate the thinking of the partner pair who presented. Kit supported this talk by sharing sentence starters for the restatements.

After the second pair shared, Kit thanked the presenters and stepped in front of the chart paper. When the student pairs were presenting, no marker was used to represent their thinking. The pointer was used to indicate what they were talking about but no annotation. But after the shares, Kit carefully annotated the chart paper using color to make visible the connections between the chunks that the students saw as related (as in Figures 13.2 and 13.3).

Figure 13.2 · *Kit's annotations of the algebraic equations*

A) 3x = 6

B) (6x) = (12)

C) (6x) + (3) = (15)

Figure 13.3 · *Kit's annotations of the double number lines*

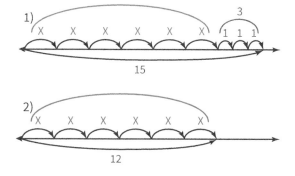

Next, Kit asked the students to make a representation on the double number line for the equation without a representation (A. 3x = 6). Here is a re-creation of one of their student's drawings (Figure 13.4).

Figure 13.4 · *Student drawing of 3x = 6 on a double number line.*

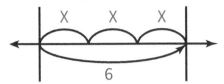

The class followed the same routine within a routine: Two student pairs shared their drawings, with one doing the talking and the other using a pointer. Kit led the class in restating and rephrasing what their classmates did.

Finally, Kit ended this routine as all Instructional Routines end, with a guided self-reflection, asking the students to think about the following questions posted on a slide:

A) Paying attention to . . . in an equation or double number line is helpful because . . .

B) When interpreting an equation or a double number line, I learned to ask myself to . . . ●

INSTRUCTIONAL ROUTINES

Instructional Routines (Kelemanik et al., 2016) are a set of highly structured routines designed to support students with learning disabilities and/or multilingual students to engage in mathematical thinking. As Kelemanik and colleagues (2016) noted, recommended practice for *both* multilingual learners and students with LD are

- ▸ Use of authentic contexts
- ▸ Use of multimodal techniques
- ▸ Rich opportunities for language use embedded in mathematics problems
- ▸ Instruction that scaffolds abstract thinking in mathematics.

Thus, designing from *both* these recommendations supports a wide range of students. At this point in the book, many of the students with disabilities we have so far met have also been multilingual. This is an example of how designing from the margins can support everyone, as well as support students who may be marginalized in multiple ways.

Instructional Routines are specifically designed to support student engagement in the Standards of Mathematical Practice (SMPs) or to allow students to engage in complex cognitive work. This routine is structured to support students to engage in SMP 7: *Look for and make use of structure.* What connects the double number lines to the equations are that they both represent the same mathematical structure, just in different modalities. The students who saw the equivalent jumps of 6 across two number lines connected that to 6*x*. They saw the jumps on the number line as a chunk, as a smaller unit that had mathematical meaning, and matched it to the symbolic representation that made the most sense with it. Kit made that even clearer when they color-coded the chunks the students saw across representations.

Each Instructional Routine uses a consistent structure with the goal of freeing up students' mental resources to think mathematically instead of thinking, "Wait, what do I do next?" Key features of every routine are

1. Articulation of a math practice goal
2. Math problem and individual think time
3. Partner work (with sentence starters)
4. Full group discussion of ideas with purposeful connections between representations (and often teacher annotations)
5. Individual reflection on math practice goal

In our interview, Kit stressed the importance of *strategic coaching* in turn and talks. They told me that before they started with these routines, they would tell middle school students to turn and talk. The students would turn to each other and both talk at each other at the same time. Kit felt students needed more explicit coaching in how to communicate about math. The use of sentence frames was critical to support students who are feeling anxious about what to say, as well as students who have difficulty getting started. They also support students who have challenges with social cues. Kit also shared how the support of sentence frames helps them as a learner with ADHD. They noted that having a combination of ADHD and perfectionist tendencies, getting started sometimes feels impossible, even with just saying a sentence about a math problem. A sentence frame can give permission to get started, and help students know that they are on the right track.

Turn and talks are one of five essential strategies (Table 13.1) embedded in the Instructional Routines. These strategies are research supported and critical elements of all math teaching.

Table 13.1 • *Essential strategies of Instructional Routines*

Essential strategies	Description	How Kit uses this strategy
Annotation	Teacher visually represents student's verbalized student thinking.	Kit uses color to represent students' verbal description of how they connected the equations to the number lines.
Ask-yourself-questions	Prompts designed to get students to think metacognitively without dictating a particular process or strategy.	Kit asks the students: • "Ask yourself: 'How are the number lines similar/different?'"
Four Rs (repeat, rephrase, reword, and record)	Teaching moves that support student mathematical talk. **Repeat:** Teacher calls on a student to exactly repeat another student's idea. **Rephrase:** Teacher calls on a student to say the student's idea in a slightly different way. **Reword:** Teacher rephrases the student's idea. **Record:** Teacher writes down student language.	Kit had students both repeat and rephrase the students who shared in front of the class. They also reworded student strategies when annotating the number lines and equations.
Sentence starters and frames	Teacher provides part of a response to help students find the words for what they want to say.	As student pairs were working, Kit displays "I noticed . . . so I connected" ". . . matches . . . because . . ."
Turn and talks	Students are asked to turn and talk with a partner.	Kit started with some individual think time and then had students work in pairs. During the whole group share, they have the students turn and talk whenever there is a juicy mathematical idea to process.

SOURCE: Essential strategies from Kelemanik & Lucenta (2022).

Understanding how variables work

Not only was Kit thinking about student engagement, but they were also thinking deeply about the mathematics they were teaching. When students in sixth grade start working with variables, they often do not understand what the variable means or that $6x$ means six groups of x (whatever x is). The algebraic representation of $6x + 3 = 15$ is abstract to students, completely symbolic. This disconnect between symbols and sense-making can create years of confusion for algebra unless it is addressed through meaningful experiences (for more, see "Unpacking a Core Idea: Algebraic Thinking I" on p. 224).

To help students understand how the variable works, Kit used double number lines, a strategy of representing variables as jumps on a number line developed by Cathy Fosnot and Bill Jacob (2010). Especially for students who have already done plenty of work with number lines for whole number operations, double number lines can help kids solve equations because they can see the relationships between quantities and equivalencies. This intentional development of a model as a tool for thinking comes from research in realistic mathematics education (RME), focused on helping students not just understand particular mathematical models but also to internalize them so that they can become a tool for thinking (Van Den Heuvel-Panhuizen, 2003).

This representation of variables on number lines might be new to you. When I first looked at them, I wanted the jumps of x to be somehow completely different than the jumps where you know the value (like the jumps of 1). But having worked with this representation, I see how it makes it concrete the number of jumps, as well as equivalency. Did you notice that the same two numbers (3 and 6) were repeated in the equations? Kit did this intentionally so that students can't "number grab" with the 3 or the 6 because those same numbers are repeated in multiple equations. Because of Kit's number choices, students must make sense of the difference between a 6 as a whole number versus 6 groups of the variable x. Kit also designed the task so that students would see the difference between $6x$ and $6x + 3$ and be able to think about the differences between a known number (3) and a variable (x).

THE IMPORTANCE OF CONNECTING REPRESENTATIONS

Mathematics is fundamentally multimodal. Mathematics is about how numbers *and* space operate. Many of the most challenging problems in mathematics at the research level are on mapping number to space, for example, three-dimensional space. Universal Design for Learning (UDL) calls for using multiple modalities to support student learning in all content areas.

I have argued that multimodality is central to mathematics teaching and learning and thus particularly important. Despite this centrality, it can be very challenging for students to understand mathematical representations and how numeric, symbolic, and visual representations connect. Children learning how to count need to connect a quantity of objects to a number. Learning addition means both understanding the natural action of combining two quantities and how to represent that action as $a + b = c$. I appreciate, then, how the Connecting Representations Instructional Routine directly addresses this pedagogical problem.

> **Mathematics is fundamentally multimodal. Mathematics is about how numbers *and* space operate.**

But this approach is not the only way to address helping students see connections across representations. I would argue that thus far in this book, we have seen three different, but complementary, approaches to this problem. In the cognitively guided instruction (CGI) tradition, children begin in the realm of the visual using story problems (Carpenter et al., 2015). Students begin with drawings and manipulatives, whether solving how many marshmallows were added to a cup of hot chocolate or how much each child will get if 4 children split 13 brownies. Because students begin by drawing their own representations to solve problems, they will understand those representations. Understanding of more abstract representations, such as equations, usually comes later. Students who can direct model a mathematical problem can be encouraged to write an equation to describe it, moving between mathematical representations. I recommend this approach for students just learning a new topic because students are in control of which representations they want to use.

A second, more structured, approach comes from realistic mathematics education (RME). In Chapter 9, I detailed how Dina designed a sequence of activities using RME theory of mathematical models to help all her students construct understanding of the number line. The process begins with students solving problems in a real -life context that lends itself to the model and then having the teacher use the model to visually represent student strategies. Finally, students should take up the model as a tool for thinking, as Jeremy did with the tower blocks (arrays) for multiplication in Chapter 10. This approach works well when a mathematical model is both particularly important in mathematics (like number lines and arrays) and can be confusing to students initially so they are unlikely to use it to solve problems without a nudge.

Connecting representations comes at the problem a different way. This routine teaches students how to analyze two kinds of representations to see how they work. This approach is particularly useful as we move into algebra, where students need to move between equations, concrete situations, graphs, functions, and other representations. This scaffolded practice in seeing structure, in making use of it (SMP 7), is particularly invaluable as they move forward in mathematics.

CONNECTIONS TO PEDAGOGY

You might have noticed that this Instructional Routine is more highly structured than anything else I have shared so far in the book. So is this Instructional Routine explicit instruction? Doabler and Fien (2013) defined explicit instruction as having the following features:

(a) the teacher modeling a new concept or skill,

(b) the teacher providing guided practice opportunities,

(c) the teacher checking for student understanding,

(d) the teacher providing academic feedback, and

(e) the students engaging in independent practice.

Which do you see in Kit's teaching using this routine? I see every element except the first. Kit structures everything *except* they do not tell students how to solve this complex problem. Not only does Kit structure activity so that students have to do the talking, students have to do the thinking! I consider Instructional Routines as *guided strategy development*, in which student thinking is heavily scaffolded but students are still free to think. In fact, the structure itself is designed to support student thinking!

STUDENTS REFLECTING ON ROUTINES

Kit asked students in their class that year what they thought about Instructional Routines, specifically connecting representations. Here are some student responses:

▸ "We do lots of talking with your partners and they help me catch my mistakes in problems, and that isn't something I did often in elementary school."

▸ "I like that instead of all our heads facing the teacher, they were turned to each other. That felt really good."

▶ "Mr. Golan doesn't talk all class like some teachers."

▶ "The matching A to B talk and reflect strategy helped me learn because it helped me use visual learning and everything gets explained many times."

▶ "It helped me understand stuff and breaks apart the hard stuff."

These student reflections are amazing. They provide evidence that Kit's strategy was successful with the most important experts: kids. One student even validated Kit's strategy to decenter their own talking, noting that Kit doesn't talk all class, like other teachers. What particularly strikes me is the student who reflects on the importance of heads facing other students, not the teacher, saying, "That felt really good."

In reflecting on this routine, Kit loved how talk in the classroom went from mostly teacher to mostly students. Structuring the talk in small segments was useful, where kids listen for a little, talk for a little, create something, and then talk again. Kit told me, "There's no huge chunk of time where students have a chance to get off task, or to fall behind everybody else, right? Because we're all sort of doing the same thing. But it's in these structured, smaller moments." This kind of structure is different from *guided inquiry* such as in Ms. Rey's classroom (Chapter 12), when students make most of the choices about how to engage. Learning the structures of Instructional Routines gives us more options in our pedagogical tool kits.

> Structuring the talk in small segments was useful, where kids listen for a little, talk for a little, create something, and then talk again.

REFLECTION QUESTIONS

1. What do you notice and wonder about this Instructional Routine? What would you ask Kit if they were here?

2. This routine has lots of structure to support student discussion. How might that benefit students who need support with language?

3. Have you seen students struggle with connecting different representations? Which representations seem tricky to students?

UDL Math Connections

Engagement	Representation	Strategic action
Kit is designing to increase student engagement in mathematical talk and problem solving. They structure talk with individual thinking time, turn and talks, and structured whole group shares. They also provide language support such as sentence frames.	This Instructional Routine is designed to get students to develop strong understandings about how mathematical representations are related.	Students are asked to reflect on their own knowledge and to develop the habit of asking themselves "ask yourself questions," which can develop their metacognition.

Unpacking a Core Idea: Algebraic Thinking I

Algebra has often been described as generalized arithmetic. It allows us to generalize $a \times b = b \times a$, if we already understand that $5 \times 3 = 3 \times 5$ (the commutative property of multiplication). All the work we invest in students' understanding of multiple ways to do whole number computations can be leveraged to develop strong understanding of how algebra works. We can begin quite early discussing these kinds of ideas with students in elementary school. When students come up with mathematical conjectures, such as "any number times one is the same thing," we can explore their ideas and name them (the identity property of multiplication). These kinds of generalizations prepare students for algebraic thinking. It also prepares students for making and supporting conjectures (a mathematical hypothesis), one of the Standards of Mathematical Practice (SMP2).

Algebraic thinking can be supported in the elementary grades by open-ended tasks that allow students to decompose and recompose numbers. In the tiles problem done by the second graders in Chapter 6, students had to determine multiple ways to tile the frame, which included thinking about equivalency and the equal sign. This is an algebra problem!

One of the trickiest things about algebra are the abstract symbols, particularly the concept of variables and the equal sign. Students often think that the equal sign means "the answer comes next," not that it represents equality in quantity on either side. Students can explore problems such as $4 + 5 = b + 6$, which can help students develop stronger understandings of the equal sign as meaning equivalence, not the answer comes next (Carpenter et al., 2003). It can also develop *relational thinking*, when students use what they know about number to find the answer to b; for example, a student might notice that 6 is one more than 5, and so b must be one less than 4. Students with learning disabilities in a third-grade class were able to develop and express their relational thinking about the equals sign after a consistent exposure to these kinds of problems (Foote & Lambert, 2011). In this lesson, Kit uses double number lines to help students see the equivalence in the equations (Fosnot & Jacob, 2010). Other methods are balance models and algebra tiles.

Variables are extremely tricky. When we teach students about these symbols in ways that do not connect to real-life and/or representations, mathematics starts to lose meaning for students. Students often think of variables as holding the place of one number, not of ANY number (Van de Walle, et al., 2017). This concept of variability becomes particularly important when students get to graphing equations and the line represents all the possible values. Students who may take longer to understand abstract ideas should have plenty of opportunities to develop their understanding of variables through multiple visual representations, as Kit does here.

Learn More:

Carpenter, T. P., Franke, M. L., & Levi, L. (2003). *Thinking mathematically: Integrating arithmetic and algebra in elementary school*. Heinemann.

Foote, M. Q., & Lambert, R. (2011). I have a solution to share: Learning through equitable participation in a mathematics classroom. *Canadian Journal of Science, Mathematics and Technology Education, 11*(3), 247–260. https://doi.org/10.1080/14926156.2011.595882

Fosnot, C. T., & Jacob, B. (2010). *Young mathematicians at work: Constructing algebra*. Heinemann.

Van de Walle, J., Bay-Williams, J., Lovin, L., & Karp, K. (2017). *Teaching student-centered mathematics: Developmentally appropriate instruction for grades 6–8* (3rd ed.). Pearson.

CHAPTER 14

RETHINKING ASSESSMENT FOR EQUITY

IN THIS CHAPTER, WE WILL . . .

- Visit with my multiplication intervention group as I implement dynamic assessment
- Follow a middle school math teacher as he redesigns assessment in his inclusive classroom
- Explore how to use assessment to better understand complex learners, as well as to help learners better understand themselves

IN MY INTERVENTION with Franco and Jeremy, fourth and fifth graders who needed extra support in multiplication (Chapter 10) we worked with towers of connecting cubes to represent multiplication. After a few sessions, I felt so confident that they had made progress understanding multiplication that I decided to give them a second assessment using the same first few problems as the first assessment. On that first assessment, Jeremy had not solved any problems, and Franco had solved one (5 × 5). Neither had shown any written work. But now I felt that they would both rock it using their new strategies of skip counting and repeated addition.

As the boys started the assessment, I was watching Franco. I beamed as he used repeated addition to solve multiple problems he missed the first time. He went from 1 out of 6 correct in the first assessment to 5 out of 6 in the second one. Even more importantly, he went from answers with no written work to showing his mathematical thinking. He solved 5 out of 6 problems, and even his wrong answer had a valid strategy; he just lost count. Figures 14.1 and 14.2 show Franco's first and second assessments.

Figure 14.1 · *Franco's first assessment*	**Figure 14.2 ·** *Franco's second assessment*
2 x 4 (2	2 x 4 ⁻8
5 x 5 ⫫25 +1	5 x 5 ⁻25 1⫫5 5+5 +5 +5 +5 = 25
6 x 10 69	6 x 10 ⁻60 6 X 10 =6 ⫫ ⟶ = 10+10+ 10+10+10+10 = 60
4 x 2 ,2	4 x 2 =8 4 X 2 = 8
3 x 7 ⫫28	3 x 7 = 21 2X4 4X2 = 42 7+7 +7 = 21
8 x 9 2 0	8 x 9 9+9+9 +9 +9 +9 +9 +9 +9 = 30 ? =30 ?

Pleased, I turned to look at Jeremy and immediately worried. Jeremy, usually jovial and relaxed, seemed incredibly tense. His legs were jittering up and down, and his face looked very stressed. I walked over and knelt down next to him. I saw that he had written a correct answer to the first one (2 × 4) but nothing else.

I asked if he wanted to draw anything; he shook his head "no." I asked if he wanted to use his fingers; he shook his head "no." I asked if he wanted to use blocks, and again, "no." I felt terrible. I had been so confident that my intervention had worked. I saw the increase in knowledge and confidence in Franco, but I didn't know what had happened with Jeremy. Figures 14.3 and 14.4 show Jeremy's first and second assessments. I see that Jeremy is doing less guessing, but I am definitely not seeing the beautiful multiplicative thinking I had seen in our sessions.

Figure 14.3 · *Jeremy's first assessment*	**Figure 14.4** · *Jeremy's second assessment*
2 x 4 87	Solve. Show your strategies. 2 x 4
5 x 5 24	5 x 5
6 x 10	6 x 10
4 x 2 26	4 x 2 = 4
3 x 7 10	3 x 7
8 x 9 18	8 x 9

After the assessment was collected, I gathered the boys together. I decided that I needed to be more explicit about how the work we were doing was connected to these bare number problems. I took a blank copy of the assessment and cut each problem into a strip. I grabbed the first one, 2 × 4. I wrote on a whiteboard "2 towers of 4." I drew a picture of 2 towers of 4. I asked what the equation was for this situation. Franco answered right away, "2 times 4," but Jeremy seemed unsure. I wrote up the equation and asked again, "What is this in towers?" Jeremy started to get a spark in his eyes and grabbed some blocks to build it. For the rest of the session, the boys solved the problems on the assessment by translating it into "tower talk," as they called it. Once he made this connection, Jeremy solved every one of these problems.

In our very next session one week later, I decided to try an assessment again but this time with more support so that I could really learn what Jeremy knew. This assessment used equivalent problems (problems of the same difficulty levels assessing the same factors). This time, I sat the boys together (along with a third boy who wanted to use blocks as well) and made sure all had plenty of blocks. Figure 14.5 shows them at work using blocks to solve problems.

Figure 14.5 · *Multiplication group using blocks for assessment #3*

Franco's score was the same as his assessment the previous week, but Jeremy went from $\frac{1}{6}$ to $\frac{5}{6}$, the same jump in score that Franco had. Jeremy's assessment (Figure 14.6) has no written work, but I saw that he used the blocks to build towers for each problem. ●

> **Think About It**
>
> So what does Jeremy know about multiplication? What does this story make you wonder about assessment?

Figure 14.6 ·
Jeremy's third assessment using blocks

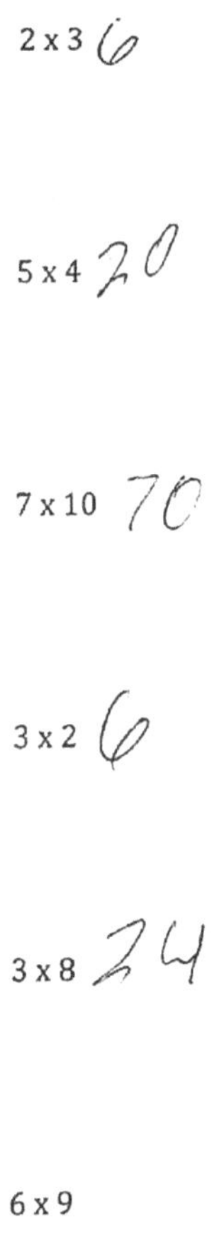

2 x 3 *6*

5 x 4 *20*

7 x 10 *70*

3 x 2 *6*

3 x 8 *24*

6 x 9

The purpose of assessment is for us to learn what children know rather than what they don't know. Imagine me reporting to Jeremy's classroom teacher. Which is more helpful for her? If I tell her that he only got one right or that he got 5 out of 6 correct when given blocks? The second is much more helpful because now she knows how to support him. She knows that he understands the basic concept of multiplication and can do it when supported with blocks (see Figure 14.6).

In this chapter, we will explore assessment. Assessment is a major barrier for disabled and neurodiverse students in mathematics. In my interviews, assessment comes up again and again as a place that stresses students (and teachers!) out. In my research in Luis's classroom in Chapter 2, when I asked students for a time that math was challenging, 5 out of 9 students discussed anxiety around testing. Students told me how it felt to take a math test:

"I would understand, but I'll get too nervous and forget something. . . . Cause when you are kind of nervous, you, forget things . . . it is just like, I should know this, wait, I forgot about this, should I remember? I just like get kind of nervous." (Ana)

"For some reason on tests I tend to like, panic and then if I like study something I for . . . it is like I blank out completely. So, with tests, I don't test well." (Desi)

These two students, both girls with an Individualized Education Program (IEP) for a learning disability, describe the process very similarly. This process begins with stress, panic, and feeling nervous. When you feel those things, you forget or "blank out." This process is very similar to the hypothetical process at the heart of math anxiety (Ashcraft & Moore, 2009). Ashcraft and Moore proposed that when a person with math anxiety solves a math problem, particularly under stressful conditions, the anxiety interferes with working memory, which is necessary to solve mathematics problems.

These authors proposed that this leads kids to underperform on tests of mathematics because of what they term the *affective drop* (Ashcraft & Moore, 2009).

> Ashcraft and Moore proposed that when a person with math anxiety solves a math problem, particularly under stressful conditions, the anxiety interferes with working memory, which is necessary to solve mathematics problems.

I notice that Ana starts with "I would understand." This girl makes a bold claim: she knows the mathematics, but test situation doesn't allow her to show what she knows. This statement reminds me of watching Jeremy, his legs shaking, stare at the mostly blank assessment. This issue is not about whether these students understand the math, it is about how assessment feels. Students are expected to remember in a situation in which they feel anxiety, stress. They feel that stress because doing well on the tests IS important to them. And that level of anxiety directly affects their ability to show what they know.

We seem to have a vision of assessment as always assessing the individual alone, without supports, as if what we can do alone with no tools is what matters. Dynamic assessment is a more flexible kind of assessment that allows us to adapt assessments to more accurately show what children know when using tools and interacting with others (Vygotsky, 1978). These adaptations can vary, from encouraging students to use manipulatives, to allowing students to work as a group, to giving students verbal prompts. It is not about what the child can do without tools because tools are part of mathematics.

The same is true about working with others. Dynamic assessment has been explored to better understand what students with disabilities or low achievement in math actually know (Peltenberg et al., 2009; Storeygard et al., 2010). In one study, students with intellectual disabilities showed understanding of concepts of ratio, above what their teachers predicted, even though they had not been taught the topic (Heuvel-Panhuizen, 1996). This written assessment was designed to be accessible, with items embedded in real-life contexts that involve ratio, not the symbolic notation of ratio.

In the Disability Rights Movement, there have been decades of critique of the idea that knowledge or competence should be assessed alone, focused on deficits. Instead, we can learn about what we can do with support, with community, with tools. Opening up assessment practices is a powerful way to bring disability rights into our math classrooms!

> **In the Disability Rights Movement, there have been decades of critique of the idea that knowledge or competence should be assessed alone, focused on deficits.**

As we work to make assessment practices more effective and less harmful for students, I pose the following two questions to guide our work:

Assessment Accessibility Check

- ▶ Is the assessment practice helping teachers understand and teach complex learners?
- ▶ Is the assessment practice helping students understand themselves as math learners?

The term "complex learners" can be used with all of our students; every one of us is variable and complex. However, one reason that assessment is such a barrier is that students with disabilities are often particularly complex to assess. Language in assessments can be tricky. Assessments can be stressful when you feel you have failed at them in the past. And students' understanding can be variable across math topics and in the specific context of the assessment. Great assessments allow us to see and understand complexity, such as the three interview tasks on counting in Chapter 3.

How would we use these questions to evaluate my work with Jeremy and Franco? Well, the simple assessment I had designed did give me important information on Franco's math strategies and understanding. But it only seemed to bring out stress for Jeremy. I needed to not only offer blocks but also help him see how he could use blocks on the assessment, as well as in our session. Once he made this connection, the assessment gave me useful information and helped him understand himself as a math learner.

MOVING TOWARD EQUITABLE ASSESSMENT IN A MIDDLE SCHOOL CLASSROOM

Of course it is not only students who dread assessments. Many teachers also find assessment the most challenging part of our job. Mr. Jay, who in Chapter 4 showed us how to use both inquiry and more explicit kinds of instruction, was also experimenting with assessment in his classroom.[4] When I asked him what he was trying to change about assessment, he told me a story (Figure 14.7).

---

[4] These data were collected and analyzed with the assistance of my colleagues Marilyn Monroy Castro and Rebeca Mireles-Rios.

Figure 14.7. • *Mr. Jay working with a student*

During the state exam a few years ago, a girl in his seventh-grade class who was an excellent math student called him over, a frantic look in her eye. She pointed to a problem and asked her teacher, "What should I do?" Mr. Jay could not answer, but he could see that she had solved everything but just had a final subtraction problem to find the difference between 16 and 8. He had never seen her have any difficulty with such a problem. Mr. Jay could not answer, and so he just said, "I know you can figure it out." But he felt concerned.

He described two very important problems with this kind of assessment. First, it had his student, usually calm and collected, extremely stressed out. She was so stressed that she could not remember how to solve a problem that she usually could solve. That it was a subtraction problem, something usually that she would do without thinking, concerned him. That sense of stress, of anxiety, was a big problem all by itself. Mr. Jay sees his job as a middle school math teacher to interrupt the deep dive students at that age generally take in their enjoyment of math (Gottfried et al., 2007). Mr. Jay told me:

> My kids just freeze and blank out under this pressure of this test—
> they're anxious and they can't think and there's this huge roadblock
> for them. . . . I try to tell them, take a walk, get some air. Because right
> now, you're just all in your head. I mean, that's fear—it's fight or flight
> where the brain turns off.

What Mr. Jay is describing brings me back to the description of math anxiety, when anxiety takes up the working memory that students need for thinking about mathematics (Ashcraft & Moore, 2009). It also reminds us that high-achieving students experience math anxiety as well, particularly in stressful testing situations.

Mr. Jay's second problem was that this high-stakes state exam was not an accurate measure of what his student knew. This combination—that current assessments were both inaccurate and stressful—led Mr. Jay to do a revamp of his assessment practices. He decided, "Math tests did not have to be the same as they were for me in middle school. They could change for the better."

Mr. Jay's Formative Assessments

Mr. Jay already had some assessment practices that worked for him that he wanted to keep in place. Observation was his most important assessment tool. As he told me, "Each kid in my class is a different puzzle, like a math problem all on their own." Mr. Jay knows his students, and he knows that each one is working on something different. He is able to learn about students through observations, and he focuses on different things for different students.

> **"Each kid in my class is a different puzzle,
> like a math problem all on their own."**

Mr. Jay also collected student work, and each day after class, I would see him looking through it. This process, along with observations, always informed the way that he taught class the next day. Mr. Jay would also frequently have students do a short problem at the end of class, an exit ticket, particularly if he had a sense that the students were not sure about a particular kind of problem. He would then collect these and analyze. An exit ticket often served to give him precise information for the class as a whole, which helped him know whether he should move on or return to the topic the next day.

Across all of these items, Mr. Jay paid close attention to student strategies. Student strategies were a frequent topic of conversation in class. To help students refine and remember their strategies, Mr. Jay asked them to make their own strategy charts in their notebook. This process became a touchstone assessment item, with Mr. Jay asking students to share their strategies, so they could discuss their efficiency. If a student started using a strategy of another student, they would include it in the notebook as well.

Rubrics for Guided Inquiry Tasks

As we explored in Chapter 4, Mr. Jay and his students did weekly Visual Pattern Tasks. He decided that he wanted to give students a better sense of what he was looking for in their participation in these tasks, to give some strategic feedback. He also wanted to make sure that student effort in these tasks was reflected in student grades. He created a simple rubric:

Level	Student actions on Visual Pattern Task
1	Student redraws the pattern
2	Student continues the pattern to the next few terms
3	Student finds the number of squares in Term 43
4	Student writes an expression to solve for any term

This rubric was useful in focusing students on the next step in their problem-solving process, as well as in helping them understand what the next step in their own development was. In my observation of the visual task, which I describe in Chapter 4, every student in the inclusive class met the expectation of Level 4 for that visual pattern (although many skipped Level 3). My observation came late in the school year, and clearly, the students had been given feedback and had taken it up. Their strategic development was supported by this rubric.

Rethinking Tests and Quizzes

In the second year I was observing in his classroom, Mr. Jay made a dramatic change in how he did tests and quizzes in his class. He moved from tests and quizzes that assess individual knowledge to collaborative tests and quizzes. He typically put students into random groups of three. The students worked together on the assessment, with each student writing down answers on their own sheet of paper. They are graded based on the answers on their own paper, yet the students are encouraged to talk and discuss as much as they like. In addition, students can always retake any part of a test or quiz.

In collaboration with the resource room teacher, Mr. Jay also let students with IEPs choose to take the unit tests in the resource room. The students, particularly at the beginning of their first year in his class in seventh grade, chose this option. This approach worked for them, Mr. Jay believed, because it boosted their confidence as they began to engage in the high academic expectations of seventh-grade math, with the shift toward a more abstract mathematics of algebra. Most students decided during the year to take the quizzes in class with the rest of the students. In interviews, one of the students with an IEP told us that she didn't feel she needed to go to the resource room after the first few tests. Her decision was based on the group format of the assessments; this made her feel comfortable enough that she could get help if necessary. I love how empowered this student felt to make decisions about her own testing accommodations.

Mr. Jay's work aligns closely with mastery-based grading, particularly how students can retake tests and quizzes until they demonstrate mastery of the concept (Townsley & Schmid, 2020). For Mr. Jay, I think his redesign is most closely connected to how assessment feels. He constantly connected his practices of assessment to not only what kind of data it collects but also to how it might make his students feel.

STUDENT AND TEACHER RESPONSE

Both Mr. Jay and his students were pleased with this shift in assessment. Mr. Jay believes that it shifted assessments from "gotcha" moments into situations in which students really learn. He told me,

> I think at this level, a math test should be a learning opportunity rather than something that will bring a kid down. I mean, a kid will feel like, oh now I'm an F, you know. So I feel like if I can make it a learning opportunity, I let kids take group tests.

In a focus group of his seventh-grade students, I asked what they thought of group tests and quizzes. They told me it was better than taking tests alone, because you

- "Feel more confident in a group."
- Feel "secure."
- "Sometimes I forget, they remind me, it is like backup."
- "If you don't know something the people around you might know it, better together."
- "Your group has to agree on it."

So do Mr. Jay's assessment practices answer my Assessment Accessibility Check questions?

- Is the assessment practice helping teachers understand and teach complex learners?
- Is the assessment practice helping students understand themselves as math learners?

I would argue yes. He is learning about his students through observation, student work, and student strategies. He also learns about what they are capable of in small groups. The students can learn more about themselves through these assessment practices, in their strategy notebooks, the rubrics on the visual tasks, and the group tests/quizzes. One final way in which students develop self-understanding is the retake option. When students can look over their assessments and make their own decisions about what they want to try again on, they are learning about what they know and about what they need to continue to work on.

EXPANDING ASSESSMENT THROUGH CHOICE

As I reflect on Mr. Jay's transformation from a traditional grading system to one in which students can give and receive help on most items, I want to also consider additional assessment practices that support neurodiverse students. In their book *Choosing to See* (2021), Pam Seda and Kyndall Brown connected mathematics teaching practices to racial equity and culturally relevant teaching. In their chapter on Releasing Control, they discussed using quizzes that give the student autonomy through choice. Here is their example of an elementary choice "Totally Ten" quiz, where students pick options for their assessment.

Elementary Totally Ten Quiz

Directions: You may choose problems from any category to total a score of 10. You may pick only two problems from the Score 2 section. For example, you may choose two Score 2 problems and one Score 6 problem. The choice is yours! For extra credit, you may earn a maximum score of 12. *Show all work* on a separate piece of paper.

Score 2 Evaluate: 25 + 32 Evaluate: 45 − 27 Evaluate: 17×26
Score 4 Create an addition problem that will result in the following answer: 833 Create a subtraction problem that will result in the following answer: 211 Create a multiplication problem that will result in the following answer: 544
Score 6 Create a division word problem that will result in the following answer: 13
Score 8 Create a problem for each operation (addition, subtraction, multiplication, and division) that will result in the following answer: 242

SOURCE. Adapted from Seda and Brown (2021, pp. 152–153).

> ## Think About It
>
> How might a Totally Ten quiz feel different from a traditional quiz for a student? Could that matter in their score? What would we learn from such a quiz?

This kind of assessment would allow students to make choices that would help us know what they actually know. I can think of students who would jump right to Score 8, the most challenging problem, because the creative aspect better suits them. Yet students who feel more comfortable with computation also have options in Score 2. This kind of assessment also develops student strategic competence. Whenever we ask students to make choices (about what strategy to use, which problems to do, or how to work in class), we are developing their self-understandings about themselves as math learners. They are learning through their choices. When we do not provide choices, we are deciding for them what works best for them—and we may be wrong!

REFLECTION QUESTIONS

1. Have you experienced assessment in math as a barrier as a student or a teacher? What kind of assessments?

2. Are there assessment practices in this chapter that you would want to try? Which one?

3. Chose one assessment you use in your work and ascertain how it does on the Assessment Accessibility Check:

   - Is the assessment practice helping teachers understand and teach complex learners?

   - Is the assessment practice helping students understand themselves as math learners?

UDL Math Connections

Engagement	Representation	Strategic action
One of Mr. Jay's issues with his previous assessment practices was how they made his students feel. As he tries new practices, he is constantly checking to see how students feel about the new assessment practices.	Multiple kinds of assessment allow Mr. Jay to see students from different points of view. Rachel learned that Jeremy demonstrated more knowledge of multiplication when assessment was multimodal.	Mr. Jay sees assessment as a barrier to students. He is seeking to redesign his classroom in both how he learns about his students and how he gives them feedback. Assessment is redesigned to develop students' strategic self-knowledge.

Unpacking a Core Idea: Algebraic Thinking II

For many learners, algebra is a series of steps that students follow without understanding the why. Algebra can be a very different experience if sufficient attention is paid to making sure students see connections between abstract equations and concrete representations.

Recognizing and describing repeated patterns is a core idea in algebra. Visual Pattern Tasks (https://www.visualpatterns.org/), as Mr. Jay uses in this chapter and in Chapter 4, are an excellent way to help students generalize abstract equations from concrete geometric patterns. Students are asked to generalize across each case to describe the growing pattern using symbolic language. Students then have a reason to use notation such as parenthesis, coefficients, and exponents—they need them to mathematically describe the patterns they are noticing.

Visual Pattern Tasks ask students to make conjectures about how the pattern is growing, predict the next cases, generalize how it is growing, and determine which equation describes it. This kind of thinking is critical for mathematics. One wonderful feature of visual patterns is that students come up with different ways to chunk the pattern, which leads to different equations. They can then discuss whether these equations are equivalent. Discussing how to write the same formula in different ways can strengthen student understanding of simplifying expressions, which otherwise can seem abstract. Students can even graph visual patterns to further strengthen their understanding across representations.

Learn More:

Van de Walle, J., Bay-Williams, J., Lovin, L., & Karp, K. (2017). *Teaching student-centered mathematics: Developmentally appropriate instruction for grades 6–8* (3rd ed.). Pearson.

CHAPTER 15

REIMAGINING MATH GOALS IN INDIVIDUALIZED EDUCATION PROGRAMS

IN THIS CHAPTER, WE WILL . . .

- Follow along as Suzanne, a special education teacher, redesigns her students' math Individualized Education Program (IEP) goals
- Investigate concerns about math IEP goals
- Explore MATHS goals (Measurable, Ambitious, Toward access, High-leverage, and Stakeholders included) as Rachel reimagines goals for a former student

IT ALL STARTED in a meeting with Suzanne Huerta (Figure 15.1), a fifth-grade special education teacher, and her math coach Jody Guarino, after a visit to her special education classroom. In the class visit, her students were exuberant and positive about the mathematics they were doing around fractions. Suzanne had started class with the following question:

What do you know about $\frac{3}{8}$ths?

Students then all shared something that they knew about $\frac{3}{8}$ths. Students were clearly developing relational understanding about fractions (see Figure 15.2). I loved how the task was challenging, yet so open that everyone had something to share.

Figure 15.1 • *Suzanne Huerta, special education teacher*

SOURCE: SUZANNE HUERTA

Figure 15.2 · *Suzanne's chart of student responses to "What do you know about $\frac{3}{8}$ths?" (names removed)*

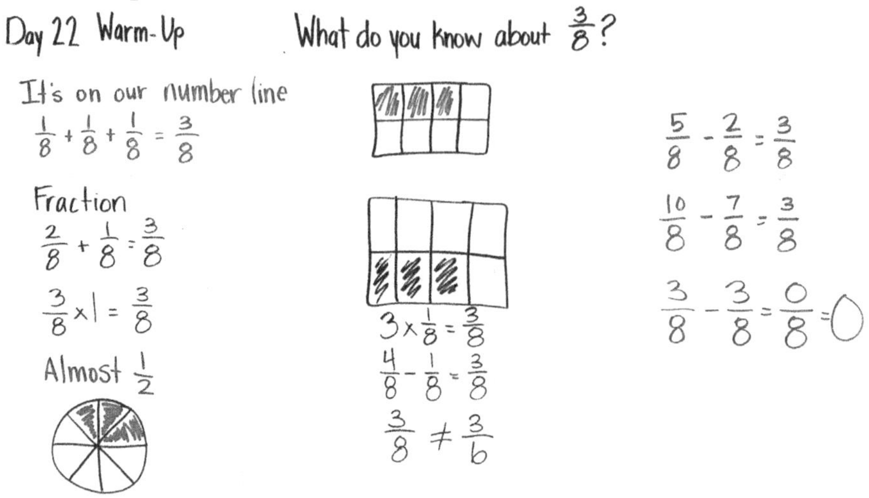

Day 22 Warm-Up   What do you know about $\frac{3}{8}$?

It's on our number line

$\frac{1}{8} + \frac{1}{8} + \frac{1}{8} = \frac{3}{8}$

Fraction

$\frac{2}{8} + \frac{1}{8} = \frac{3}{8}$

$\frac{3}{8} \times 1 = \frac{3}{8}$

Almost $\frac{1}{2}$

$\frac{5}{8} - \frac{2}{8} = \frac{3}{8}$

$\frac{10}{8} - \frac{7}{8} = \frac{3}{8}$

$\frac{3}{8} - \frac{3}{8} = \frac{0}{8} = 0$

$3 \times \frac{1}{8} = \frac{3}{8}$

$\frac{4}{8} - \frac{1}{8} = \frac{3}{8}$

$\frac{3}{8} \neq \frac{3}{6}$

SOURCE: Reprinted with permission from Suzanne Huerta.

Think About It

What do these students know about fractions? Can you name at least five pieces of knowledge that they have about fractions?

She then posed the following story problem about making cakes, which she situated within an upcoming school event:

> Students want to bake 6 cakes. Each cake takes a $\frac{1}{3}$rd of a cup of sugar. How much sugar do they need?

Students were excited to share their thinking on this story problem (a Multiple Groups Fraction Problem). Their work showed strong understanding of fractions, including the relational thinking at the heart of fractional understanding.

As we debriefed, Suzanne wanted to shift the conversation toward a major problem she had not yet been able to solve: Math IEP goals, or the individualized yearly goals on her students' IEPs, legal documents that provide accountability for student growth. She shared how as her instruction had changed toward sense-making, her IEPs and related data collection became more and more disconnected from the real work of the class. Students now expressed displeasure at being pulled out of problem solving to do small-group work on math goals and/or collect data for those goals, often a worksheet.

For Suzanne, these IEP goals no longer reflected her goals as a math teacher. Her goals were for students to make sense of mathematical problems, for them to persevere through challenges, and to develop strategies that they could use to make sense of any problems. She wanted them to begin to know themselves as math learners, and to know how to problem solve. She wanted to design goals around the Standards of Mathematical Practice (SMP), particularly SMP 1: *Make sense of problems and persevere in solving them.*

As we ended the meeting, we decided to work together on revising the way she designed and collected data for her students' IEP goals in math. Suzanne picked three students who both (a) needed updated math IEP goals and (b) needed more support as they engaged in the kind of challenging grade-level fraction story problems Suzanne gave to her class. She wrote a general goal, which I include here with no specific details that might connect it to an individual student, even though her individualized goals may include slightly different kinds of problems and/or strategies.

> By [date], when given a story problem [whole numbers or a fraction], student will demonstrate use of some of these three strategies [restating the problem in their own words, creating a representation, and revising their strategy when needed] to make sense of a problem and persevere in solving the problem in $\frac{4}{5}$ trials as measured by teacher evaluation of student work/data collection.

Suzanne has always made sure her students understand their IEP goals, meeting regularly with them to discuss progress. Suzanne sat down with each of these students, first discussing what was going well for each student in math and what felt challenging. They also discussed each student's previous math goals. Suzanne presented the new goals to the students, who were all excited about focusing on the kind of story problems they did in class. Together, they made sure that each individual goal had strategies that the student wanted to work on during problem solving. Suzanne told them that she would be collecting data by looking at their work samples during class, as well as by taking notes in an observation document she had made (each with the specific strategic goals for each student; Table 15.1).

Table 15.1. · *Suzanne's IEP data collection tool*

Date	[Student] was able to restate "what the problem was about" in their own words when asked by a teacher.	[Student] attempted multiple strategies or methods to solve problem, evidenced by student work samples, and/or observations.	[Student] used representations, visuals, or diagrams in their solution, evidenced by student work samples.
Teacher notes			

During these conversations, one student even asked to create an additional math goal on a specific math content (skip counting by fives), which Suzanne was happy to add!

As Suzanne worked to put data collection for these goals into practice, she was pleasantly surprised at how "embedded" (her word) this data collection was in her everyday practice. Most days she did a story problem with the students (like the multiple groups problem with the cakes), and she always asked a few students to restate what the problem was about before students went off to work. She made sure to ask the students with this new IEP goal at least once a week to do so, and she kept track of their growth in restating the problem.

When I asked her how it was going, she told me, "It is helping the students, because they are explaining their thinking so much more." This was both because she was asking more questions and paying more attention to *how* they solved the problems, but also because students knew it was their IEP goal and thus believed that it was important. She also said:

> I feel like, for once, I am enjoying working on a goal. Usually in the past I would hand a worksheet to them, give it to me when you are done, then I would find the percentage they got correct. But now I feel like I am developing relationships with my students, not just what they do or do not know, but *how* they know it.

With this shift, Suzanne is working on what really matters to both her and her students. The IEP work is aligned with her daily work as a teacher, and the students and teacher both agree on the importance of this goal. ●

IEP MATH GOALS

Every student who qualifies for special education in the United States who needs academic support has an IEP. (Students who need accommodations and/or services but not specialized academic instruction are given a 504 plan.) IEP goals are often made by the students' previous teachers, although we always have a chance to update annual goals during a school year. The goals Suzanne's students had originally were typical of IEP math goals across the country: focused on computation and procedures. Goals like the following:

> By (date), when given 25 multiplication double digit by single digit numbers, the student will multiply 1-digit numbers by 2-digit numbers using the standard algorithm with 80% accuracy in 4 out of 5 trials.

I hear all the time from educators about their issues with IEP math goals like this one. I hear that IEP goals are too narrowly defined on computation, algorithms, and memorization, often on below-grade-level skills. Because IEP goals are legally binding, we as educators are required to follow them. Since the reauthorization of the Individuals with Disabilities Education Act (IDEA) in 1990, IEP goals need to be standards based. The purpose is to make sure that the child with an IEP is given access to grade-level content, and that the goals for that child are ambitious. This requirement stems from far too many IEPs that repeated the same low-expectation goals year after year.

An IEP goal can make inclusion for students challenging or impossible, as some goals are so disconnected from classroom practice that students need to be taken out of class for instruction on their IEP goals. Another issue is that often students have little understanding of their own IEP goals. Some districts control IEP goal writing, giving teachers pull-down lists created by a company rather than individually created for each student. Yet despite these problems, IEP goals can be a road map to make sure special education students actually receive the specially designed instruction they are promised.

ADVOCATING FOR IEP GOALS

Paulo Tan is a former math teacher and a current Disability Studies in Education professor. He is also the parent of a child with a disability. I share here his reflection on a contentious IEP meeting for his son as they wrote a new IEP math goal, written in an article about transforming math IEP goals (Tan, 2017). In this article, he connected IEP goals to developing mathematical mindsets such as developing a positive relationship toward math. Noting that the vision for an IEP meeting is of collaboration between families and educators, he noted that

> the vision is often lost in the process of developing achievable short term and discrete goals. This disconnection is often caused by the hyper-focus on remediating skill deficits. [T]he lead special educator teacher felt it was important for one of the IEP mathematics goals to have my son, who was in 5th grade, correctly identify one-digit numbers in a field of two. As a math educator and a parent who had 11 years of experience and understanding of my son's general knowledge, I expressed to the teacher, that my son was way beyond identifying and recognizing numbers. . . . Nevertheless, the argument went back and forth for some time as they were unconvinced of my claims. The stalemate eased once I steered the team to our common vision and our previous conversations about powerful math mindsets. (Tan, 2017, p. 35)

If we can align math IEP goals with our visions of equitable mathematics, IEP goals can shift from being a barrier to being a tool for equity (Tan, 2017).

REVISING OUR UNDERSTANDING OF IEP GOALS

According to IDEA, the main purpose of IEP goals is to "meet the child's needs that result from the child's disability to enable the child to be involved in and make progress in the general education curriculum" (IDEA, Section 1414 [d][1][A][i][II]; cited in Yell et al., 2016). Thus, implementing standards-based goals is not simply using content standards to provide the language of IEP goals but a larger process of increasing access and participation for students with disabilities in the general education curriculum that follows these standards. Bateman and Linden (2006) suggested:

> Don't clutter IEPS with detailed goals and objectives for all the content standards in the general curriculum. Instead, focus on the accommodations and adjustments an individual child needs for appropriate access to participation in the general curriculum. Goals should be prioritized and deal with large, important areas. (Bateman & Linden, 2006, pp. 15–16)

This seems like great advice—choose goals based on how much they afford access to the general education curriculum. We understand, then, standards-based IEPs as both a document and a process that should work toward the student's access and participation in the general education curriculum.

> We understand, then, standards-based IEPs as
> both a document and a process that should work
> toward the student's access and participation
> in the general education curriculum.

Another way to make IEP goals more inclusive and yet standards based is to incorporate Universal Design for Learning (UDL) principles into their design so that students who communicate and learn in different modalities are better included. Caruana (2015) advocated moving away from language that limits the modalities in which students can access and respond to information. For example, she noted the following standard from the Common Core State Standards (CCSS): "Tell and write time in hours and half-hours using analog and digital clocks." She proposed that for an IEP goal, this standard should be shifted to the following: "Communicate the time in hours and half-hours using analog and digital clocks." This shift allows students who use augmentative and alternative communication (AAC) systems to meet the standards. Our goals should be as flexible and multimodal as our instruction.

PROPOSING MATHS GOALS

Integrating my experience as a teacher with this recent work on making IEP goals more accessible and more directed toward inclusive practice, I propose MATHS goals (see Table 15.2).

Table 15.2 · *MATHS Goals*

Measurable	This goal can be measured in a way that is valid and reliable, as well as manageable for the teacher collecting data.
Ambitious	This goal believes in the potential of this child to engage in meaningful mathematics and sense-making.
Toward access	Focusing on this goal will increase the child's access to and participation in the general education classroom/curriculum.
High-leverage focus	Focusing on this goal will pay off big for the child. Investment in this concept, skill, or practice will provide dividends in the future. There are two categories of these: 1) high-leverage content goals (the core ideas of mathematics) and 2) high-leverage mathematical practices goals (how students engage).
Stakeholder input	This goal has been developed in collaboration with the student, their family, and the general education teacher.

REVISING AN IEP GOAL WITH MATHS

As I was writing this chapter, I began thinking a lot about one of my students when I was a classroom teacher. Jose entered my class as a fifth grader. He was 10 years old, from a Puerto Rican family who had lived for several generations in the United States, and he had an IEP for a specific learning disability. Jose was shy, taking a long time to warm up to new people or situations. He loved animals and cared expertly for the menagerie in our classroom. Although able to decode text, he seemed to have trouble remembering and understanding what he read.

In mathematics, his previous classroom had focused exclusively on memorization of facts and procedures, which seemed to make him unsure about the problem solving in my class. Jose had memorized some procedures such as the algorithm for addition (which he could do successfully) and the algorithm for subtraction (which he mostly could not do). I wasn't sure what he understood about concepts in math, such as place value, as he was hesitant to talk about math with adults, even in a one-on-one situation. Jose seemed to have particular difficulty when I presented him with a word problem or rich task as he expected me to tell him what operation to use.

I knew that Jose had not had enough experience in making sense of problems for himself, and to me, this was the *most* important habit I could teach him. He also needed to learn the fifth-grade curriculum, which focused heavily on fractions and equivalence. I wasn't sure if he had significant difficulty understanding the concepts of fractions, or if he was not given any exposure in previous grades, but at that time, he had difficulty identifying equivalent fractions or drawing fractions.

Jose's math IEP goal when I received him as a student was simple and procedural:

> Given a set of numbers, Jose will solve two-digit subtraction problems with regrouping with 80% accuracy in $\frac{4}{5}$ trials.

This goal did not seem right. First, it was not important enough. Subtraction didn't seem like the most high-leverage use of Jose's time as a fifth grader, not when the curriculum of fifth grade is so focused on fractions, ratios, and equivalence. The goal was written about subtraction because that was an area of need found on Jose's assessment, not because subtraction was the *most* important thing for Jose to focus on. Of course, I wanted to teach Jose everything, but I knew I needed to focus, particularly on writing IEP goals. So I decided to make sure Jose knew how to use a calculator for subtraction, perhaps embed some subtraction work into the class, and move forward with the ambitious goal of fractional understanding.

Reimagining a Core Ideas MATHS IEP Goal

Based on my assessments, I found that Jose was not yet able to identify equivalent fractions, including for $\frac{1}{2}$. This seemed like a really important place mathematically to invest time as he started fifth grade as equivalence matters with fractions AND with algebra. It is a core idea; investing in his understanding of this concept should facilitate his progress in not only fifth-grade math but also with math in all subsequent grades. I wrote this goal as a first-draft annual goal:

> Given a fraction, Jose will generate two equivalent fractions and explain why the fractions are equivalent.

I like this goal. I think it is ambitious, supports access, and is high leverage. But is it measurable? Not yet. But before I tackled that, I first thought through how I would help Jose develop this understanding. What is the progression at work here? Well, probably we would engage in the following three steps:

1. Identify equivalent fractions (not produce them, but recognize them). Given that Jose is so shy, I think that beginning with equivalent fractions in multiple forms (number line, area models, set models, and numbers) and allowing him to choose without talking would be a good place to start. From this, I can learn about what representations make sense to him. I would start with benchmark fractions like $\frac{1}{2}$, $\frac{1}{4}$th, and $\frac{1}{3}$rd).

2. The next step would be generating equivalent fractions. I would like him, if I gave him $\frac{1}{2}$, to be able to generate two equivalent fractions by drawing, writing the fractions, or saying them. Again, I would focus on benchmark fractions.

3. The last step would be Jose explaining why the fractions are equivalent. This would be a stretch for Jose, not only for his understanding of fractions but also for his comfort with mathematical talk. But it is important to push him as long as it is truly an area to invest. In this case, I would be pushing Jose to talk about a complex area of mathematics (fractions are so complicated to talk about!). I really believed that this would be an important goal for him and have tons of benefits down the line.

So I can see how I would facilitate this, but how do I translate this sequence into IEP speak and make it specific and measurable? Here is my second draft, with annual objectives:

> Annual goal: Given a fraction with a denominator of 2, 3, 4, 5, 6, 8, 10, 20, or 100, Jose will generate two equivalent fractions by writing a fraction and/or drawing a model, and he will explain verbally or in writing why the fractions are equivalent in 3 consecutive trials.
>
> First objective: Given familiar sets of cards with multiple representations (number line, area models, set models, and as numbers) of fractions with denominators of 2, 3, 4, 5, 6, 8, or 10, Jose will be able to identify pairs of equivalent fractions with 90% accuracy.
>
> Second objective: Given 4 fractions with a denominator of 2, 3, 4, 5, 6, 8, 10, or 20, Jose will generate two equivalent fractions for each fraction verbally or in writing with 90% accuracy.

I chose to use percent accuracy for the two objectives because then you would not have to present the same task five times (to assess four out of five trials). I think that 90% accuracy would be sufficient as just one error would be more computational than a conceptual error. I would be convinced that Jose "had it" if he met that standard. But for the annual goal, I used trials because that is a complex task that has two different behaviors (generate and explain) so I wanted to be sure he did have the idea by assessing at more than one time.

Throughout the goals, I was careful to outline the specific conditions under which Jose would be assessed, including the denominators I would use, which gradually get more complex as the year progresses. By including 100 in the final goal, I would be setting Jose up for understanding percentages and decimals.

Is this a MATHS goal? It is now **Measurable**. It is **Ambitious** because it asks Jose to do the mathematics needed for his grade level and to explain it, but it is designed so that it gives him the support needed to read the goal. The goal is **Toward access** because fractions are so much of the focus in fifth grade that this goal (especially compared with subtraction) allows his focus to be on understanding what is happening in his class. Although some might argue that these standards are third grade, they are the third-grade standards that support maximum engagement in fifth grade. And lastly, it is **High leverage** because so is the topic of fractions. Equivalency matters tremendously throughout mathematics. A strong foundation in fractions could make a big difference for Jose. Since this is a retrospective exercise, I cannot include **Stakeholders**.

Reimagining an SMP MATHS IEP Goal

I still wanted to design another IEP goal for Jose, one that would support him to engage more in mathematical problem solving. As I mentioned, when I met Jose, he had trouble starting problem solving, waiting for me to tell him what operation to use (which I never did). He did not know yet that he could figure it out on his own. I have found this to be a HUGE problem for students with disabilities often because they have spent years being told what procedures to use. After being trained in that fashion, it is extra challenging for a student to engage in solving complex problems without a predetermined solution path.

So for the first few weeks of Jose's fifth-grade class, I had one math-related focus and one focus only. I would walk up to him as he worked in class and ask, "Can you tell me about what you are doing," and "Does it make sense to you, yes or no?" When I first asked him this second question, he looked at me as if I had two heads. He didn't really know what I meant—how is math supposed to make sense? Eventually he grew to understand that I expected him to make sense of the math. And he had to know, at the minimum, whether he understood it. And if he shook his head, I learned to ask, "What can you do?" I had also learned that for Jose, my explanations were not helpful. There was something about talking to the teacher about math that was super-stressful to him. Through discussions about what he could do when he was stuck, we got to a place in which he would (a) ask one of his friends or (b) draw a picture to figure out a problem. In sum, Jose had difficulty starting problems, making sense of them, and figuring out ways to persevere when challenged. And we were beginning to work out together what he could do when stuck.

So let's try to translate this into an IEP goal. The behavior I want is for Jose to (a) after reading a problem, try to make sense of that problem; (b) represent the problem; and (c) try different strategies when he got stuck until he found one that worked. This is trickier to assess than the content goal. I decided to use work samples and self-assessment rubrics to measure his progress.

I started thinking about involving the student in self-assessment rubrics for IEP goals through conversations with Dustin Townsend, a special education teacher in Iowa who has been experimenting with collaborative rubrics to assess the SMPs for students with disabilities in secondary special education. Table 15.3 shows a self-assessment rubric I designed for Jose based on the strategies that worked for him.

Table 15.3 · *Student Self-Evaluation Rubric*

Yes/No for each day.	Mon	Tue	Wed	Thur	Fri
Today I **read the problem multiple times** until it made sense to me.					
Today I **restated the problem in my own words**.					
Today I **drew a picture** of the problem.					
Today I **asked friends for help** so that I could hear their strategies.					
What worked best for me today?					

The great thing about this strategy is that now Jose is more involved, and that means (*surprise!*) more learning! The SMPs are about developing the habits of mathematicians, and they involve metacognition.

I could also validate Jose's self-assessment by using student work samples to provide another data source (called "triangulation" in research). On the plus side, that is no extra work for me or Jose, and it does not mean that I need to pull him aside or in any way interrupt his day for assessment. For Jose, who is shy and needs time to do his work, this is a benefit.

I planned to check on his progress in meetings with Jose to look over the data. If he is not growing, then he probably needs more explicit support engaging in these strategies, such as more scaffolded support talking with his friends about math, or perhaps some questions to ask himself about the problems to get him thinking.

So let's try to translate this into IEP speak. The behavior I want is for Jose to

1. After reading a problem, try to make sense of that problem
2. Represent the problem
3. Try different strategies when he gets stuck until he finds one that works

To make it measurable, we need to make it very clear.

Annual goal:

> Given a story problem that is relevant to Jose's interests, Jose
> will demonstrate use of strategies to make sense of problems and
> persevere (including restating the problem in his own words, creating
> a representation, and revising his strategy when necessary) as
> measured by student self-assessment rubric and teacher evaluation of
> student work in four out of five consecutive opportunities.

Is this a MATHS goal? It is **Measurable**. The measurement seems right because I use two different sources of data. It is **Ambitious** because it asks Jose to grow in a core practice of mathematics (SMP 1). The goal is **Toward access** because engaging in problem solving is the core of his general education mathematics class. And lastly, this goal is **High leverage** because problem solving is just that. The more we engage in problem solving in math, the better we get at problem solving (which IS math!). And it certainly met the challenge that I had discussed at student-led conferences with Jose's family, helping him develop confidence in his problem solving skills **(Stakeholder Input)**.

CHALLENGING SYSTEMS

As I end this book, it seems fitting we end with IEP goals, an aspect of our work that is rarely done alone. I include Stakeholders because we can only make our goals better if families are involved. In some settings, even individual special education teachers have little control over the process of designing IEP goals. Many of my readers are general education math teachers, who may feel tangential to the goal writing process (despite the legal requirement that you be involved!). Some teachers feel the IEP goals are written by the legal department, not by teachers at all. The best IEP goals are deeply collaborative: between teachers with different expertise, between teachers and students, between families and schools.

While in this book I have focused on what is within your control as teachers in your classroom, many of these issues will require us to challenge and transform unjust systems. Just as in our classrooms, we can figure out what is narrow about the systems we work within. What is working for our users? What are the barriers for our families, students, and teachers? And how can we open up systems and practices to make them more accessible?

> While in this book I have focused on what
> is within your control as teachers in your
> classroom, many of these issues will require us
> to challenge and transform unjust systems.

We can rethink disability, rethink mathematics, but we will also have to rethink our schools and systems to make them truly inclusive for all.

REFLECTION QUESTIONS

1. What have been your experiences with IEP goals in math?

2. If you had a magic wand and could change one thing about your students' IEP goals in math, what would it be?

3. Could you make that change happen? Who would you need to work with to get it done?

UDL Math Connections

Engagement	Representation	Strategic action
An IEP goal on the SMPs focuses attention on engagement in meaningful problem solving. Working together, teachers and students can problem solve and increase student participation in problem solving and mathematical discussion.	Focusing IEP goals on Core Ideas creates more time and space to work on the most important ideas. Allowing for flexibility in how students show what they know in a goal allows for more access for a wider range of students.	The IEP goals shift toward developing students' self-knowledge about how they solve problems. Using self-assessment rubrics Involves students in understanding their own learning.

Unpacking a Core Idea: Fractional Equivalence and Ordering

Once students begin to understand how fractions work through fraction story problems, they will begin to develop understandings of fractional equivalence. Students generally start with the benchmark fractions; just as they generally learn $\frac{1}{2}$ first, they learn what is equivalent to $\frac{1}{2}$. Equivalence is a core idea as it underlies everything else they do with fractions, decimals, and percentages. As a classroom teacher, I had students create a page of equivalent fractions, decimals, and percentages in their math notebook, adding additional fractions as they learned about them. For some students, this page became an important resource to develop fluency with benchmark equivalencies.

Students will develop their own strategies for finding equivalent fractions, particularly thinking about the ratio between the numbers. So to find an equivalent fraction for $\frac{1}{2}$, students might start by doubling the numerator and the denominator to $\frac{2}{4}$s, then again to $\frac{4}{8}$ths, and so on. If they need to simplify, the same knowledge that the ratio stays the same is helpful. Some of my students used a ratio table to keep track of what they were doing.

$$\frac{1 \mid 2 \mid 4 \mid 8}{2 \mid 4 \mid 8 \mid 10}$$

$$\text{So } \frac{1}{2} = \frac{8}{10}$$

Comparing and ordering fractions is a closely related skill, also using students' developing relational understanding of fractions. An important model for this is a number line. Students can play games or do activities in which they puzzle out which fractions are more or less than others and place them on a number line (or a clothesline!). Important strategies students develop are

- Recognizing fractions that are equal to 1
- Recognizing fractions that are greater than 1
- Comparing just the size of the pieces (denominators)

- ► Comparing just the number of pieces you have (numerators)
- ► Relational thinking about both the size of the pieces and the number of pieces you have
- ► Thinking about equivalent fractions to compare

How would students order this set of cards? Which of the above strategies might they use?

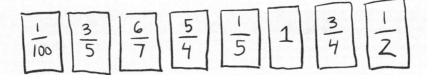

APPENDIX A: CORE IDEAS IN K–8 MATHEMATICS ALIGNED WITH TEACHING PRACTICES

Core idea (page number)	Teaching Practices
Counting (p. 126)	1:1 Interview (Ch. 3, pp. 48–49)
	Counting Collections (Ch. 7, pp. 116–123)
Number Sense/Place Value (p. 119)	Counting Collections (Ch. 7, pp. 116–123)
	Choral Counting (Ch. 7, pp. 115–116)
	CGI Story Problems (using multiples of ten, particularly Measurement Division with tens) (Ch. 8, pp. 127–136, 174–175)
Early Addition and Subtraction (p. 138)	CGI Story Problems (all addition and subtraction problem types) (Ch. 8, pp. 127–136, 138–139)
Addition and Subtraction Fact Fluency (p. 155)	Rekenrek Number Strings (Ch. 9, pp. 141–143, 152)
	Math Games (Ch. 10, pp. 170–172)
Multidigit Addition and Subtraction (p. 156)	CGI Story Problems (using multidigit numbers) (Ch. 8, pp. 127–136, 138–139)
	Unit: Measuring for the Art Show (Fosnot, 2020) (Ch. 9, pp. 143–152)
	Number Strings (Ch. 9, pp. 146–149)
Early Multiplication and Division (p. 174)	Tower Tasks (Ch. 10, pp. 159–170)
	CGI Story Problems for Multiplication and Division (Ch. 10, pp. 174–175)
Multiplication Fact Fluency (p. 176)	Math Games (Ch. 10, pp. 170–172)
	Number Strings (Ch. 11, pp. 177–186)
Multidigit Multiplication and Division (p. 190)	CGI Story Problems for Multiplication and Division (using multidigit numbers) (Ch. 10, pp. 174–175)
	Number Strings (Ch. 11, pp. 177–186)

Fractional Equivalence and Ordering (p. 256)	Which One Doesn't Belong Fraction Talk (Ch. 1, pp. 4–5, 256–257)
	What Do You Know About [fraction] (Ch. 15, pp. 241–242, 256–257)
	Comparing Fractions (Ch. 15, pp. 256–257)
	CGI Story Problems on Equal Sharing and Multiple Groups (Ch. 12, pp. 196–200, 210–211)
	Percentage Number String (Ch. 11, pp. 186–188)
Operations With Fractions (p. 210)	CGI Story Problems on Equal Sharing and Multiple Groups (Ch. 1, pp. 2–12; Ch. 12, pp. 196–200, 210–211)
Algebraic Thinking (p. 224, p. 240)	Double Number Lines (Fosnot & Jacob, 2007)(Ch. 11, pp. 186–188; Ch. 13, pp. 213–219, 224)
	Visual Pattern Tasks (Ch. 4, pp. 52–59; Ch. 15, pp. 235, 240)
	Open Middle Task (Ch. 6, pp. 94–96)

APPENDIX B: BARRIERS AND SUPPORTS IN MATH CLASS FROM A NEURODIVERSE PERSPECTIVE

Read the narratives below written by people with learning disabilities (such as dyslexia or dyscalculia). Think about the following questions:

- ▶ What supports learning in math for this student?
- ▶ What are the barriers to learning math for this student?

	Narrative	What supports learning in math for this student?	What are the barriers to learning math for this student?
1	Math is "hard" because of how boring and time-consuming it is. Homework usually consists of doing the same problem forty times in a row! Then tomorrow, we will do forty more of the exact same problem, except with one extra digit of complexity thrown in. The pages march by, an endless procession of mind-numbing paperwork, a treadmill of uninteresting problems. . . . What I fail to understand is that the "harder" classes are where math becomes far more interesting. Instead of forty dull problems, they give you five interesting ones. Instead of pointless drills, you can begin to see how to use math as a tool. They finally give you a pile of two-by-fours and let you start nailing things together. (Memoir by Shamus Young, 2011, p. 119)		

	Narrative	What supports learning in math for this student?	What are the barriers to learning math for this student?
2	Learning . . . just learning real quick. It takes me time. I could tell you that it takes me a while to learn, especially in Math. It's my worst subject. It could take me weeks to learn one single thing. There's a lot of subjects I can learn, then I forget it, real quick, do it again, learn again. To me, it's just learning it at that moment in an hour, and hour and a half, the class we have. It takes a couple of classes for me to get to know the subject. . . . It's really weird how I'm labeled with a learning disability, but when it comes to a subject, I click onto things that interest me coz I know, I know already, I know what's going on, I know what happened. It just clicks and I'm like one of the main students raising their hands and discussing it with the teachers. (Interview with Santiago, in Connor, 2007, pp. 205, 209).		
3	Soon after entering fourth grade the truth became apparent. While I could recite the numbers and the multiplication tables that I had memorized, they were only symbols with numerical names that didn't mean anything to me. I didn't understand the concepts behind them. Faced with the daily onslaught of progressively more difficult mathematical concepts, I could no longer deny there was a problem. I started to shut down completely. I found myself unable to cope, and for the first time I became clearly aware of the fact that I didn't get things my classmates did. I began to feel less and less comfortable at school. I felt anxious that someone would find out I couldn't understand everything. I always felt the most vulnerable during the math portion of the day. (Memoir by Samantha Abeel, 2005, p. 22)		

(Continued)

(*Continued*)

	Narrative	What supports learning in math for this student?	What are the barriers to learning math for this student?
4	If the teacher came into the classroom snarling and spouting facts in rote fashion, with no explanation of the core meanings, my disabilities flared and I failed. But in subjects such as physics, biology, and algebra, taught using multisensory methods by kind, enthusiastic teachers, I had nearly perfect grades. (Memoir with Dr. Abraham Schmitt, 1994, p. 118)		
5	I first noticed there was something different about my brain in primary school. Dyscalculia was not a recognised condition at the time, certainly not at any of the schools I attended. As soon as I was expected to detach visual aids from maths, it became a problem for me. I could understand maths when I could see the things to count, even my fingers. Removing this, broke my fragile relationship with maths. No one understood why I could not grasp these supposedly simple concepts. My memory of this time was there were a lot of teachers who just didn't understand why I could excel in certain subjects and fail stunningly in anything related to maths. (Blog by LozMac, 2018)		
6	By eighth grade, I had learned the correct math procedures but still needed extra time. In that class we were doing "rapid math," which provoked terrible anxiety in me and which I would do almost anything to avoid. The task in this exercise was to complete an entire page of calculations in five minutes. I would sneak the book home the night before, answer all the questions, and then write the answers in my book lightly in pencil; in class the next day, all I had to do was copy over my answers. This was the only way I could complete the exercise in the allotted time. Though I had done the work (at home), I felt like a fraud. (Memoir by Barbara Arrowsmith-Young, 2013, p. 21)		

	Narrative	What supports learning in math for this student?	What are the barriers to learning math for this student?
7	Among the advantages [of LD] was a better understanding at a young age of my limitations and weaknesses. Though this might not sound like much of an advantage, one must remember that every person has their own weaknesses and limitations. I was able to realize, for example, that to get through math, I should draw out the problems. This system let me visualize what I was trying to do. (Garret Day, in Rodis et al., 2001, p. 99)		

Memoirs written by and with people with learning disabilities/dyslexia/dyscalculia:

Abeel, S. (2005). *My thirteenth winter: A memoir*. Scholastic.

Arrowsmith-Young, B. (2013). *The woman who changed her brain: How I left my learning disability behind and other stories of cognitive transformation* (Reprint ed.). Simon & Schuster.

Schmitt, A., (1994). *Brilliant idiot: An autobiography of a dyslexic*. Good Books.

Young, S. (2011). *How I learned*. CreateSpace Independent Publishing Platform.

Collections of narratives written by individuals with learning disabilities:

Connor, D. J. (2007). *Urban narratives: Portraits in progress; life at the intersections of learning disability, race, and social class*. Peter Lang.

Rodis, P., Garrod, A., & Boscardin, M. L. (2001). *Learning disabilities and life stories*. Allyn and Bacon.

Blog posts:

LozMac (2018, January 8). *Smart thick kid—Living with dyscalculia*. OxGadgets. https://www.oxgadgets.com/2018/01/living-with-dyscalculia.html

REFERENCES

Abeel, S. (2005). *My thirteenth winter: A memoir*. Scholastic.

Ahmed, I., & Chao, T. (2018). Assistive learning technologies for students with visual impairments: A critical rehumanizing review. *Investigations in Mathematics Learning*, *10*(3), 173–185. https://doi.org/10.1080/19477503.2018.1463005

Akhavan Tafti, M., Hameedy, M. A., & Mohammadi Baghal, N. (2009). Dyslexia, a deficit or a difference: Comparing the creativity and memory skills of dyslexic and nondyslexic students in Iran. *Social Behavior and Personality*, *37*(8), 1009–1016. https://doi.org/10.2224/sbp.2009.37.8.1009

Alfieri, L., Brooks, P. J., Aldrich, N. J., & Tenenbaum, H. R. (2011). Does discovery-based instruction enhance learning? *Journal of Educational Psychology*, *103*(1), 1–18. https://doi.org/10.1037/a0021017

Amalric, M., Denghien, I., & Dehaene, S. (2018). On the role of visual experience in mathematical development: Evidence from blind mathematicians. *Developmental Cognitive Neuroscience*, *30*, 314–323. https://doi.org/10.1016/j.dcn.2017.09.007

Annamma, S. A., Ferri, B. A., & Connor, D. J. (2018). Disability critical race theory: Exploring the intersectional lineage, emergence, and potential futures of DisCrit in education. *Review of Research in Education*, *42*(1), 46–71. https://doi.org/10.3102/0091732X18759041

Arnoux, P., Furukado, M., Harriss, E., & Ito, S. (2011). Algebraic numbers, free group automorphisms and substitutions on the plane. *Transactions of the American Mathematical Society*, *363*(9), 4651–4699. https://doi.org/10.1090/S0002-9947-2011-05188-3

Arrowsmith-Young, B. (2013). *The woman who changed her brain: How I left my learning disability behind and other stories of cognitive transformation* (Reprint ed.). Simon & Schuster.

Artiles, A. J., Harry, B., Reschly, D. J., & Chinn, P. C. (2002). Over-identification of students of color in special education: A critical overview. *Multicultural Perspectives*, *4*(1), 3–10. https://doi.org/10.1207/S15327892MCP0401_2

Ashcraft, M. H., & Moore, A. M. (2009). Mathematics anxiety and the affective drop in performance. *Journal of Psychoeducational Assessment*, *27*(3), 197–205.

Attree, E. A., Turner, M. J., & Cowell, N. (2009). A virtual reality test identifies the visuospatial strengths of adolescents with dyslexia. *CyberPsychology & Behavior*, *12*(2), 163–168. https://doi.org/10.1089/cpb.2008.0204

Baroody, A. J. (2003). The development of adaptive expertise and flexibility: The integration of conceptual and procedural knowledge. In A. Baroody & A. Dowker (Eds.), *The development of arithmetic concepts and skills: Constructing adaptive expertise* (pp. 1–33). Routledge.

Baroody, A. J., Purpura, D. J., Eiland, M. D., & Reid, E. E. (2015). The impact of highly and minimally guided discovery instruction on promoting the learning of reasoning strategies for basic add-1 and doubles combinations. *Early Childhood Research Quarterly*, *30*, 93–105. https://doi.org/10.1016/j.ecresq.2014.09.003

Bateman, B. D., & Linden, M. A. (2006). *Better IEPs: How to develop legally correct and educationally useful programs* (J. Donovan & T. Kinney, Eds.; 5th ed.). IEP Resources, Attainment Company.

Battey, D., Neal, R. A., Leyva, L., & Adams-Wiggins, K. (2016). The interconnectedness of relational and content dimensions of quality instruction: Supportive teacher–student relationships in urban elementary mathematics classrooms. *The Journal of Mathematical Behavior*, *42*, 1–19.

Bauman, H. D. L., & Murray, J. J. (2014). *Deaf Gain: Raising the stakes for human diversity*. University of Minnesota Press.

Bay-Williams, J., & Kling, G. (2019). *Math fact fluency: 60+ games and assessment tools to support learning and retention*. ASCD.

Bellos, A., & Harriss, E. (2015). *Patterns of the universe: A coloring adventure in math and beauty* (Illustrated ed.). The Experiment.

Berry, R. Q. III. (2008). Access to upper-level mathematics: The stories of successful African American middle school boys. *Journal for Research in Mathematics Education*, *39*(5), 464–488.

Bibby, T. (2002). Shame: An emotional response to doing mathematics as an adult and a teacher. *British Educational Research Journal*, *28*(5), 705–721. https://doi.org/10.1080/0141192022000015543

Boaler, J., & Greeno, J. G. (2000). Identity, agency, and knowing in mathematics worlds. In J. Boaler (Ed.), *Multiple perspectives on mathematics teaching and learning* (pp. 171–200). Ablex.

Boaler, J., & Sengupta-Irving, T. (2016). The many colors of algebra: The impact of equity focused teaching upon student learning and engagement. *The Journal of Mathematical Behavior*, *41*, 179–190. https://doi.org/10.1016/j.jmathb.2015.10.007

Bottge, B. A. (1999). Effects of contextualized math instruction on problem solving of average and below-average achieving students. *Journal of Special Education*, *33*(2), 81–92.

Bottge, B. A., Heinrichs, M., Mehta, Z. D., & Ya-Hui Hung. (2002). Weighing the benefits of anchored math instruction for students with disabilities in general education classes. *Journal of Special Education*, *35*(4), 186–200.

Bottge, B. A., Ma, X., Gassaway, L., Toland, M. D., Butler, M., & Cho, S. J. (2014). Effects of blended instructional models on math performance. *Exceptional Children*, *80*(4), 423–437. https://doi.org/10.1177/0014402914527240

Bottge, B. A., Rueda, E., Serlin, R. C., Hung, Y.-H., & Kwon, J. M. (2007). Shrinking achievement differences with anchored math problems: Challenges and possibilities. *Journal of Special Education*, *41*(1), 31–49.

Bottge, B. A., Stephens, A. C., Rueda, E., LaRoque, P. T., & Grant, T. S. (2010). Anchoring problem-solving and computation instruction in context-rich learning environments. *Exceptional Children*, *76*(4), 417–437.

Bushart, B. (n.d.). *Numberless word problems*. https://numberlesswp.com/

Butterworth, B. (2010). Foundational numerical capacities and the origins of dyscalculia. *Trends in Cognitive Sciences*, *14*, 534–541.

Cameron, A., & Fosnot, C. T. (2008). *Muffles' truffles: Multiplication and division with the array* (Illustrated ed.). FirstHand.

Canobi, K. H. (2009). Concept-procedure interactions in children's addition and subtraction. *Journal of Experimental Child Psychology, 102*,131–149. https://doi.org/10.1016/j.jecp.2008.07.008

Cantor, P., Osher, D., Berg, J., Steyer, L., & Rose, T. (2019). Malleability, plasticity, and individuality: How children learn and develop in context1. *Applied Developmental Science, 23*(4), 307–337. https://doi.org/10.1080/10888691.2017.1398649

Carpenter, T. P., Fennema, E., Franke, M. L., Levi, L., & Empson, S. B. (2015). *Children's mathematics: Cognitively guided instruction* (2nd ed.). Heinemann.

Carpenter, T. P., Franke, M. L., & Levi, L. (2003). *Thinking mathematically: Integrating arithmetic and algebra in elementary school.* Heinemann.

Caruana, V. (2015). Accessing the common core standards for students with learning disabilities: Strategies for writing standards-based IEP goals. *Preventing School Failure: Alternative Education for Children and Youth, 59*(4), 237–243. https://doi.org/10.1080/1045988X.2014.924088

Codina, C. J., Pascalis, O., Baseler, H. A., Levine, A. T., & Buckley, D. (2017). Peripheral visual reaction time is faster in deaf adults and British sign language interpreters than in hearing adults. *Frontiers in Psychology, 8*. https://www.frontiersin.org/articles/10.3389/fpsyg.2017.00050

Connor, D. J. (2007). *Urban narratives: Portraits in progress; life at the intersections of learning disability, race, and social class.* Peter Lang.

Cortiella, C., & Horowitz, S. H. (2014). *The state of learning disabilities: Facts, trends and emerging issues.* National Center for Learning Disabilities. http://www.hopkintonsepac.org/wp-content/uploads/2015/12/2014-State-of-LD.pdf

Craig, M., Dewar, M., Turner, G., Collier, T., & Kapur, N. (2022). Evidence for superior encoding of detailed visual memories in deaf signers. *Scientific Reports, 12*(1), Article 1. https://doi.org/10.1038/s41598-022-13000-y

De Clercq-Quaegebeur, M., Casalis, S., Vilette, B., Lemaitre, M. P., & Vallée, L. (2018). Arithmetic abilities in children with developmental dyslexia: Performance on French ZAREKI-R Test. *Journal of Learning Disabilities, 51*(3), 236–249. https://doi.org/10.1177/0022219417690355

Demirkaya, P. N., & Bakkaloglu, H. (2015). Examining the student-teacher relationships of children both with and without special needs in preschool classrooms. *Educational Sciences: Theory & Practice, 15*(1), Article 1. https://doi.org/10.12738/estp.2015.1.2590

Demir-Lira, Ö. E., Suárez-Pellicioni, M., Binzak, J. V., & Booth, J. R. (2019). Attitudes toward math are differentially related to the neural basis of multiplication depending on math skill. *Learning Disability Quarterly, 43*(3), 179–191. https://doi.org/10.1177/0731948719846608

Desoete, A., & De Craene, B. (2019). Metacognition and mathematics education: An overview. *ZDM, 51*(4), 565–575. https://doi.org/10.1007/s11858-019-01060-w

Devine, A., Hill, F., Carey, E., & Szűcs, D. (2018). Cognitive and emotional math problems largely dissociate: Prevalence of developmental dyscalculia and mathematics anxiety. *Journal of Educational Psychology, 110*(3), 431–444. https://doi.org/10.1037/edu0000222

Doabler, C. T., & Fien, H. (2013). Explicit mathematics instruction what teachers can do for teaching students with mathematics difficulties. *Intervention in School and Clinic, 48*(5), 276–285. https://doi.org/10.1177/1053451212473151

Dolmage, J. (2015). Universal design: Places to start. *Disability Studies Quarterly, 35*(2), Article 2. https://doi.org/10.18061/dsq.v35i2.4632

Dowker, A. (2019). *Individual differences in arithmetical abilities*. Psychology Press.

Dunn, C., Rabren, K. S., Taylor, S. L., & Dotson, C. K. (2012). Assisting students with high-incidence disabilities to pursue careers in science, technology, engineering, and mathematics. *Intervention in School and Clinic, 48*(1), 47–54. https://doi.org/10.1177/1053451212443151

Durkin, K., Star, J. R., & Rittle-Johnson, B. (2017). Using comparison of multiple strategies in the mathematics classroom: Lessons learned and next steps. *ZDM, 49*(4), 585–597. https://doi.org/10.1007/s11858-017-0853-9

Eide, B., & Eide, F. (2012). *The dyslexic advantage: Unlocking the hidden potential of the dyslexic brain* (Reprint ed.). Plume.

Empson, S. B., & Levi, L. (2011). *Extending children's mathematics: Fractions & decimals: Innovations in cognitively guided instruction*. Heinemann.

Erenberg, S. R. (1995). An investigation of heuristic strategies used by students with and without learning disabilities. *Learning Disabilities: A Multi-Disciplinary Journal, 6*(1), 9–12.

Everatt, J., Steffert, B., & Smythe, I. (1999). An eye for the unusual: Creative thinking in dyslexics. *Dyslexia, 5*(1), 28–46. https://doi.org/10.1002/(SICI)1099-0909(199903)5:1<28::aid-dys126>3.0.CO;2-K

Faulkner, V. N., Crossland, C. L., & Stiff, L. V. (2013). Predicting eighth-grade algebra students with individualized education programs. *Exceptional Children, 79*, 329–345.

Fletcher, G., & Zager, T. (2021). *Building fact fluency: A toolkit for multiplication & division facilitator's guide*. Stenhouse.

Flores, M. M., & Milton, J. H. (2020). Teaching the partial products algorithm using the concrete-representational-abstract sequence. *Exceptionality, 28*(2), 142–160. https://doi.org/10.1080/09362835.2020.1772070

Foote, M. Q., & Lambert, R. (2011). I have a solution to share: Learning through equitable participation in a mathematics classroom. *Canadian Journal of Science, Mathematics and Technology Education, 11*(3), 247–260. https://doi.org/10.1080/14926156.2011.595882

Fosnot, C. T. (2007). *Measuring for the art show: Addition on the open number line*. Heinemann.

Fosnot, C. T. (2010). The landscape of learning: A framework for intervention. In C. T. Fosnot (Ed.), *Models of intervention in mathematics: Reweaving the tapestry*. National Council of Teachers of Mathematics.

Fosnot, C. T., with various contributors (2020). *Contexts for learning mathematics*. New Perspectives on Learning Series. Heinemann.

Fosnot, C. T., & Dolk, M. (2001). *Young mathematicians at work: Constructing number sense, addition, and subtraction*. Heinemann.

Fosnot, C. T., & Jacob, B. (2010). *Young mathematicians at work: Constructing algebra*. Heinemann.

Fosnot, C. T., & Uittenbogaard, W. (2007). *Minilessons for extending multiplication and division.* Heinemann.

Franke, M. L., Kazemi, E., & Turrou, A. C. (2018). *Choral counting & counting collections: Transforming the preK-5 math classroom.* Stenhouse.

Freitag, E. (2021, May 18). What do teachers really need to do to support unfinished learning in math? *Medium.* https://ebfreitag.medium.com/what-do-teachers-really-need-to-do-to-support-unfinished-learning-in-math-2f5013994a9f

Freudenthal, H. (1991). *Revisiting mathematics education: China lectures.* Springer.

Geary, D. C. (2004). Mathematics and learning disabilities. *Journal of Learning Disabilities, 37,* 4–15.

Geary, D. C., Hoard, M. K., Nugent, L., & Byrd-Craven, J. (2008). Development of number line representations in children with mathematical learning disability. *Developmental Neuropsychology, 33*(3), 277.

Gottfried, A. E., Marcoulides, G. A., Gottfried, A. W., Oliver, P. H., & Guerin, D. W. (2007). Multivariate latent change modeling of developmental decline in academic intrinsic math motivation and achievement: Childhood through adolescence. *International Journal of Behavioral Development, 31*(4), 317–327. https://doi.org/10.1177/0165025407077752

Gutierrez, R. (2002). Enabling the practice of mathematics teachers in context: Toward a new equity research agenda. *Mathematical Thinking and Learning, 4*(2–3), 145–187.

Hamraie, A. (2017). *Building access.* University of Minnesota Press. https://doi.org/10.5749/j.ctt1pwt79d.7

Hatano, G., & Inagaki, K. (1986). Two courses of expertise. In H. Stevenson, H. Azuma, & K. Hakuta (Eds.), *Child development and education in Japan* (pp. 262–272). W. H. Freeman/Times Books/Henry Holt.

Hemmings, B., Grootenboer, P., & Kay, R. (2011). Predicting mathematics achievement: The influence of prior achievement and attitudes. *International Journal of Science and Mathematics Education, 9*(3), 691–705. https://doi.org/10.1007/s10763-010-9224-5

Hickendorff, M., Torbeyns, J., & Verschaffel, L. (2019). Multi-digit addition, subtraction, multiplication, and division strategies. In A. Fritz, V. G. Haase, & P. Räsänen (Eds.), *International handbook of mathematical learning difficulties: From the laboratory to the classroom* (pp. 543–560). Springer International. https://doi.org/10.1007/978-3-319-97148-3_32

Horn, I. S. (2008). Turnaround students in high school mathematics: Constructing identities of competence through mathematical worlds. *Mathematical Thinking and Learning, 10*(3), 201–239.

Hughes, C. A., Morris, J. R., Therrien, W. J., & Benson, S. K. (2017). Explicit instruction: Historical and contemporary contexts. *Learning Disabilities Research & Practice, 32*(3), 140–148. https://doi.org/10.1111/ldrp.12142

Hunt, J., & Ainslie, J. (2021). *Designing effective math interventions* (1st ed.). Routledge.

Hunt, J., & Empson, S. (2014). Exploratory study of informal strategies for equal sharing problems of students with learning disabilities. *Learning Disability Quarterly, 38*(4), 208–220. http://ldq.sagepub.com/content/38/4/208.short

Hunt, J. H., Silva, J., & Lambert, R. (2019). Empowering students with specific learning disabilities: Jim's concept of unit fraction. *The Journal of Mathematical Behavior*, *56*, 100738. https://doi.org/10.1016/j.jmathb.2019.100738

Hunt, J. H., Tzur, R., & Westenskow, A. (2016). Evolution of unit fraction conceptions in two fifth-graders with a learning disability: An exploratory study. *Mathematical Thinking and Learning*, *18*(3), 182–208.

Hurst, C., & Huntley, R. (2018). Algorithms · · · Alcatraz: Are children prisoners of process? *International Journal for Mathematics Teaching and Learning*, *19*(1), 47–68.

IDEO. (2012). *Design thinking for educators* (2nd ed.).

Imm, K., Lambert, R., Moy, E., Vitale, N., & Raman, S. (2024). Beyond the rhetoric of "re-imagining": Using design thinking to create with and for teachers. *Mathematics Teacher Educator 12*(2), 111–132.

Immordino-Yang, M. H., & Damasio, A. (2007). We feel, therefore we learn: The relevance of affective and social neuroscience to education. *Mind, Brain, and Education*, *1*(1), 3–10.

Indar, G. K. (2018). An equity-based evolution of universal design for learning: Participatory design for intentional inclusivity. *Proceedings of UDL-IRM International Summit 2018*. https://www.learningdesigned.org/sites/default/files/Done_INDAR.EDIT_.DH_.JEG%20copy.pdf

Ing, M., Webb, N. M., Franke, M. L., Turrou, A. C., Wong, J., Shin, N., & Fernandez, C. H. (2015). Student participation in elementary mathematics classrooms: The missing link between teacher practices and student achievement? *Educational Studies in Mathematics*, *90*, 341–356. https://doi.org/10.1007/s10649-015-9625-z

Jackson, A. (2002). The world of blind mathematicians. *Notices of the AMS*, *49*(10), 1246–1251.

Jackson, H. G., & Neel, R. S. (2006). Observing mathematics: Do students with EBD have access to standards-based mathematics instruction? *Education and Treatment of Children*, *29*(4), 1–22.

Johnson, N. C., Turrou, A. C., McMillan, B. G., Raygoza, M. C., & Franke, M. L. (2019). "Can you help me count these pennies?": Surfacing preschoolers' understandings of counting. *Mathematical Thinking and Learning*, *21*(4), 237–264. https://doi.org/10.1080/10986065.2019.1588206

Kelemanik, G., & Lucenta, A. (2022). *Teaching for thinking: Fostering mathematical teaching practices through reasoning routines*. Heinemann.

Kelemanik, G., Lucenta, A., & Creighton, S. J. (2016). *Routines for reasoning: Fostering the mathematical practices in all students*. Heinemann.

Krähenmann, H., Opitz, E. M., Schnepel, S., & Stöckli, M. (2019). Inclusive mathematics instruction: A conceptual framework and selected research results of a video study. In D. Kollosche, R. Marcone, M. Knigge, M. G. Penteado, & O. Skovsmose (Eds.), *Inclusive mathematics education: State-of-the-art research from Brazil and Germany* (pp. 179–196). Springer International. https://doi.org/10.1007/978-3-030-11518-0_13

Kubicek, E., & Quandt, L. C. (2021). A positive relationship between sign language comprehension and mental rotation abilities. *The Journal of Deaf Studies and Deaf Education*, *26*(1), 1–12. https://doi.org/10.1093/deafed/enaa030

Kurz, A., Elliott, S. N., Lemons, C. J., Zigmond, N., Kloo, A., & Kettler, R. J. (2014). Assessing opportunity-to-learn for students with disabilities in general and special education classes. *Assessment for Effective Intervention*, *40*(1), 24–39. https://doi.org/10.1177/1534508414522685

Lambert, R. (2015). Constructing and resisting disability in mathematics classrooms: A case study exploring the impact of different pedagogies. *Educational Studies in Mathematics*, *89*(1), 1–18. https://doi.org/10.1007/s10649-014-9587-6

Lambert, R. (2017). "When I am being rushed it slows down my brain": Constructing self-understandings as a mathematics learner. *International Journal of Inclusive Education*, *21*(5), 521–531. https://doi.org/10.1080/13603116.2016.1251978

Lambert, R. (2019). Political, relational, and complexly embodied; experiencing disability in the mathematics classroom. *ZDM*, *51*(2), 279–289. https://doi.org/10.1007/s11858-019-01031-1

Lambert, R. (2021). The magic is in the margins: UDL math. *Mathematics Teacher: Learning and Teaching PK-12*, *114*(9), 660–669. https://doi.org/10.5951/MTLT.2020.0282

Lambert, R., Greene, Q., & Lai, V. (2022). #DeleteDeficitThinking: Strategies to name and challenge deficit thinking in Universal Design for Learning. In R. D. Williams (Ed.), *Handbook of research on challenging deficit thinking for exceptional education improvement*. IGI Global.

Lambert, R., & Harriss, E. (2022). Insider accounts of dyslexia from research mathematicians. *Educational Studies in Mathematics*, *111*(1), 89–107. https://doi.org/10.1007/s10649-021-10140-2

Lambert, R., Imm, K., Schuck, R., Choi, S., & McNiff, A. (2021). "UDL is the what, design thinking is the how:" Designing for differentiation in mathematics. *Mathematics Teacher Education and Development*, *23*(3), 54–77.

Lambert, R., McNiff, A., Schuck, R., Imm, K., & Zimmerman, S. (2023). "UDL is a way of thinking"; theorizing UDL teacher knowledge, beliefs, and practices. *Frontiers in Education*, *8*. https://www.frontiersin.org/articles/10.3389/feduc.2023.1145293

Lambert, R., Nguyen, T., Mendoza, M., & McNiff, A. (2022). Addressing agency and achievement in a multiplication intervention. *Insights into Learning Disabilities*, *19*(1), 79–101. https://eric.ed.gov/?id=EJ1341312

Lambert, R., & Sugita, T. (2016). Increasing engagement of students with learning disabilities in mathematical problem-solving and discussion. *Support for Learning*, *31*(4), 347–366. https://doi.org/10.1111/1467-9604.12142

Lambert, R., Sugita, T., Yeh, C., Hunt, J. H., & Brophy, S. (2020). Documenting increased participation of a student with autism in the standards for mathematical practice. *Journal of Educational Psychology*, *112*(3), 494–513. https://doi.org/10.1037/edu0000425

Lambert, R., & Tan, P. (2020). Does disability matter in mathematics educational research? A critical comparison of research on students with and without disabilities. *Mathematics Education Research Journal*, *32*, 5–35. https://doi.org/10.1007/s13394-019-00299-6

Lamon, S. J. (2007). Rational numbers and proportional reasoning: Toward a theoretical framework for research. *Second Handbook of Research on Mathematics Teaching and Learning*, *2*, 629–668.

Lewis, K. E., & Lynn, D. M. (2018). Against the odds: Insights from a statistician with dyscalculia. *Education Sciences*, *8*(2), 63. https://doi.org/10.3390/educsci8020063

Liljedahl, P. (2020). *Building thinking classrooms in mathematics, grades K–12: 14 teaching practices for enhancing learning* (1st ed.). Corwin.

Linton, S. (1998). *Claiming disability: Knowledge and identity*. NYU Press.

Lockhart, P. (2009). *A mathematician's lament: How school cheats us out of our most fascinating and imaginative art form*. Bellevue Literary Press.

LozMac (2018, January 8). *Smart thick kid—Living with dyscalculia*. OxGadgets. https://www.oxgadgets.com/2018/01/living-with-dyscalculia.html

Lyon, G. R., Shaywitz, S. E., & Shaywitz, B. A. (2003). A definition of dyslexia. *Annals of Dyslexia, 53*(1), 1–14. https://doi.org/10.1007/s11881-003-0001-9

Marian, V., & Shook, A. (2012). The cognitive benefits of being bilingual. *Cerebrum: The Dana Forum on Brain Science*, 13.

McFarland, L., Williams, J., & Miciak, J. (2013). Ten years of research: A systematic review of three refereed LD journals. *Learning Disabilities Research & Practice, 28*(2), 60–69. https://doi.org/10.1111/ldrp.12007

Meyer, A., & Rose, D. H. (2005). The future is in the margins: The role of technology and disability in educational reform. In D. H. Rose, A. Meyer, & C. Hitchcock (Eds.), *The universally designed classroom: Accessible curriculum and digital technologies* (pp. 13–35). Harvard University Press.

Meyer, A., Rose, D. H., & Gordon, D. T. (2014). *Universal Design for Learning: Theory and practice*. CAST Professional Publishing. http://udltheorypractice.cast.org/

Moeller, K., Fischer, U., Link, T., Wasner, M., Huber, S., Cress, U., & Nuerk, H. C. (2012). Learning and development of embodied numerosity. *Cognitive Processing, 13*(Suppl 1), S271–S274. https://doi.org/10.1007/s10339-012-0457-9

Moschkovich, J. (1999). Supporting the participation of English language learners in mathematical discussions. *For the Learning of Mathematics, 19*(1), 11–19. https://doi.org/10.2307/40248284

Moschkovich, J. (2012). Mathematics, the common core, and language. *Teachers College Record, 96*(3), 418–431.

NAEP Office of Special Education Programs, Individuals with Disabilities Education Act (IDEA) (2023). database. https://data.ed.gov/dataset/idea-section-618-data-products

Naraian, S. (2017). *Teaching for inclusion: Eight principles for effective and equitable practice*. Teachers College Press.

Nasir, N. S., Snyder, C. R., Shah, N., & Ross, K. M. (2013). Racial storylines and implications for learning. Human Development, 55(5–6), 285–301.

National Academies of Sciences, Engineering, and Medicine. (2018). *How people learn II: Learners, contexts & cultures*. National Academy Press.

National Governors Association Center for Best Practices & Council of Chief State School Officers. (2010). *Common Core State Standards for Mathematics*.

National Mathematics Advisory Panel. (2008). *Foundations for success: The final report of the National Mathematics Advisory Panel*. U.S. Department of Education.

Oliver, M. (2009). The social model in context. In T. Titchkosky & R. Michalko (Eds.), *Rethinking normalcy: A disability studies reader* (pp. 19–30). Canadian Scholars' Press.

Osher, D., Cantor, P., Berg, J., Steyer, L., & Rose, T. (2020). Drivers of human development: How relationships and context shape learning and development 1. *Applied Developmental Science*, *24*(1), 6–36. https://doi.org/10.1080/10888691.2017.1398650

Peltenburg, M., Van Den Heuvel-Panhuizen, M., & Doig, B. (2009). Mathematical power of special-needs pupils: An ICT-based dynamic assessment format to reveal weak pupils' learning potential 1. *British Journal of Educational Technology, 40*(2), 273–284.

Peters, G., De Smedt, B., Torbeyns, J., Verschaffel, L., & Ghesquière, P. (2014). Subtraction by addition in children with mathematical learning disabilities. *Learning and Instruction, 30*, 1–8.

Purpura, D. J., Baroody, A. J., Eiland, M. D., & Reid, E. E. (2016). Fostering first graders' reasoning strategies with basic sums: The value of guided instruction. *The Elementary School Journal, 117*(1), 72–100. https://doi.org/10.1086/687809

Rittle-Johnson, B., Loehr, A. M., & Durkin, K. (2017). Promoting self-explanation to improve mathematics learning: A meta-analysis and instructional design principles. *ZDM, 49*(4), 599–611. https://doi.org/10.1007/s11858-017-0834-z

Rittle-Johnson, B., Schneider, M., & Star, J. R. (2015). Not a one-way street: Bidirectional relations between procedural and conceptual knowledge of mathematics. *Educational Psychology Review, 27*(4), 587–597. https://doi.org/10.1007/s10648-015-9302-x

Robertson, S. M., & Ne'eman, A. D. (2008). Autistic acceptance, the college campus, and technology: Growth of neurodiversity in society and academia. *Disability Studies Quarterly, 28*(4). http://dsq-sds.org/article/view/146/146

Rodis, P., Garrod, A., & Boscardin, M. L. (2001). *Learning disabilities and life stories*. Allyn and Bacon.

Rogowsky, B. A., Calhoun, B. M., & Tallal, P. (2015). Matching learning style to instructional method: Effects on comprehension. *Journal of Educational Psychology, 107*(1), 64–78. https://doi.org/10.1037/a0037478

Rose, T. (2017). *The end of average: Unlocking our potential by embracing what makes us different* (Reprint ed.). HarperOne.

Schmitt, A. (1994). *Brilliant idiot: An autobiography of a dyslexic*. Good Books.

Schneps. (2007). Visual learning and the brain: Implications for dyslexia—Schneps—2007—Mind, brain, and education. *Mind, Brain, and Education, 1*(3), 128–139. https://onlinelibrary-wiley-com.proxy.library.ucsb.edu:9443/doi/abs/10.1111/j.1751-228X.2007.00013.x

Schwartz, D. L., Tsang, J. M., & Blair, K. P. (2016). *The ABCs of how we learn: 26 scientifically proven approaches, how they work, and when to use them* (Illustrated ed.). W. W. Norton.

Seda, P., & Brown, K. (2021). *Choosing to see: A framework for equity in the math classroom*. Dave Burgess Consulting, Inc.

Sengupta-Irving, T., & Enyedy, N. (2015). Why engaging in mathematical practices may explain stronger outcomes in affect and engagement: Comparing student-driven with highly guided inquiry. *Journal of the Learning Sciences, 24*(4), 550–592. https://doi.org/10.1080/10508406.2014.928214

REFERENCES

Shalev, R. S. (2007). Prevalence of developmental dyscalculia. In D. B. Berch, & M. M. M. Mazzocco (Eds.), *Why is math so hard for some children? The nature and origins of mathematical learning difficulties and disabilities* (pp. 49–60). Paul, H. Brookes.

Siegler, R. S. (2007). Microgenetic analyses of learning. In *Handbook of Child Psychology*. American Cancer Society. https://doi.org/10.1002/9780470147658.chpsy0211

Silva, J. M. (2021). Through an equity lens: Teaching practices for children who are bilingual with learning disabilities during mathematics discussions. *Insights into Learning Disabilities*, *18*(2), 187–209.

Simmons, F. R., & Singleton, C. (2006). The mental and written arithmetic abilities of adults with dyslexia. *Dyslexia*, *12*(2), 96–114. https://doi.org/10.1002/dys.312

Sinha, T., & Kapur, M. (2021). When problem solving followed by instruction works: Evidence for productive failure. *Review of Educational Research*, *91*(5), 761–798. https://doi.org/10.3102/00346543211019105

Skiba, R. J., Horner, R. H., Chung, C. G., Karega Rausch, M., May, S. L., & Tobin, T. (2011). Race is not neutral: A national investigation of African American and Latino disproportionality in school discipline. *School Psychology Review*, *40*(1), 85.

Storeygard, J., Hamm, J., & C. T. Fosnot. (2010). Determining what children know: Dynamic versus static assessment. In C. Fosnot (Ed.), *Models of intervention in mathematics: Reweaving the tapestry*. National Council of Teachers of Mathematics.

Tan, P. (2017). Advancing inclusive mathematics education: Strategies and resources for effective IEP practices. *International Journal of Whole Schooling*, *13*(3), 28–38.

Tan, P., & Kastberg, S. (2017). Calling for research collaborations and the use of dis/ability studies in mathematics education. *Journal of Urban Mathematics Education*, *10*(2), 25–38.

Taylor, H., & Vestergaard, M. D. (2022). Developmental dyslexia: Disorder or specialization in exploration? *Frontiers in Psychology*, *13*. https://www.frontiersin.org/articles/10.3389/fpsyg.2022.889245

Thelen, E. (2005). Dynamic systems theory and the complexity of change. *Psychoanalytic Dialogues*, *15*(2), 255–283. https://doi.org/10.1080/10481881509348831

Tournaki, N., Bae, Y. S., & Kerekes, J. (2008). Rekenrek: A manipulative used to teach addition and subtraction to students with learning disabilities. *Learning Disabilities: A Contemporary Journal*, *6*(2), 41–59.

Townsley, M., & Schmid, D. (2020). Alternative grading practices: An entry point for faculty in competency-based education. Competency-Based Education, 5(3), e01219. https://onlinelibrary.wiley.com/doi/full/10.1002/cbe2.1219

Truman, J. V. (2017). *Mathematical reasoning among adults on the autism spectrum: Case studies with mathematically experienced participants* [Thesis, Education: Faculty of Education]. http://summit.sfu.ca/item/17501

Tzur, R., Johnson, H. L., Hodkowski, N. M., Nathenson-Mejia, S., Davis, A., & Gardner, A. (2020). Beyond getting answers: Promoting conceptual understanding of multiplication. *Australian Primary Mathematics Classroom*, *25*(4), 35–40. https://eric.ed.gov/?id=EJ1285740

U.S. Department of Education, Institute of Education Sciences, National Center for Education Statistics, National Assessment of Educational Progress (NAEP). (2013). *2013 Reading and Mathematics Assessment.* https://www.nationsreportcard.gov/reading_math_2013/#/

Van de Walle, J., Bay-Williams, J., Lovin, L., & Karp, K. (2017). *Teaching student-centered mathematics: Developmentally appropriate instruction for grades 6–8* (3rd ed.). Pearson.

Van Den Heuvel-Panhuizen, M. (1996). Assessment and realistic mathematics education. *CD-β Wetenschappelijke Bibliotheek, 19.* https://dspace.library.uu.nl/handle/1874/1705

Van Den Heuvel-Panhuizen, M. (2003). The didactical use of models in realistic mathematics education: An example from a longitudinal trajectory on percentage. *Educational Studies in Mathematics, 54*(1), 9–35. https://doi.org/10.1023/B:EDUC.0000005212.03219.dc

Van Der Auwera, S., Torbeyns, J., De Smedt, B., Verguts, G., & Verschaffel, L. (2022). The remarkably frequent, efficient, and adaptive use of the subtraction by addition strategy: A choice/no-choice study in fourth- to sixth-graders with varying mathematical achievement levels. *Learning and Individual Differences, 93*, 102–107. https://doi.org/10.1016/j.lindif.2021.102107

Von Károlyi, C., & Winner, E. (2004). Dyslexia and visual spatial talents: Are they connected? In T. M. Newman, & R. J. Sternberg (Eds.), *Students with both gifts and learning disabilities: Identification, assessment, and outcomes* (pp. 95–117). Springer US. https://doi.org/10.1007/978-1-4419-9116-4_6

Vygotsky, L. S. (1978). *Mind in society.* Harvard University Press.

Vygotsky, L. S. (1993). *The collected works of L.S. Vygotsky: The fundamentals of defectology (abnormal psychology and learning disabilities)* (R. W. Rieber & A. S. Carton, Eds.). Springer US. https://www.springer.com/gp/book/9780306424427

Waitoller, F. R., & King Thorius, K. A. (2016). Cross-pollinating culturally sustaining pedagogy and universal design for learning: Toward an inclusive pedagogy that accounts for dis/ability. *Harvard Educational Review, 86*(3), 366–389.

Webb, N. M., Franke, M. L., Ing, M., Wong, J., Fernandez, C. H., Shin, N., & Turrou, A. C. (2014). Engaging with others' mathematical ideas: Interrelationships among student participation, teachers' instructional practices, and learning. *International Journal of Educational Research, 63*, 79–93. https://doi.org/10.1016/j.ijer.2013.02.001

Wei, X., Lenz, K. B., & Blackorby, J. (2013). Math growth trajectories of students with disabilities: Disability category, gender, racial, and socioeconomic status differences from ages 7 to 17. *Remedial and Special Education, 34*(3), 154–165.

Wei, X., Yu, J. W., Shattuck, P., McCracken, M., & Blackorby, J. (2013). Science, Technology, Engineering, and Mathematics (STEM) participation among college students with an autism spectrum disorder. *Journal of Autism and Developmental Disorders, 43*(7), 1539–1546. https://doi.org/10.1007/s10803-012-1700-z

Wilson, M. (2018, September 24). The untold story of the vegetable peeler that changed the world. *FastCompany.* https://www.fastcompany.com/90239156/the-untold-story-of-the-vegetable-peeler-that-changed-the-world

Woodward, J. (2004). Mathematics education in the United States: Past to present. *Journal of Learning Disabilities, 37*(1), 16–31.

REFERENCES

Yell, M. L., Katsiyannis, A., Ennis, R. P., Losinski, M., & Christle, C. A. (2016). Avoiding substantive errors in individualized education program development. *TEACHING Exceptional Children*, *49*(1), 31–40. https://doi.org/10.1177/0040059916662204

Young, S. (2011). *How I learned*. CreateSpace Independent Publishing Platform.

Zhang, D., Xin, Y. P., Harris, K., & Ding, Y. (2014). Improving multiplication strategic development in children with math difficulties. *Learning Disability Quarterly*, *37*(1), 15–30. https://doi.org/10.1177/0731948713500146

INDEX

**JENNIFER M. BAY-WILLIAMS,
JOHN J. SANGIOVANNI, ROSALBA SERRANO,
SHERRI MARTINIE, JENNIFER SUH,
C. DAVID WALTERS, SUSIE KATT**

Because fluency is so much more than
basic facts and algorithms.
Grades K–8

**MARIA DEL ROSARIO
ZAVALA,
JULIA MARIA AGUIRRE**

Discover innovative equity-
based culturally responsive
mathematics instruction that
unlocks the mathematical
heart of each student.
Grades K–8

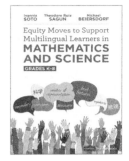

**IVANNIA SOTO,
THEODORE RUIZ SAGUN,
MICHAEL BEIERSDORF**

Focus on the literacy
opportunities that multilingual
students can achieve when
language scaffolds are
taught alongside rigorous
math and science content.
Grades K–8

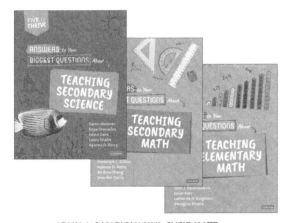

**JOHN J. SANGIOVANNI, SUSIE KATT,
LATRENDA D. KNIGHTEN, GEORGINA RIVERA,
FREDERICK L. DILLON, AYANNA D. PERRY,
ANDREA CHENG, JENNIFER OUTZS, KAREN MESMER,
ENYA GRANDOS, KEVIN GANT, LAURA SHAFER**

Actionable answers to your most pressing
questions about teaching elementary math,
secondary math, and secondary science.

Elementary, Secondary

**CHRISTA JACKSON, KRISTIN L. COOK,
SARAH B. BUSH,
MARGARET MOHR-SCHROEDER,
CATHRINE MAIORCA, THOMAS ROBERTS**

Help educators create integrated STEM
learning experiences that are inclusive for all
students and allow them to experience STEM
as scientists, innovators, mathematicians,
creators, engineers, and technology experts!

Grades PreK–5 and Grades 6–12

CM23841706

A Sage Company

Helping educators make the greatest impact

CORWIN HAS ONE MISSION: to enhance education through intentional professional learning.

We build long-term relationships with our authors, educators, clients, and associations who partner with us to develop and continuously improve the best evidence-based practices that establish and support lifelong learning.